Desert Indian Woman

Desert Indian Woman

◇ Stories and Dreams

Frances Manuel and Deborah Neff

Danny Lopez, *Tohono O'odham Language Consultant*

The University of Arizona Press

TUCSON

The University of Arizona Press
© 2001 The Arizona Board of Regents
First printing
All rights reserved
∞ This book is printed on acid-free, archival-quality paper.

Manufactured in the United States of America
06 05 04 03 02 01   6 5 4 3 2 1

Library of Congress Cataloging-in-Publication Data
Manuel, Frances Sallie, 1912–
Desert Indian woman : stories and dreams /
Frances Sallie Manuel and Deborah Lyn Neff.
p. cm.
ISBN 0-8165-2007-0 (cloth) — ISBN 0-8165-2008-9 (pbk.)
1. Manuel, Frances Sallie, 1912–   2. Tohono O'Odham
Indians—Biography.   3. Tohono O'Odham Indians—
Folklore.   4. Tohono O'Odham Indians—Social life
and customs.   I. Neff, Deborah Lyn, 1954–   II. Title.
E99.P25 M32   2001
979.1004′9745—dc21
2001017112

British Library Cataloguing-in-Publication Data
A catalogue record for this book is available from the
British Library.

Publication of this book is made possible in part by
the proceeds of a permanent endowment created with
the assistance of a Challenge Grant from the National
Endowment for the Humanities, a federal agency.

This book is dedicated to my beloved son, Floyd, and to my dear grandson, John Antone, who recently passed on. And to the children who are coming.
— Frances Manuel

I think if I could sit down and tell you EVERY-
THING that happens to me since I was a little girl,
you could have a BIG, BIG STORY about things.
But I don't tell, I mean, I'm not SURE! And if I did
tell you something, somebody might say this is not
true, ya know, that's why I just forget things. A lot
of things happen to me, a lot of things I feel, a lot of
things I dream, a lot of things I IMAGINE. But I never
did tell anybody. Up to this day I hear things and I see
things. It's not for ME to tell, it's not in ME! But it's
nothing, anyway. I just hear the air, and the sound,
or the dreams . . . or even I hear my own heartbeats.
[thoughtfully] I like that, though.
    —Frances Manuel, 1987

There are very few people I take seriously.
My grandmother is one of them.
    —Jose Fendenheim, 1988

Contents

Illustrations

Preface

I want to thank my girls, and Floyd. And all my grandchildren and great-grandchildren. Of course Floyd isn't the oldest, but he's going first. And then Juanita, Mildred, Florence, Linda, Christy, and the grandchildren.

We don't have a word for "thank you." The word *Jios o 'a s-m-ho'igel* means "Thank you, Lord" in O'odham. [Laughing] Once I was saying it to my husband, and he says, "I didn't give it to Jesus, I gave it to you!"

When I first met Debbie, she was one of those people that helps at the schools and gets somebody to talk to the kids. I think I did it for ten years. I don't know whether she hears what I tell to the little kids, and I don't know from that what she hears about it, and that caught her ear and she started asking questions. And pretty soon it got easier to talk about things. It's hard to talk to a person about things like that, but it got easier. And we talked about writing a book.

Writing the book?[1] Sometimes it was hard and sometimes it's easier. I guess all people are like that. Sometimes it is easier to talk about something. It's written in your head and you just talk about it. Sometimes it's hard, you have to think hard before you get the words in. Sometimes you don't feel like talking. Sometimes it makes me sad, sometimes it makes me mad. And sometimes you ask yourself, "Why am I doing this?" All those things go into that. I wonder if any of these writers feel that way. They must. . . . Working together? Sometimes it's very good to sit across from each other and talk about it, makes you feel good, makes you strong. Sometimes you don't feel anything—it's not there. And sometimes you talk about things and you have a future. You go on from there. So I thank Debbie for being patient. Thank her with all my heart.

The book? It's all there, nothing is made up.

Frances Manuel
San Pedro, Arizona

Frances and I have been working on this book since 1981, but she began tell-
ing me her story years before. We used to tell each other stories while we were
driving back and forth from Tucson to San Pedro—about a forty-minute trip.
Frances had homes in both places. Sometimes we'd play hooky from work, stop-
ping in the desert at a place that looked good to us when we had time to kill,
and go for a walk among the giant saguaros, mesquite trees, cholla, and prickly
pear cactus. We would sit on a rock on the side of a hill, and Frances would
talk to me about her life and about the living things in the desert that her
people, the Tohono O'odham, used to eat and use for medicine. That was when
I was working with Indian Education in the Tucson public schools, from 1979
to 1981. Frances's niece, Alberta, introduced us, for I was the "Project Specialist
in Cultural Awareness," and Frances is a basket weaver.

I used to pick up Frances in town to take her for basket-weaving demon-
strations in the elementary schools. Sometimes she would tell the children a
story about a rainbow, a little story she read somewhere. It's about a little girl
and boy who used to play together in an Indian village, one which I imagined
to be like San Pedro a long time ago, when Frances was a child.

> *A long time ago a boy and a girl were growing up together, and every day they*
> *would play together. He taught her to hunt and to play ball, and she taught him*
> *how to cook and make baskets. The two children used to play all day together in*
> *the desert, until one day the girl's parents decided that it was time for her to get*
> *married. The young girl would have to leave the village to live with her husband's*
> *family in a village far away, so the boy and the girl were very sad. And so the day*
> *came and they met at their favorite meeting place in the desert for one last time.*
> *They were so sad. One day the boy brought a basket of brightly colored flowers,*
> *gave it to her, and said, "When you think of me, hold these flowers up to the sun."*
> *So one day while she was thinking of him, she held the basket of flowers up to*
> *the sun. The sun picked up the colors and hurled them through the sky, making*
> *a rainbow, a beautiful rainbow. So he knew that she was thinking of him.*

I don't know why we liked that story so much! Later on, when I asked her to
tell it, she would say, "You know the story, you tell it!"

At that time, Frances was still living in town. I'll never forget this one day
I had given Frances a ride home from a basket-weaving class. We were in the
Tucson house, the high-rise government housing project where Frances lived

at the time. It was a dingy sort of place, with a lot of interesting characters milling about, and quite a few elderly. Having gotten off the elevator at the tenth floor, we were walking down the hall to her apartment. "Whoever heard of an Indian taking an elevator to her house!" Frances exclaimed, laughing from behind a five-foot-long spray of bear grass she was carrying.[2] Frances is barely five feet tall, and on the tenth floor of the Tucson House, she was a sight! We had a lot of fun in those days. Frances and I became friends very quickly, and soon talked like we had known one another for years. Before long, Frances had introduced me to her family and village, and my visits became part of her life.

It was 1981 when Frances and I began recording her life story, the year that I was preparing to leave Tucson for Madison, Wisconsin, to finish my doctorate. We had been spending lots of weekends together on the reservation that year. Many evenings we sat under the ramada, *watching the nighthawks fly toward the light. Lorenzo, Frances's longtime friend, was often with us then, and the two of them would sing O'odham songs.[3] In wintertime Frances would tell legends, the collective stories of her people, and in the summer tales or "little stories." Just about anytime, she'd tell stories she heard somewhere — at the bus stop, the hospital, or on pilgrimage to Magdalena, in Sonora, Mexico. But most of her stories were about her own experiences, what she has seen and learned in the world from her birth at Ko:m Wawhai in 1912. I would miss those stories.*

So one day in 1981 we were walking in the desert by her house, I asked Frances if she wanted to tape-record her stories for a book about her life, written in her own words. She agreed. She said:

I am very proud of being a Papago[4]
and I know where I came from and I know who I am.
That's what I want my children to be
to know who they are and where they came from

.

Ya know,
I think it's kind of a SHAME
that we don't sit our kids down and tell stories about this and that.
Maybe it's our own fault

.

but we don't have time to tell the story
  on account of SCHOOL
    on account of ACTIVITIES
on account of something else

.

Or for us we go to meetings
or we want to go to bed early
or um
maybe go to a movie . . .
if you want
to watch TV

.

We don't have TIME
to tell those stories
that's why they don't know

.

It's our fault.
  (1981)

Much of the meaning of words lies in the way words are spoken — their sounds and accompanying gestures. So when it makes sense to do so, I employ this poetic format to give the reader a sense of the original speech event.[5]

The words that are capitalized are spoken more loudly; breaks between lines indicate slight pauses (approximately half a second); and the periods, full stops. For the best effect, the sections written in poetic format should be read aloud, to evoke a sense of Frances's narrative style and the ways that she communicates meaning. Ideally, all of her words should be read in your mind as if you are reading out loud. This will help to provide a sense of the rhythms *of Frances's narrative style, rendering digressions into song and story more accessible. Her dialect does not illustrate a mere lack of familiarity with English grammatical structure. In some cases, Frances may retain grammatical structures carried over from the Tohono O'odham language into English. (An example is Frances's use of "he" and "she" interchangeably in contexts where gender is not marked in the O'odham.)*

The influence of Frances's original language can also be seen in her deep inhalations and her use of loudness and pitch to communicate emphasis. Her O'odham worldview is, of course, expressed even in the English — for example,

*speaking in the present tense when talking about the deceased, or giving ani-
mation to a pot or pan. As you read Frances's words, perhaps you will feel the
connectedness that her dreams, songs, and legends share with everyday life as
they bring images and people from faraway times and places into the present.
Perhaps you will enter another world of meaning.*

The Book

*Frances's story is a life history of a Native American woman growing up on the
U.S.-Mexican border during a time of drastic change. Its overall themes concern both creativity and loss, and thus carry a powerful message for our times.
For the reader less interested in lengthy introductions and an afterword, these
can be skipped or read later; Frances's words stand on their own.*

Because Frances's words were spoken, *she did not rethink, edit, or rephrase
them for the book; her words are written the way they were spoken the first
time. Frances has a skill that many people from oral cultures have: to speak
words in meaningful phrases and progressions without having to write them
down. Frances has trusted me with these words and has allowed me to present
them on the written page. I consider this a great gift, and I have recorded and
arranged them with as much care as possible. But I don't speak for her. Most
of what the reader wishes to know about how the book was written can be
found within the commentaries and appendices. Historical and other contex-
tual material appears in the notes to each chapter.*

*Frances's story was told to me, with nods of agreement and the implicit
understandings of our long acquaintance.[6] But I could see right from the beginning that much of Frances's text had been rehearsed—told before, almost
verbatim. Gradually, I became less visible, and Frances got used to the small
tape recorder between us. Sometimes Lorenzo or one of Frances's grandchildren was present, too, and became part of the story. There were also segments
that were taped by Frances alone at her home, when she felt like speaking to
me or to her would-be audience through the tape recorder.*

*The text includes recordings from over thirty sittings; these were transcribed
verbatim. I have arranged the material chronologically, which was Frances's
wish, careful to keep embedded legends, songs, reflections, and journeys to
other times and places in their original contexts. Other than moving sections
around, editing was minor. Frances's style of telling stories, including her col-*

loquial English, is retained. Some of the original repetition is kept as well, because Frances commonly uses repetition for emphasis. My comments within the text are bracketed or italicized. I tried to keep my comments to a minimum during the tape-recording process, but we often chatted back and forth as we wound down our sessions; the sporadic sections written in interview format reflect this process. Spaces within the text indicate a new topic from the same tape sequence. A diamond-shaped ornament connotes a new tape or a change in voice—from Frances's to mine or vice versa.

It has not been common practice to credit the native speaker with coauthorship of life histories.[7] Over one hundred collaborative works about Native Americans have been written in the "as told to" format, with the non-Indian as sole author.[8] We have departed from this tradition on the basis that oral tradition is literature.[9] *Furthermore, we have shared authorship functions throughout our work, negotiating the style of presentation and what is to be included. Frances spoke and allowed her text to be tape-recorded. I transcribed the tapes, arranged and edited them, and provided commentary. Frances read and commented upon each draft, and answered my questions as we went along.[10]*

Most of what we recorded is included here, pieced together from thirty-five tapes. We have arranged the text into five parts. The chronological ordering of the parts reflects Frances's wishes and the general order in which topics were covered. Frances's detailed reflections on her life appear toward the end, as they did in the telling. The first three parts constitute Frances's life history, whereas the final two parts consist of her beliefs and reflections about her life. They are titled "S-koksonagk (Many Pack Rats), 1913–1930: Growing Up"; "San Pedro to Tucson: Marriage and Family, 1941–1981"; "Homecoming: San Pedro, 1981–Present"; "God and I'itoi: Speeches from the Heart"; and "Reflections: Things That Connect." Each part is introduced and/or followed by commentary. A more extensive Afterword closes the text, describing some of our more recent experiences together, with a brief social-historical summary. Two appendices end the book. The first concerns the process of recording, writing, and collaboration. The second is a summary outline of the subjects covered in the taped conversations.

Frances and I chose to make the tape recordings in English because English is our shared language. This is also the case with several of Frances's grandchildren who are in my age group and do not speak O'odham.[11] All of the songs and several narrative pieces were performed in Frances's native lan-

guage, O'odham, and are recorded here in both languages. The transcriptions and translations, done primarily by Frances's son-in-law Danny Lopez but also Professor Ofelia Zepeda, follow the Tohono O'odham lexicon developed by Albert Alvarez and Kenneth Hale.[12] We are particularly grateful to Danny Lopez for taking on the time-consuming and difficult task of recording and translating the songs and other O'odham sections, so that this work can join the work of others in upholding the value of reading and writing the O'odham language. I am grateful that I had the opportunity to throw ideas around with Robert Brightman during the early stages of conceptualizing the book at Wisconsin. His enthusiasm stimulated my awareness of the magic of the spoken word, and influenced the approach to oral literature taken here. Thanks, too, to Hazel Salzman, for the tapes, and to Becky Moser for her help in locating Frances's grandfather, Ge Wu:lo.

This book could not have been written without the assistance and support of Frances's family. I am grateful to her grandchildren, James and Jose Fendenheim, for their inspiration and support over the many years that we spent growing up together on the reservation in our twenties, and to Amelia Quiroga and Sonya Banks for being there when they were small, so I could watch Frances help raise them. Special love to Big John, who passed on just before the book went to press. Our book has benefited from the insightful suggestions of John Fendenheim and Mildred Antone on earlier drafts. Frances's daughters have provided friendship and support over the years, so many thanks to Juanita Fendenheim, Florence Lopez (and her husband, Danny), Mildred Antone, Linda Sanchez (along with her husband, Pancho), and Christy Manuel. To the kind people of San Pedro—thanks for putting up with me and my occasional entourage. How could I thank Hector Gonzalez for his ongoing encouragement and mentoring in Tucson? There are many more—Patti Hartmann at the University of Arizona Press, our copy editor, Beth Wilson, Emory Sekaquaptewa, Brian Parks, Deborah Johnson, Kim Matthews, and Rebecca Cortez each placed his or her special mark on the work. Finally, I thank Frances for bringing me into her family and for becoming my teacher. Any mistakes or omissions in the book are, of course, my own.

Deborah Neff
Tucson, Arizona

Introductions

I have not been the only one who has been privileged to hear Frances's stories. Her family and her students have heard them, too. Frances loves to tell them! When Frances was a child, more formal storytelling events took place in O'odham households on cold winter nights, when stories were related in vibrant words that came alive with gesture and emotion. Sometimes they were told over many nights, remaining unfinished by day. Frances called them speeches, for they were teachings. "Oh, I hated to be preached!" she says. In recent years there has been a resurgence of interest in the collective stories of O'odham elders and the tribe has orchestrated storytelling events. Told more informally around the hearth and kitchen table, pieces of the life stories of O'odham elders continue to be related to families and friends in O'odham households.

The first tape that Frances recorded about her life was at the request of her close Milga:n friend, Hazel Salzman, in the 1970s, a few years before we met. Hazel moved away, and when I wrote to tell her about our book, she generously sent me the four tapes they had recorded together.[1]

The first subject Frances spoke about with Hazel was the Tohono O'odham Wi:gita, an ancient and elaborate religious ritual performed to bring rain and to put the world in order. The Wi:gita is one of the core rituals of the old religion, a rain ceremony observed in the summer months between mid-July and mid-August, during the summer monsoons in the Sonoran desert. A cornerstone of Tohono O'odham religion and ritual, it is still performed today to "pull down the clouds."[2] I asked Frances to talk about it, and she recorded her response for me in O'odham, sitting alone on her bed in 1981.

As Frances tells it, Hazel had taken her to the Heard Museum in Phoenix, and they started talking about the Nawacu, a sacred person who once lived among Frances's people. Here Frances relates a story about powerful, sacred beings, called Slanted-eyed Buzzard and Nawacu, who rescue a young girl from the top of a mountain. The story is a shortened version of a much longer one, "a little story," mixed with song, commentary, and message. Frances be-

gins in O'odham with a phrase her grandfather would use when he delivered wise words in speech and story.

We:s ha'icu 'o 'i- hab cu'ig. We:s ha'icu 'o 'i- hab cu'ig. 'I:ya t-ki:dag 'ed. Pi 'at ha'icu, pi 'at ha'icu 'am hu o paḍc.

[Everything is based here, everything is based here, here in the home. May nothing, may nothing disturb it.]

Cem 'añ hekid 'am we:maj, k 'am hasko hema ñeid g nawacu pigcul matĭ 'am hema 'o'oho, k 'ia 'u'apa k 'am ñ-ce:gid. K 'am ñ-kakke hegai Milga:n 'oks, "No 'id wuḍ 'em- kachina?" Kuñ 'am 'a:gid mac pi 'edgit hegai mo hab 'e-a'aga kachina, k 'asba wuḍ hegai mac hab 'a'aga nawacu. Kut 'ab ha'icu 'i-ñ-kakke 'ab 'amjiḍ g nawacu, kuñ hab 'a:g mac pi 'am hu hekid 'a'aga 'am toñiabk 'ed, 'amai s-he:pĭ c-eḍ. Kut gm hu 'u:pam me: k 'am hu hebai 'am 'ep mel k 'u'acug hegai 'o'ohon matkĭ g Ruth Underhill 'am 'o'oho k 'am ñ-kakke mas hab masma 'an ha'icu 'o'ohonas mañ hab masma ha'icu s-ma:c. Kuñ hab 'a:g mant pi 'am hu has 'o si cei nopi hegam matp 'am ha'icu 'a:gid gm hu hasko wuḍ ki:kam c 'am 'a gawul masma s-ma:c g Ho'okĭ 'a:gida. Matp heḍai 'am 'i-ha'icu a:gid, c hab masma 'am hab s-ma::c g ha'icu 'a:gida, k ha:icu pi hab masma 'o 'e-ka: mañ hab masma ha'icu ka: k 'am

[I always went around with her (Hazel), and she saw a picture of the Nawacu that someone drew, and she brought it over and showed it to me. And she said, "Isn't this your Kachina doll?" And I told her that we don't have Kachina dolls, but that is one of our effigies, symbols. And she started to ask me things about it, and I told her that we don't talk about it in the summer, only in winter. So she left, and sometime later she got the book that Ruth Underhill wrote and asked me if what was in the book was the way I knew it.[3] I told her that I really would not be able to say, because they are from different places and so they might tell their stories differently; their Ho'oki a:gida[4] would be different. Whoever told those stories, well, that would be the way they told their stories; some things would not be the way I heard them, but that is all right. And then she asked

'a s-ape. K 'am 'ep ha'icu ñ-kakke
'ab amjiḍ g nawacu, k si s-ap 'ab
'o'ohonas. K hab si masma hab ma:s
mo hab cem ma:s g nawacu 'am
wi:gida c-eḍ. Kunt hab 'i-ñ-a: mant
'am 'o hema 'a:gǐ hegam mo wuḍ 'aṣ
'al ṣopol ha'icu 'a:gida hab 'elidc mo
pi gewkdag. Mañ 'am ha'icu 'a:gid
k 'am 'o'ohon g nawacu, hegai du'ag
mo am 'e-a'aga heg 'eḍa ha'icu
'a:gida, heg 'eḍ Ho'okǐ 'a:gida, mat
has masma 'ab 'i-wuha, mat g
nawacu 'ab 'i-huḍuñ hegai 'uwǐ.

me again about the Nawacu, the
likeness of it was very good. It
looked like long ago when they
had the Wi:gita ceremony, this is
how they looked. After a while I
decided to tell one of the shorter
stories, thinking perhaps that
maybe the stories are not as powerful.[5] And so I told the story, and
she was able to draw the Nawacu,
the mountain as it was in the story,
the Ho'oki a:gida, the way they
appeared, and how the Nawacu
helped the girl down.]

Kutp hab 'e-a:g hegai Milga:n 'oks
mac hab t-wua kc 'am ha'icu ha-
a:gid g 'a'al, mac 'am ha-daḍsp c
'am ha-a:gid 'idam ha'icu 'a:gida,
kutp hab 'e-elid mo g 'a'al si has
ha-elid 'idam ha'icu 'a:gida. K
'eḍa pi hab masma hemu. Wecij
hemajkam 'o hegai taccu mat 'am 'o
daḍkc g 'o'ohon 'ab 'o ñeidat, wa:m
hegam 'o'ohon mo si s-ta-kakaima.
An 'at 'o 'u'ukcid g 'o'ohon c pi 'o
ṣa'i dagito. Hekǐ hu 'at 'am 'o 'i-t-
daḍs k 'am 'o ha'icu t-a:gǐ, hegam
ha'icu 'a:gida ke we:s ha'icu mo 'ab
we:nags g Ho'okǐ 'a:gida. Hemu
'at we:s ha'icu huhug, pi 'o 'am hu
'e-a'aga.

[She thought that we tell these
stories to children, that we set
them down and tell them these
stories, and she probably thinks
that the children think these stories
are very important. Yet this is not
what it is like these days. Young
people prefer to read books, to sit
and read them, especially when
they are about things very interesting. They will hold onto a book
and not let it go. Long ago it was
not like this. Long ago they would
set us down and tell us the stories,
the stories and all the things that
are connected to them, the Ho'oki
a:gida. And now they are all gone,
they are no longer told.]

Kuṣ ha'i g cecioj am cem s-ho:ntam
'i:da 'uwǐ. Kuṣ 'am hu hebai 'am

[Some young men were interested
in marrying this girl, but she didn't

'e-nam hegam Mawid c Juḍumĭ
k 'am 'e-we:m ñeñio, k 'am hema
na:to g kuawul bayoka. Kuts 'am
'a'ad g we:mgal maṣ wuḍ Ban,
maṣ ha'icu s-wohocud, k 'am meḍ
'am cem ma: g bayoka hegai 'uwĭ.
"Id 'ats 'o ma: g Mawid k 'ats 'o
m-ho:nt." Kuts 'am meḍ 'am cem
ma: g bayoka g 'uwĭ kuts 'oya pi bei.
Kuṣ hegai 'uwĭ gm hu 'aṣ si da'ic
hegai bayoka. Kuṣ ṣa'i ha'as kuts
'am jiwa g we:nagac hegai 'uwĭ k
hab kaij, "Dagitoñ! Mat 'o 'i-na:to
g 'e-cu'i k 'am 'o ha'icu ñ-hidol nt
'o ñ-gegusid k 'o hi." Kuts 'oya 'am
'i-bagat g Ban k hab kaij, "Nt 'o
meḍ k 'o 'a:gĭ g Juḍumĭ c Mawid
kut 'ab 'o 'i-hihi k 'io m-mua k 'io
bei hegai 'uwĭ." Ha'ap 'aṣ kaij c gm
hu me.

Kuts gm hu 'ep ha'icu cikp hegai
'uwĭ k 'am hu hebai kuṣ hab
'a:g g 'e-we:nag maṣ 'am wo'o kc
'e-ulñihogid, "Wamgiñ! Ab 'o hihim
hegam mats 'io m-mua. Wamgiñ!"
Kuṣ 'am 'aṣ i-si -wo'o hegai cioj kuṣ
'oya hab 'ep kaij g 'uwĭ, "Ṣa:cu 'ap
'a:g kc hab 'e-ju:kc. Tṣ 'o m-mua! Pi
'ap 'am hu 'i-e-nakog. Mapt 'o has
'o 'i-e-juñk 'o 'e-do'ibio." Kuṣ hab
hahawa kaij hegai cioj, "Am okĭ 'a
woho mokĭ s-ñ-mu'am hegam."

like any of them. Sometime later
Mountain Lion and Bear met to
talk, and they made a string of
beads out of the fruit of the *kuawul*
[wolfberry].[6] They sent their relative to the Coyote, one who was so
trusting, and he ran over there to
try to give it to her: "This is what
Mountain Lion wants to give to
you, and he wants to marry you."
He tried to hand it to her, but she
would not accept it. She just threw
it away. After a while her brother
said, "Leave her alone, so she can
finish her grinding and make my
meal for me so I can leave!" And
so Coyote became angry and he
said, "I'm going over to tell Bear
and Mountain Lion, and they will
come and kill you and take her."
He said this and left.]

[After a while the girl went on
with what she was doing, and
then she looked up and said, "Get
up! And take a look at those who
said they were going to kill you.
Come on, get up, they are arriving, those who are going to kill
you!" But the brother didn't say
anything. Finally, after a while she
said, "What are you going to do?
Why are you just like this? They
are going to kill you! You are not
even trying to get ready to prepare
yourself so that you may save your-

self!" "I doubt they will really kill
me," he said.]

◇

And they retreat and don't kill him. But one day they were talking among
themselves. . . .

Am hu hebai kuṣ hab kaij hegai
S-ha'ahamakam 'am Siwlokĭ wui,
"Kutt has 'o ju: hegai 'uwĭ?" Kuṣ
hab kaij g S-ha'ahamakam, "Kutt
hig 'am 'o si has ju: nopi pi hema
s-t-ho:ntam." Kuṣ 'eḍa g Siwlokĭ 'ab
si kaiham g Mawid k 'am 'a hekaj
'aṣ meḍk 'am bei hegai 'uwĭ maṣ
'am hebai 'oimmeḍ. Kutṣ 'am bek
meḍk k gn hu dai heg da:m du'ag
maṣ wuḍ Waw S-da:pk. Kuṣ 'an hia
daha g 'uwĭ natṣ pi pi 'ap 'i-huḍ.
Kuṣ 'eḍa gḍ hu g ki:kam 'an hiu cem
ga:g hegai 'uwĭ.

[And one day this person said,
"What shall we do with her?" He
said to Whirlwind, "Why don't we
do something to her because she
is so hurtful by not wanting any
one of us?" Yet it was the way that
Whirlwind was a very trusting person, and he ran over and took her.
He took her to this place called
Waw S-da:pk, Slippery Cliff Face,
and he put her right on the edge
of it. There she sat and sat, she sat
for some time. And over there they
began searching and searching for
her. Each evening the people would
gather and discuss things, and try
to figure out what happened to
her.]

Mat hekid pi 'o himad g jewed,
mat pi'an hu ha-oksig, pi 'an hu
ha-kelig, pi 'an hu ha-wecij hemaj-
kamk, pi 'an hu ha-'a'aligk. Maṣ
hab cu'ig 'ab hebai g keli napaḍk
ki' ṣon 'ab. Kuṣ hab kaij, "Kut has
hig 'e-ju: mamt 'o 'a:gĭ g t-nawaj,
kowaḍk wuikam ñuwĭ mo heg pi
me:kculid g jewed, 'e-weco 'uliñc

[We always say that the Earth
would not be moving [time would
not be passing], and so there
would be no old age, there would
be no youth, no children. And so
it was. And there in this place was
an old man sitting in the corner
of the house, and he said, "Why
don't you all ask our friend, the

ha'icu ñeid k hebai ha'icu 'am
'a cem si 'a'agĭ, pegi, k heg 'am
cecga. Mt 'o 'a:gĭ kutp hems heg 'o
'e-nako mat 'o ce:. Ñia, kuṣ woho
'am 'i-a:gid kutṣ 'am hahawa himk
'am 'i-u:gka gn hu 'u:gk him. Ṭṣ
'am 'i-hud tṣ 'am 'ep 'e-hemapa.
"Kuṣ hab kaij," ṣa g wepo mant
s-mai mokĭ hebai has cu'ig. Bo g
'uwĭ ṣuak heg 'abai Waw S-da:pk,
ga hu mo 'ab si s-mu'uk, 'ab 'o g
'uwĭ ṣuak. Kutp hud 'i-hegai kc
'an daha." Ñia, kut 'amjid 'am 'ep
cem 'a'aga mat has masma 'ab 'o
'i-huduñ, has masma 'an 'o bei, k
'am 'a 'ep pi 'e-ma:c k gm hu 'apṣ
'i-pi 'e-ma:c. Pegi, k hab kaij, hega
'e:p keli, "At has hig 'e-ju mo wa:j hu
ki: g t-nawaj si'al ṣon 'abai kc hab
wud nawacu. Heg 'at 'o 'e-nako mat
'o 'i-huduñ. Kut 'a s-e-mai mat has
masma 'ab 'o 'i-hudun."

Slanted-eyed Buzzard? He travels
across far spaces on this Earth, he
travels above it and has the Earth
beneath him and sees everything.
Whenever something is approach-
ing us, he sees it first. Tell him, and
perhaps he will be able to find her."
And so immediately they told him.
Buzzard took off right away, and
he flew, he flew up high. When
it became evening, they again
gathered, and he said, "I think I
have found out where she is. There
is a woman crying over there at
Waw S-da:pk, Slippery Cliff Face,
way up there at the highest points,
there is a woman crying. It is likely
that it is her." And so they began
to try to figure out how they were
going to get her down from there.
Again they were not sure what they
were going to do. And again this
one, the old man, said, "Our friend
lives over there to the east, that
one, the Nawacu; tell him, and he
will be able to get her down. He
will be able to figure something
out."]

"Hu-hu, hu-hu," 'am hahawa sikod
memda k 'e-nako. Amjid 'am wo:p,
pi hekid 'ampṣ 'i-him g nawacu, cem
hekid 'aṣ ṣa jejwokim, mo g kawyu.
Pegi, 'i-wo:p k ga hu hahawa dada
k' am hahawa 'a:gid mo 'an daha
waw ku:g 'ab, mo 'ab 'i-si s-mu'uk.
Ñia, k 'am 'a cem hekĭ hu ce: k 'am

[Early the next morning a runner
ran over there to where Nawacu
lived. He was laying there with
his back to him. And he said to
him, "They extend you greetings as relatives, those who live
in the west. And they ask if you
would feel for them and go over

me:, ta'i meḍajc, 'u:pam meḍk 'am
hebai t-am napaḍwa k 'im hu mawa
'e-huaṣamĭ 'eḍ k 'am 'i-wuhas g
wapko kai k'am hiaṣ. Na:nko 'e-wua
k'am hu hebai t-am hahawa ṣoṣonc:

there." And he proceeded to tell
him what happened. He didn't say
anything. Again he told him what
had happened. Again he didn't
say anything. After a while he said
it again: "They extend greetings
of kinship to you, those people,
those people who are like me,
those living in the west. And if you
go and help us, we are at a ter-
rible loss as to what to do." Finally,
he began to rise very slowly. "Go
ahead and get ready so we can
leave and go see them." "Hebihu,"
he ran about getting himself ready.
And then they began running
from there. They ran and arrived
there, and he directed him to the
place and said, "She is sitting up
there at the highest point." And he
ran backward, he said, "Hebihu,
hebihu." He had already seen her
up there. After a while he slumped
down on the ground and reached
into his bundle and pulled out the
gourd seeds.[7] He dropped them
down on the ground and then was
kind of going about, and then he
began:]

Gaḍ wa-wai wuṣñe
Gaḍ wa-wai wuṣñe
Ṣ-am 'i-wuṣñe
Ṣ-am 'i-wuṣñe
Ya s-bem kainak ñe:ka
Ya s-bem kainak ku:kai

[Over there the plant grows
Over there the plant grows
It grows
It grows
Singing so loudly
Hooting so loudly
It comes out.]

Ñia, tṣ'am 'i-wu:ṣ g wako.

[And gourd plants began to grow.]

Gaḍ wa-wai wuṣñe
Gaḍ wa-wai wuṣñe
Ṣ-am 'i- wuṣñe
Ṣ-am 'i- wuṣñe
Ya s-bem kainak ñe:ka
Ya s-bem kainak ku:kai

Ñia, tṣ wu:ṣañ k 'ab ces k 'ab ces k
gn hu 'a'ahe g waw s-mu'uk kutṣ
'am 'ep ñei:

[And it began to grow upward, it climbed onto the rock, it grew and grew and reached the very top, and he continued,]

Gaḍ wa-wai wuṣñe
Gaḍ wa-wai wuṣñe
Ṣ-am 'i- wuṣñe
Ṣ-am 'i- wuṣñe
Ya s-bem kainak ñe:ka
Ya s-bem kainak ku:kai

Ñia:, t gn hu 'a'ahe hegai 'am
himk. Ñe, t-ab ces waw t-ab k gn
hu 'a'ahe. T-heg 'ab 'ab 'i-e-keiṣ k
'ab 'i-huḍ. Ab 'i-huḍñim k 'ab hi
'oic 'i-huhugim k 'ab "i-huḍñim g
wapko. K'ab him k'ab him k 'i-hu
'i-huḍ. Pi 'am hu hebai ṣa'i 'a:gas
mas hab 'i-kaij "Thank you, 'a g
Jios o 'a:s-m-ho'igel." Am 'i-we:mt,
pi 'am hu ṣa'i 'a:g. Ñia, t-gam hu
hahawa 'ep me: g Nawacu 'u:pam.

[The plant reached her, and she stepped on it and began to climb down. She climbed down, and after her came the gourd plant that was growing. She climbed all the way down, and it doesn't say if she said "Thank you," or whether she said anything to him, like she was happy about being able to come down. The Nawacu then took off running; the Nawacu never just walks, he is always kind of running, like the Milga:n (Americans) say, "jog."]

*Gm hu hahawa 'ep ki:dag. Mu'i
ha'icu 'am has 'e-wua 'am ha-ṣa:gid
mo 'am ki:dag. Pegi, k'am hu hebai
mo hab kaij hegai cioj, "Pegi,
ñ-sikol, bant hi 'o ñ-ju: k 'o him
k'im hu 'o ñ-ul huḍñig ta:gio. Am
him k'am hebai ñt 'am 'o bet. Kupt
bo 'e-a:gad heg 'o wuḍ ñ-si:s. Kut
g ñ-wepo cu'igam 'am 'o ñ-ka:k
'am 'o wu:ṣ g cekiṭoidaj k hab wuḍ
'a:ga mat 'am 'o ha-ceggia g O:bĭ.
'o 'aigo." Pegi, k hab 'ep hi kaij 'aigo
hegai 'uwĭ, "Pegi, ñ-si:s, bant hab 'a
'ep hi ñ-juñ k 'im 'o him k ga hu 'o
ñ-ul si'alig ta;gio. Kut hemo 'i-me: g
ma:sig nt 'ab o 'i-ceṣ. Kut g ñ-wepo
cui'igam o ñeid k ga:m 'o 'i-me:,
hekaj 'e-tonlidk he'es gm o 'i-me:."
Matp hekĭ hu hab 'e-wua g 'u'uwĭ,
s-si'alim k o wa:migk o 'iam, a 'u'im
g wihog, ciolim o 'u'im, o wa'igam g
su:dagĭ. Matp hascud 'i ha-cikpan.
Nam ñeid g hu'u mo 'ab 'i-cecṣag
si'al ke:k. Heḍai 'amps hia 'i-ñeid.
Im hab huḍñig ta:gio 'e:p mat 'an
hebai o ka: mat o 'i-gei g hu'u. Am o
ñei, bo hia masma hab cu'ig, ñ-idañ
'am m-a:gid.*

[And then, as time went on, the
people continued to live and different things happened. And so
it was that one day the two sat
and the boy said to his sister, "I'm
going to go do this, I'm going to
go over there to the west, and I will
face that direction. I will run to
that direction and I will fall in and
I will make a resounding noise.
And you will say, 'That is my older
brother who made that resounding
noise.' And those who are like me
will hear me and there will be certain things they must do. It will be
the sound that will tell them they
must get ready to go to war with
whomever, the enemy." And so
she said, "Well, my older brother,
I guess I will also do the same. I
will face the east and as soon as the
morning comes, I will rise. And
those who are like me will see me
and will begin to run, and then it
will become fully morning. They
will see me and will say, 'That is
my sister, my relative, and she is
coming.'" And so that is the morning star that rises there. How many
of you have seen it, how many of
you rise early in the morning and
so are able to see the star as it rises,
that one which is the female star?
She is the one who is like us.]

These old stories were given to the people in the Beginning and are considered sacred. For Frances, they teach values, admonishing us to respect the wisdom of our elders, and not to gossip. Most important the legends teach how to live on this Earth with respect for what our Creator gave to us in the Beginning. Breaking into song, Frances sings the plants into being. They come alive through the powerful presence of her engagement in the storytelling performance.

In spite of her family's extreme pride in not wanting to marry Mountain Lion, Whirlwind hides the girl on top of a mountain to protect her from the wrath of Bear and Mountain Lion. An old man, respected for his wisdom, decides to send a runner for Nawacu, their friend who lives in the East. Like the story of Jack and the Beanstalk [Frances makes this comparison], Nawacu creates the vine of a gourd plant. He brings her down, and the people are able to return to living again. Following her brother's lead, the girl becomes a star, the Morning Star. And now it is the two, the brother and sister stars, who exist to help the humans by telling them when to run and go to war and when to get up and grind corn, to do their work.

Hemu matt ge'e 'an bei g Milga:n himdag k heg 'ab ñeid maṣ ha'icu wuḍ clock. Maṣ hekĭ hu g O'odham hab masma kc g ma:sidag 'ab ñeid, heg 'e-e:kdag 'ab ñeid, heg taṣ 'ab ñeid mo hebai 'i-jujcu kc he'es wuḍ 'i-himdam. Hemu 'ac pi hab masma kc clock, calendar 'ab ñeid, am s-ma:c mat hekid 'o 'i-e-change g seasons, mat hekid 'o 'i-kekiwa g taṣ, hekid 'o 'i-u:pam hi g taṣ, kuc heg 'ab ñeid, hekid wuḍ 'o 'i-full moon-kad. Mac cem hekid ha'icu haba cu'ig, we:s ha'icu haba cu'ig. Mat hekid 'an 'i-dada g Milga:n k 'in t-bei. Naṣ pi woho mat mu'i ha'icuikaj 'am 'i-t-we:mt g Milga:n

[Now today we have chosen to accept many of the ways of the Milga:n and so we look at the clock where the O'odham before were not like that, they simply looked to the dawn, light; he looked to the shadows, he looked to the sun, and where it was situated and how much it had traveled. Today we are not like that. We watch the clock and the calendar and we know when the seasons will change. We know when the sun will change positions on the horizon. We look to it to see when there will be a full moon. It is like that, everything is there. Whenever the Milga:n ar-

k 'eda 'ep pi whoho mas 'am 'aṣ
'i-t-we:mt. Mat 'aṣ t-ho'iged k 'am
'i-t-we:maj, 'am 'a ha'icu taccu.
T-jeweḍga, mo heg taccu. Mat hekid
'an 'i-dada g Milga:n k'am t-maṣca
g ñi'oki k 'am t-maṣca g 'o'ohona,
'am t-maṣca g kuinta. Mu'i ha'icu
'am t-maṣca. Pegi, kuc heg 'am si
'oid c heg hab si elid mo heg wuḍ
si hegai. Ba kaij g keli 'o'dham,
"Mat keid ha'icu 'ab 'o i-me; kutt
'o '-ñe:ñ k 'an 'o t-bei k hab 'o cem
masma mo heg wuḍ t-himdag, mo
heg wuḍ hegai. Am cem si gawul
t-jujcu, macc 'in hab cu'ig. Hekid
'i-mac hekid 'in 'aṣ hihim c pi ma:c
g 'o'ohona kc pi ma:c g Milga:n
ni'oki. Heg 'a 'i-s-ma:c mat hascu
'ab 'i-t-ma mat heḍai t-na:to.

rived here and took us . . . , well,
it is true that they helped us with
many things. Yet it is not true that
he was doing all this to be help-
ful just because he felt for us—he
wanted something in return for his
help, our land that is here. When
the Milga:n came, he taught the
English language, he taught us
how to write, he taught us how to
count, he taught us many things,
and so we really follow all these
things. We think they are very important. And it is like the old men
have said, whenever something
new comes along, it will take us,
change us; we will accept it and
actually believe that it is our own
way of life. That is the way this is;
it is something we have taken on,
and it actually tries, or we try to
change ourselves, like this, the way
we are now. And now it is such that
we no longer exist without knowing the English language, without
knowing how to write. We don't
exist now only knowing what our
Creator gave us when he made us.]

Mat heḍai 'i-t-na:to mo 'am hab
kaij. Mat 'ab na:to g jeweḍ k 'an
ce: mat 'ab na:to g da:m ka;cim k
'ab ce: 'ab we:maj si 'e-i-gi:giaḍat k
'in dagito. Pegi, kut 'am himk 'am
hebai 'i-ceka kut 'am pi dodolmui.
Pegi, kut 'am na:to g tokiṭoḍ kut

[This is what he said. He made
the Earth and he made the sky
and he placed them there, and
he tied them together and placed
them there. At one point the Earth
was not tame, it was wild; and so
he made the spider and he made

'am wijinat kut heg hekaj 'am si wupuls k 'am dagito. Pegi, kut 'am dodolmat g jewed. Pegi, kut 'am da:m na:to g do:da'ag cu:cam k 'ab ma: g cekitoidag. Am da:m na:to g us ke:kam k 'ab ma: g cekitoidag k 'ab ma: g himdag. Am da:m na:to g jewedo meddam k 'ab ma: g cekitoidag k 'ab ma: g himdag. Ñe, mu'i ha'icu 'am hab cui'ig. Kut hemowa mat 'o s-kaihog heg hekaj mo mu'i ha'icu 'e-da:m hab cu'ig.

ropes, with it he tied them together securely, the Earth and the sky, and so the Earth was now tame. And upon the Earth he made the living things to stand upon it, and to them he gave a conscience, thought, and he gave them a way of life. And upon it he made *'u:s ke:kag*, living plants, trees, and he gave it thought and he gave it a way of life. And upon it he made *'u'uwhig da'adam'*, the birds that fly, and he gave them thought, and he gave them a way of life. And upon it he made *'jewedo memeda-dam*, the ones that run on the ground, and he gave them thought, and he gave them a way of life. And so there are many things that were made. There are many things that were made on the Earth, and if you are interested in hearing it all, there are many things to be said, that is what we were told. And so it happened when the Milga:n came, he put us in schools, and from then on it has felt as if we are not free. We feel as if we are not free in the sense that we are not the same way we were back when the Earth was first put here. Back when the land that was of the O'odham, belonged to the O'odham, when it was all desert. Back when we could be however we wanted. Today when we want to live in a particular place, they will tell us, "This is not your district."[8] And sometimes when we want to do something, they will tell us to ask for permission from some district or village representative. Yet this was not our way; we don't know how to do all this because it is not our way of life. The voting that goes on—we don't know how to vote because we don't fully understand it, again because it is not our way of life.]

K ʼaṣaba hemu geʼe haʼicu gm hu ʼi-t-waːkĭ g Milgaːn heg hekaj mo ʼab hema hab kaij mo haba masma mo ʼab hema t-oic keːk k hab kaij, "Dahiwañ," "Kekiwañ," "gam hab him," "ʼi-g hab hiːm." Pegi, kutp ʼam ʼa cem hekid hab kaij kuc ʼam hab t-juñhim. Hegai taṣ ʼab ñeid, cal- endar ʼab ñeid mat hascu wuḍ ʼo taṣkad kut hebai has ʼo cuʼikad. Mo hekĭ hu pi hab masma, kutt ṣaba pi has ʼo t-ju. Hekĭ ʼatt hu ʼam eḍa ʼi-waː, geʼe ʼam ʼeḍa ʼi-waː. Atp hu ʼi-cem t-Milgaːncud cʼeḍa pi maːc Milgaːn ñiʼokĭ.

[But now the Milgaːn has gotten us to accept many things. Perhaps it is true, as someone once said, that there is someone standing be- hind us and tells us to stand, we stand; tells us to sit, we sit; tells to go that way; tells us not to move. It seems that we are always being told what to do. We are constantly looking at the clock, looking at the calendar, looking to see what day it is and where we must be. Long ago it was not like this. But now what are we to do? We have now taken on so much of the other way of life; we are trying to be Milgaːn, yet we don't even know the English language well.]

Idam ʼañ hab ha-aːg ʼaʼal no hab hi g ha-geʼegeḍga. ʼAm ʼa hekĭ hu s-maːc nopı ʼam hekı hu ʼam ʼaːgĭm, ʼam ʼa hekı hu kaː. Amp hems pi

[I am mostly telling this to the children because the adults al- ready know, someone has already told you this. It may not have been

hab kai-dam ka:, hema hab 'o cei,
"Pi 'o hab hi ce'is, bac hi masma
ka:." K 'am 'a s-ape 'e:p.

told exactly like this one. Someone
might say, "This is not the way,
this is the way we heard it," but
that is fine.]

I'll say this first in O'odham.
We;peg 'am b 'o cei 'o'odham
ñi'okikaj 'ab 'amjeḍ'i:da mant hekid
i ge'eda k 'ab ka: i:da ñi'okĭ mo
hab kaij g keli o'odham, oks mat
'am t-na:to g t-na:toikam k an ce: g
jeweḍ k an da:m nato g da:m ka:cim
k ab we:nadk si wupuṣ an da:m
na:to g dodag cu:c ab ma: g himdag,
ab ma: g gewkdag, ab ma: g ceki-
toidag, am da:m na:to g us ke:g, ab
ma: g himdag, ab ma: g cekitoidag,
am da:m na:to g u'uwhig da'adam,
ab ma: g cekitoidag, ab mai: him-
dag, am da:m na:to g o'odham 'ab
ma: g cekitoidag, ab ma g: himdag,
ab ma: g gewkdag mat hascukaj o
e-ṣemac, ab ma: g ha'icu hugĭ mat
hascu o ku'ad 'o duakog an o'odham
jeweḍ da:m, hab masma i dagĭto,
t am hebai ce:k k dagĭto hegai natt
o s-cegĭtog, natt pi o cegĭtog, natt o
s-wohocudad, a natt pi o wohocu-
dad, natt o pi ha'icucud, natt o si
ha'icucud, that's the question I'll
ask.

[I'll say this first in O'odham. This
is from when I was growing up,
this is what the old men, women
would say: "When our creator
made us, and he made the Earth
and above it he made the sky and
he tied them together. And upon
it he made all the living things
and gave them a way of life and
gave them their work, their role.
And there he made the plants and
he gave them a way of life and
strength. And there he made the
flying birds and gave them their
way of life and gave them life, and
there he made man and gave him
life and gave him a way of thinking, living, and gave him capa-
bilities for him to support himself
with. He gave him food to eat so
that he may live here among the
land of the people, and this is the
way he left us. That is where things
began. This is the way he left us.
Will we remember this, or will we
forget? Will we believe it, or will
we not believe? Will we consider
it important, or will we consider it
unimportant? That is the question
I'll ask.]

Frances's Story

Frances Manuel is a Native American elder, a Tohono O'odham, or Desert Indian, as the people call themselves in English. Most Tohono O'odham live on one of three Arizona reservations totaling over two million acres, one-third the size of their land at the time of their discovery by the Spaniards in the sixteenth century. The Spaniards called the area including roughly present-day northern Sonora, Mexico, and southern Arizona, Pimería Alta. It is a seamless land that until recently knew no border. The Desert People have lived here for untold hundreds of years, gathering wild fruits and vegetables, hunting, and farming in a hot and often unpredictable desert.⁹ The Tohono O'odham language belongs to the Uto-Aztecan family, more closely related to Pima than to Yaqui and Hopi. Today most Tohono O'odham also speak English. At the time of this writing there are about twenty thousand Tohono O'odham living on three reservations and in cities in Arizona and elsewhere.

At the time of their discovery by the Spaniards and until the early decades of the twentieth century, the Tohono O'odham were an agricultural people, farming the harshest desert in North America. The weather in the Sonoran Desert can be capricious with cold nights and hot days, summer temperatures hovering over 100 degrees, torrential storms, droughts, and occasional floods. It is a vast and beautiful place, a land of wide valleys and low mountains, dominated by the giant saguaro, cholla, and prickly pear cactuses; mesquite, palo verde, and ironwood trees; creosote bush, saltbush, white bursage, and catclaw; and many species of animals and birds. Without perennial streams, the Tohono O'odham practiced flash-flood or akĭ ciñ (arroyo mouth) and de temporal (rainy weather) farming. Local summer rains collected in arroyos and ran through them onto the floodplains. Corn, beans, and squash were planted in July or August, with one harvest in October or November. Wild plants were gathered, deer and rabbit were hunted, and items were traded and exchanged. People lived in villages organized on the basis of parent and daughter villages, often migrating from summer fields to winter foothills to supplement their diets.¹⁰ By the turn of the twentieth century, many Tohono O'odham began to move out of the larger villages where they had found refuge during two hundred years of Apache wars. They returned to the scattered settlements of earlier times, isolated ranches and homesteads where they gathered wild foods,

worked their fields, celebrated harvests, and ranched, supplementing their in-
comes with wage work for Mexicans or the Milga:n (Americans). Ranching
was introduced by the Spaniards, and many Tohono O'odham living at that
time owned cattle and horses. Frances was born in Ko:m Wawhai, Arizona,
in 1912, the year after the Mexican Revolution began, and four years before
the reservation was established in 1916.[11] She soon moved with her father and
grandparents to S-koksonagk (Many Pack Rats), a farming homestead that
was a full day's ride by horse and buggy from Ko:m Wawhai, over miles of
difficult desert roads.

An only child, Frances lived an isolated childhood at S-koksonagk sur-
rounded by desert plants and animals, horses, and two aging grandparents,
with only the occasional presence of other children. Her first home there was
much like that of her ancestors, a dome-shaped brush house of mesquite covered with branches and grass, later replaced by a Mexican-style adobe structure. Playing alone, she made up games with horses, cactus, and the little birds,
developing a strong and playful imagination. Her grandmother taught her
to gather wild foods from the desert, to prepare fruits and vegetables, and to
perform the daily chores of cooking, washing, and hauling water. It was here
that she learned the ancient O'odham art of basket weaving. At S-koksonagk,
Frances learned what she calls the simple life, a way of being in the world which
has remained with her since childhood.

As she grew older, Frances watched the men in her family become increasingly involved in activities away from home, such as government wage work
and jobs on ranches and mines owned by Mexicans and the Milga:n. At boarding school, she was one of the first O'odham girls to receive an elementary education in English, at the same time forbidden to speak her native language. As
a young woman Frances relocated to San Pedro [Wiwpul, or Tobacco Weed],
the village of her husband, Jose, as was customary. It was here that Frances
bore her first three children. Frances and Jose were forced to move to Tucson to
look for work in 1941. Frances calls this "The Bad Year," one of many drought
years that decimated cattle and reduced O'odham harvests, a process compli-
cated by increasingly overgrazed land. Frances and Jose entrusted their children and fields to Jose's parents, and sent for their children later, never returning to farming. For thirty-nine years Frances performed domestic work in
town for the Milga:n, returning on occasional weekends and holidays to her
two-room adobe house in San Pedro.

When I first met her, Frances had been living in Tucson's Projects, over by Tenth Avenue and 20th Street. Before the Convention Center was built, it was just a short hop from Oracle to Main Street through downtown—she lived south in the multiethnic Tucson barrio, *and I lived north. Her husband had been gone for almost twenty-five years when we first met in 1977. Frances had been raising her six children in Tucson while cleaning houses, ironing, and selling tortillas. She started demonstrating basket weaving in Tucson schools in the 1960s, and that is how we met. In 1981 Frances retired permanently to San Pedro, where she lives today, near her daughter and several grandchildren.*

Frances's Life

Though there exists a strong tradition of storytelling among Frances's people, the life history genre—telling one's story to another person, who records it—is not part of O'odham tradition.[12] To place oneself apart as the center of attention runs counter to O'odham values of humility, and at times Frances has been uncomfortable with the process. "But I'm not so special!" she is fond of saying. Frances is very clear that the words she records pertain solely to her own experiences in the world and what she was taught by her elders. Her life and stories are not meant to be generalized to "the O'odham," but to be viewed as those of one person within a culture that allows for variations on a core set of themes, beliefs, and practices, within a world that is both traditional and rapidly changing.[13] Frances is, in some ways, not representative of other O'odham. What might be a little different about Frances is her deliberate engagement in friendship across cultures and her role as a self-conscious preserver of O'odham culture. She has conducted basket-weaving workshops and demonstrations around the nation, and has worked to revive and promote O'odham dance and music. This is in addition to her work with youth and the elderly, and her speeches and cultural presentations within the community and across the country. Frances is known among some of her people as "a person who has traveled all over."[14]

Raised by her grandparents "in the middle of nowhere," Frances has grown up to be fiercely independent even as she practices traditional values. Although the values she was raised with remain her foundation, Frances has always been an independent thinker. "As a child," she says, "I learned the Mexican ways from my father, who was working for the Mexicans at the time. He taught me to ask questions, to get answers for myself. That's why I'm so curious about everything."

I, too, have become accustomed to being outside of my cultural milieu, and have traveled around. Each of us, in her own way, is committed to communicating difference. We believe voices and lives matter. Frances and I have discovered that we are really more alike than we are different. We share the goal of telling a life story and passing it on to future generations. The combination of the two of us may be unique as life histories go; we are really close friends.[15] And Frances is not your quintessential O'odham; the quintessential O'odham does not exist. Stereotypes of Indians have been created by non-Indians.[16]

A Chronology

December 6, 1912: Frances Blaine is born to Si'al Memḍa (John Blaine) and Amelia Lopez in Ko:m Wawhai, Arizona.

1913: Frances relocates with her parents and grandparents (E-o'oho/Jose and Salomina Francisco) to a farm at S-koksonagk, Arizona.

1914: Frances's mother, Amelia Lopez, dies; cause unknown.

1927: Frances and her grandfather, E-o'oho, move to Santa Rosa Ranch following the death of Frances's grandmother, Salomina.

May 6, 1930: Frances Blaine marries Jose Manuel and moves to San Pedro, Arizona.

1941: "The Bad Year." Following a severe drought that killed most of their cattle, Frances and her husband, Jose, relocate to Tucson to look for work.

1953: Frances's husband, Jose Manuel, is killed in a hit-and-run accident in Tucson.

1981: Frances's new house is finished, and Frances moves back to San Pedro to live.

Awards and Recognition

At the request of Frances's family, we have included a list of awards Frances has received in recognition of and appreciation for her work. There is much that is not listed—for example, the fact that Frances, while raising six children as a single mother, took on three teenage foster children in the 1960s, and Frances's work with the elderly at the St. Nicholas Center. Frances has been awarded over fifteen ribbons for basket weaving, dollmaking, and cooking, and has given numerous basket-weaving demonstrations, workshops, and dance/singing performances with the Desert Indian Dancers, throughout the reservation and across the United States. The awards that hang on her walls at San Pedro include the following:

Parents and staff of San Xavier Mission and the Papago Tribe, "in appreciation for the caring love which has enlightened our children in the awareness of O'odham heritage."

Arizona-Sonoran Desert Museum Sense of Place Project, "Arizona Living Treasure—1977. Keeper of the Desert Treasure," for working to keep the unique knowledge of the Sonoran Desert alive.

Save the Children: Schuk Toak Youth Tohono O'odham Alcoholism Program, for outstanding service.

The Desert Indian Dancer Youth, for fostering pride, "Distinguished Tohono O'odham Basketweaver," 1991.

The Desert Indian Dancers of Wak, for organizing the dance group in 1988. "Because of your efforts and knowledge of O'odham culture, the youth feel good about themselves."

The American Indian Association and the Tucson Indian Center, from the Tucson Indian community, in recognition of the preservation of culture, 1987.

Part I ◈ S-koksonagk (Many Pack Rats), 1913–1930

Growing Up

[Slowly] I found the truth about my LIFE,
how I was growing up
when I found out about
the vows my grandmother made for me
.
Maybe I was about three years when I had
[softly] whooping coughs
.
And my grandmother was a
very
  very
religious person
.
She made
  a vow
and she said that
she took me to Magdalena
asked St. Francis to let me live
.
And then she said
I was gonna be a simple person
.
I lived
I was gonna be a simple person
so I am a simple person now
.
And then later on
that must be the same thing she asked for Blessed Mother
[slowly] Virgin
  Mary
to
also make me live
and in return
I was always gonna have LONG HAIR
.
SO I have long hair now.
  (1981)

My entrance into Frances's world happened gradually. In a literal sense, it didn't begin until I made that first trip with Frances from South Tucson to the reservation. Now, when I drive out to see her, the forty-minute drive is my transition from the world of the town and all of its accoutrements, a ritual sojourn into the heart of the desert. As it happens now, when I pass Old Ajo Way, I tend to breathe more slowly and fully as I take in the surrounding desert, and the mountains on all sides. Off to the left is Baboquivari, the home of legendary I'itoi, the O'odham Big Brother from the time of the Beginning. And ahead, just off to the right, Kitt Peak National Observatory, built in 1958 by the Milga:n. I start to notice little things: a plastic bag stuck to a cactus blowing in the wind, or a dead coyote lying on the side of the street. Closer to my destination, the mountains are rolling and undulating in smooth, dotted contours, with an occasional saguaro in the distance. I pass brightly decorated crosses on the side of the road, commemorating those who died there. Many people have died there, mostly in alcohol-related car accidents or hit while walking. The crosses are both beautiful and sad.

Almost there, I pause by the old San Pedro road, out of habit—that old ten-minute road whose potholes made it impassable during heavy monsoons. I turn off by Johnny's store, and feel the quiet. I turn the radio off, and open the window. As I pass her, I salute Blessed Mother on the left, noticing the familiar sights and dramatic play of light and shadow on the hill. Each landmark has its story—Jimmy's disappearing rock, the dancing cactus, the rock on top of the hill that looks like an old shelter. The village is situated in a rich ecozone of saguaro, ocotillo, sage, prickly pear, wildflowers. . . . I enter by the corral and, passing the church, reach Frances's home.

It was early winter in 1981 when Frances and I finally started tape-recording her story. The scene was typical of what would come later, Frances and I sitting at her kitchen table in San Pedro with my tape recorder between us, Frances with her hands folded on the table, ready to speak. On cool winter days like this one, there is a fire burning in the living room fireplace. Frances is wearing her customary blue calico dress and a navy blue sweater; her hair is pulled back with hairpins in the usual way—long, mostly black hair with roots of white and gray. "Is it [the tape recorder] on?" she asks. Frances talks to me, and then to the small tape recorder, switching easily to her imagined audience— her family, students, and the people who might read her book "a hundred years from now."

1 ◇ Simple Things

We were poor
.
I had no shoes
two dresses
never had anything!
I'm
very
PROUD of it so .
I'd like somebody to read it
.
[softly] after I'm gone.
    (1985)

My married name is Frances Manuel and my maiden name is Frances Blaine. I was born at Ko:m Wawhai on December sixth, 1912. Of course I didn't know then, my father didn't tell me. But one day I met up with this man who was born two days later, so I figured it out—my birthday is December sixth.[1] When my mother died, I was very young, so I never did know what a mother is—my grandmother raised me. My grandfather's Indian name was E-o'oho [Painting Himself], and later it was Jose Francisco. My grandmother was Salomina, I guess she didn't have an Indian name. My father's name was Si'al Memḍa, that's "Early Morning Runner."[2] My mother's name was Amelia.

I was raised by my grandparents in a village called S-koksonagk—Many Pack Rats.[3] We moved there in 1913. We lived in the middle of nowhere in the desert. The nearest village was about thirty miles away—I think it's now called Kwin's Well. We were very poor, but we were happy—I was happy! I didn't have any pretty clothes, I didn't have an extra pair of shoes, sometimes I didn't have any shoes! I learned to ride horses; my grandparents were old, and I didn't have any playmates. So I learned to ride horses, they were my playmates.

When I was growing up, I learned to entertain myself, I learned to talk to cactus, I talked to trees, mesquite trees, I'd talk to whatever I'd find crawling on the ground. Or I talked to birds—not that they talked back to me, but I talked to them. I talked to my horse. That was a very happy life because they didn't answer back! Nowadays you talk to someone and they talk back, sometimes they give you a smart answer and it upsets you. But at that time, there was nothing, nothing to upset me.

You may think when you read this that I was just a lonely Indian girl, but I was not. I had my own entertainment, and I was very busy. I didn't have time to get lonely because I was very busy! I talked to animals, named the cactus, named the birds, named their nests, just to entertain myself! I was thinking about my play life. When I didn't have a horse, you know what I did? I would play follow the leader. I used to go round and round and round, you know, I just played make-believe. And I would play with those barrel cactus. I would make little horses, I make little men. I make, you know, all kinds of things and just play with them. I put legs on them, too, with cactus fruit. I used to play with the weeds, too. When the weeds came out, I used to pull them up and make little ladies. The roots would be the hair, and they were my dolls. I used to make dolls sometimes out of rags, steal some of my grandmother's material and make dolls. When she got to sewing, she'd miss them and bawl me out, but I did the same thing next time. And I used to plant gardens, like little cactus, cactus with flowers. We call it '*i:swig* [hedgehog cactus],[4] and we call it *ban ce:kol* [fishhook cactus],[5] everything that blooms about this time. It would be so beautiful in front of the house. Oh, I used to have pretty gardens! My grandfather got mad at me for having all those things in front. There's a tree that I would put them around. I liked to look at them because they were so pretty.

Sometimes when I was cooking, I used to make believe—that makes it easier to do, easier to work. I used to wash on my washboard. Like I'd say, "One two three four five six seven eight nine ten eleven twelve thirteen fourteen fifteen sixteen seventeen eighteen nineteen twenty!" The clothes would be cleaner, they seem cleaner that way. I made my own entertainment, so it was never a dull life. Now, when I think back . . . [slowly, thoughtfully] I was growing up alone and never did see other things, know other things, or play with any other children.

I was an only child, but I had a half brother, Johnny, and two half sisters, Suzie and Juanita. My father had three daughters after my mother died— Marie, Pauline, and Millie—but they didn't live there. I don't know how old I was, but my father got married right after my mother died. He married this little woman [Frances's stepmother] with three children. One girl died, so I got three stepsisters. I had two uncles, my father's brothers, and some cousins—my father's sisters' sons. I don't know why, but they were always there [at S-koksonagk], training horses or doing something. I started playing with my stepsisters when I was older, about eight years old. Sometimes there would be just one and sometimes there would be two of them. The youngest one was raised by her grandmother, too, another grandmother. I saw Johnny at the rodeo some time back, he was just standing there, but he didn't see me. Later somebody said he was looking for me, but I never got to talk to him. I used to play with them when I was eight or nine. So it never entered my mind what the kids think of now, I never even thought about a car! But I would pretend I owned this horse and that horse, and pretty soon I had about twenty horses! I was pretending! Imagination! Later on, I learned about processions, you know, the fiestas of saints, and I played that, too. I made a little arch and all those pretty colors. I didn't have any ribbons—now I have a lot of ribbons. I wish I was a little girl!

I made animal dolls, too, and a little corral. And I made mud pies and little mud people. When I got tired, I would do something else. Nowadays they don't play like that. Now when they get tired of toys, they smash them. I never did that—I put them away, you know? When I was out riding, I'd count something that I'd see, the first thing I'd see. I'd see a lizard, I'd say, "Well, I saw one lizard, and I have to see ten lizards before I turn back." And that's the way I would go farther, and farther, and farther, until I saw them. Sometimes I wouldn't see ten lizards, maybe about five, or eight. And I never did count the birds because the birds were always there. Sometimes I saw a rabbit and I'd say, "Well, I have to see ten rabbits before I turn back!" You know [laughing], sometimes I didn't even see another one.

Don't get me wrong, I worked. I learned to grind the wheat on the metate, I learned to make tortillas, I learned to cook everything, I learned what there is to eat from the desert, I learned a lot of things. My grandmother must be a very wise woman—she taught me a lot. Up to this day, things she said fit into a pattern. So that's why I call her a wise woman. She was like a mother to me, I thought she was my mother until I got a little older and found out that she was my grandmother.

We'll talk about my mother. My mother came from—well, at that time they called the place Ge Pi:ckim. Well, that's what my grandmother told me.

It's near Hermosillo [Sonora, Mexico].⁶ My mother's father was Antonio
Lopez. And this lady that was in Tucson must have come to Tucson before my mother, because she was my mother's godmother. She told me she
brought her to Tucson from Mexico. So she stayed with her there, working
for people, doing washing and ironing. In October my people go to Magdalena for the pilgrimage where we worship St. Francis. So I guess my godmother brought my mother from there. My grandmother told me that one
night my father came home with this young lady, they came home on horseback. So I guess she started living there, in the place called Ko:m Wawhai.
[Slowly] And they roam around these big, wide open spaces and they finally
end up at a place called S-koksonagk. They make their farm there, they farm
there, and my grandfather farms there. That's where my mother was, and
then later a mine was opened near Ko:m Wawhai and so my father went to
work there. That's when I was coming, I guess. I was on the way.

Later on, my other grandfather and grandmother were going to Magdalena to worship St. Francis. My mother told them, "You ask for Antonio
Lopez, that's my father, and if you find him say, "*Si s-ap ñ-ta:tk.*" Well, at
that time, we didn't have a word for hello or things like that, but the Indian
word means "to think of me kindly." So my grandfather asks around, and
finally, they found him and told him [softly] that his daughter was still alive.
They lost touch when she married my father, because there was no way to
know where she is. She moved out and was way far from town on the Papago
reservation. So from then on, I guess they kept in touch. I don't know if
they told him when she was dying, my grandmother didn't talk about it.

But anyway, she went to live with my father there. He was working and at
that time there weren't many people there. Of course there were people at
the bigger villages farther up or farther down, but there was only one other
family living at S-koksonagk at that time. When I came in December, one
lady was living there, that lady was a midwife. So that's the one who delivered me. Her name was Mrs. Francisco, a relative who married my grandfather's brother. They said my mother never really got well after I was born,
she was sickly off and on. [Softly] I guess when she got worse, she told my
grandmother to take me and raise me, that maybe someday I'll be a good
helper. [Laughing, thoughtfully] I think I was, and, so, that's where I grew
up. At one time my mother asked my grandmother to look in her trunk
and get her organdy skirt and blouse out, I guess that's what she wanted to
be buried in. My grandmother told me that one night she got worse, so my

grandfather . . . [Frances' voice fades out.] Usually, if we are going to travel fast, we hitch four horses, so that's what my grandfather did, traveled all night, I guess. And, well, this is what I was told, because my father had to stay. So he got the lumber and the material, whatever they think my mother would like to wear, and took it to San Xavier Mission where there's a lady, a lady related to my grandfather, to do the sewing, and her husband made the coffin.[7] The clothes that were sewn were buried with her in her casket. At that time the coffins were beautifully made—I saw when I was grown, it's big and wide around. That man made the coffin.

My grandfather got there in the morning, and I guess they shopped around, shopped around until the evening, then worked all night on the coffin. In the morning it was finished, all those clothes were finished, and he traveled home. [Very softly] But she was already gone. That's what I was told. My grandmother was with her. She's buried between S-koksonagk and Kwin's Well, in the middle of nowhere. Sometimes I want to go there. Mildred [Frances's second daughter] said she was going to take me over there, but the roads are so bad that nobody travels over there.

Later on, I realized that sometimes when it's cloudy, I get lonely. My grandmother told me where my mother was buried. Up to this day, I don't know why, but I get lonely when it's cloudy and dark. When I was growing up, I'd saddle the horse and go to the grave of my mother, I'd sit on top of mother's grave. [Slowly, thoughtfully] It took me back to my childhood when I was a little girl, when I learned to ride horses. I remember where it was, where the grave was. And when I saw the sticks—there was a low fence, broken, and the barbed wire was still there—it made me sad, but glad, too, because all this time I wanted to go see my mother's grave. I don't know whether it made me feel good, or what, but I always did that. And I came home feeling better. And I'm planning to make a cross someday and take it over and put it there. That's how I feel about it. And wherever my mother is right now, she knows that I still remember her, I'll always remember her grave.

Later I went to Ko:m Wawhai with my husband and saw the piles of dirt that was my house where I was born. We call the place ma:s, it's like a footprint, it means "the place I was born." So I was telling him, "This is where I was born," and I said, ma:s, and he said, "Well, I guess your footprint isn't there anymore."

I guess that's when I started living with my grandmother. I was living close anyway, so I started living with my grandmother—she raised me. And I grew up. My grandmother always said I was seven months old when she [my mother] died. Later I found out I was a year and seven months, but still I was a baby. I was told that my mother said, "Be sure and put my shoes on, so that whenever I come to this world, you will hear my footsteps."

My uncle heard them. She had a petticoat, they used to called it *satín*. She has a petticoat so he could hear the skirt make noise and footsteps, you know. He was laying under the *ramada*, and he could hear her walking under the wall, footsteps, and the dogs started barking, I guess [they] chased her away. He told my grandmother in the morning, "Last night a woman came, I could hear her skirt and footsteps." Right away she thought of my mother, that one day she would come back . . . [Frances's voice fades out.]

This is about my father. My father lived there for a while while I was growing up. My father got married, but they still lived there. I loved my father, so anytime we had to go to his house, I would stand at the door until my father would make me a bean or rabbit sandwich. I don't know why, but if my father makes me a sandwich, it tastes so good! And then I'd go home. My grandmother didn't want me to do that because my stepmother didn't like me—I won't say she was mean. But I always did that until they moved away to another village, Baboquivari. He worked for a man at a plantation there—fruit trees. My father was a good gardener. He would still come to see me once in a while, maybe bring me a pair of shoes, or a piece of material so I could make myself a dress. It went on like that. And, um, and he had these children, my brother and my three sisters. One of them died. She died from drinking too much, left eight children behind.

I think my grandmother taught me every single thing that's in life. I think she was very wise. I remember her when she talked to me: If I did something wrong, I'd look around, and she'd be yelling at me, she says I had to look different when she's talking to me. Most of the time I listened, but sometimes I didn't feel like listening. I'd feel, "What is she talking about?" We'd be working, cleaning together, or I'd be working on my baskets. She'd sit and cook in the morning and she'd sit there after lunch, and then get up and do something, like work on her baskets. She always worked on her baskets. [Frances yawns] I remember she used to say, "Sit down and work on your basket!" And I used to hate it, I just wanted to go to the range or the water hole or play outside. I'd want to play, but she'd make me make baskets. I guess she figured how much time I should be working on my baskets, because she would say, "Okay, go do what you want to do!" And I'd say, "I'm gonna go riding!" Hmmm. It's a good thing we had a big pasture. The horses are there all the time and they'd come home to drink water. In the morning when they come I'll put my riding horse in the corral so he'd be there in case she lets me ride the horse. So I look forward to the time when she'd say, "Okay, go play!"

I was her leg; she called me, I'd get her water, or salt or something. Sometimes I'd be outside, and she'll be yelling for me. And then she'll say, "What's the matter with your eyes, you don't see good?" "Right there!" Sometimes James [Frances's grandson] does the same thing, I'll get so mad at him. And then when it was planting season, we used to pull the weeds, and she'd make me go over there and do something for her. If I'm lazy . . . you know it'd be hot, sometimes those little field bugs would be on our shirts, we'd be hot and it'll be all over us, and something else that bites. . . . Oh, I used to hate it. "Come on, you're slow!" she'd say. Then pretty soon she'll say, "Okay, you can go!" Off I'd go. I used to go to the water hole all the time. Like this morning I was looking at those little horses, and I said, "Oh, they are playing." I was just looking at them, and I remembered what my grandmother told me years and years ago—I remember that. I love horses. And I love to hear them, when they start walking, they make little funny noise. My grandmother used to say they say, "Brother, Brother," or "Sister, Sister," when they want something to eat, they think you are going to feed them. I don't like to hear them because sometimes I'm not going to feed them, and I feel sorry for them.

We had a lot of saddle horses. I never had one horse I called mine [that was mine], even though I'd call it mine. It was a pretty horse and it was a gentle horse—a gelding. I would have to ask my grandparents if I could ride it, because I had to do my work. I would do my work fast and then go out riding. I'd just go out riding. Sometimes the horse would be in the open range, and I'd get to miss him so much. And then pretty soon somebody would bring them in and the horse would be with them. So right away my grandmother used to get after me because I would feed him, and here he's not doing anything, he's not doing any work. I fed him hay and barley, that's all. Life went on until, as I said, things happened to me, weird things that I don't understand. Well, I do understand, but I don't know how to explain it.

One day, now this is weird. One day, I was about eleven, I went out on my horse. There were a lot of water holes filled with water, because it was the rainy season, I went looking for the horses. I knew they went out looking for the water hole, so I followed them, for some reason that was the place I traveled most every day. I knew the places in the desert, but that day I got lost. I was looking for the water hole and there was this hill by a mountain, and I looked up there and saw a form on horseback way up on top of the mountain. And I thought, "Somebody must be looking for their horse, too, from Kwin's Well," and that's all I remember. I was going back and forth, back and forth. Where is the water hole? Where are the horses? Where are they? Then finally I went to sleep on the horse. I dropped the reins and the horse was just eating away and went under a tree, and the mesquite tree hit me in my face and I woke up. I got down and took the reins, I walked a little bit. There was the water hole, I had just been going round and round it. So I went home. I knew where the horses were but I didn't want to go after them, so I just went home. I arrived at the house where we saddle our horses and took the saddle down, didn't even put it away, I just went to sleep. My grandmother came, kicking my feet, "You are sleeping under the ramada." I had a headache, I don't understand why. That's all I remember. I saw the man, I got lost, got on the horse, and went to sleep.

I still remember the position of the horse. The man was sitting with the purple shirt like Pancho Villa, I remember that's how the horse was standing up. I was about eleven when I went to sleep on that horse.[8] To this day I still think about what my grandmother said when I told her about this — that I like so much, love horses so much. She said that on that mountain there lived beautiful horses and with their power [gewkdag], they want me. That's what my grandmother said. I never did believe it, but maybe it was something. Because I can only go to this when I die. I can't do anything else when I die. I could be a horse, I could be one of those ladies who shows horses, or a trick rider. But maybe it was true, because when I was growing up, I used to get so mad. I wanted to be a boy so I could be with the horses the whole time. That's the only answer. I never took what she said seriously—maybe it's true, maybe it isn't. But when Pancho Villa was put in the park [in downtown Tucson], one time when I was sitting in the bus, I saw it. That's the way the horse looked when he was standing there. I don't know, but I looked up and there was the man. I had such a headache. It's so strange because I never had that before.

I never thought of anything like young girls would dream of. I never did! The only thing I was wishing for was I wish I was a boy! And I could go with them when they go for roundup, and camp out. To me, it looked fun, that's all. I never dreamed anything else! And I hear stories, a lot of stories about a lot of things, some things I don't even remember. But there's one story. After I got to town, I worked and met a lot of different people, different kinds of people—black, Mexican, and all those. One Mexican lady told me about this story and I thought it was very interesting. I always remember that story. Remember? This is one of the stories we always told going in the car, trying to scare each other.

These four men were going to the dance. There was a place where they dance. It was just an open space but with a fence around it, and a gate where they go in and pay ten cents to dance. These men were just there to have fun, and they saw a beautiful girl in a long dress. She was beautiful and she was a good dancer. So they were sitting, watching the dance, and one of the men said, "Look, the lady's got one foot like a horse's hoof!" But this man didn't see it, so they went on dancing, and finally the dancing was over and they found her standing on the road. They stopped and asked her where she was going, and she told them where to let her off. They went by a cemetery and she said to let her off there, so they did. And one of them looked back and saw it was nothing but a skeleton. That was the second man. And they got home the next day and this man was so curious, so he went back to where they let her off. Something happened, something just led him into the cemetery, and he found the dress on top of the grave. Friday came along, and the one that was dancing with her died. A month later the one that saw her horse hoof died, too, and I guess a few months [Frances inhales deeply][9] later, this man who saw the dress died in an accident. The only one left didn't see anything, he didn't look back, he didn't see the foot, so he was safe. So I guess it's better not to be nosy. So I remember that when she told me. I hear a lot of stories, they seem to be different; this is the way I heard it. I guess I liked it, that's why I remember it.

There's another one I liked, where this lady's husband left her. She had two kids. I guess she got mad and felt like killing the kids, so she did, she killed the two kids and threw them into the pigpen. The pigs ate the whole thing, bones and all. I guess she died, I don't know how she died, but she went to wherever the children went, and St. Peter told her she couldn't go in. He said she had to find her children's bones and show them to them before they can let her in. So she can always be heard by the river, by an old ranch, crying for her kids. A lot of people hear her crying all the time, looking for her children's bones.[10]

When we were kids, we used to tell stories, too. This was at San Pedro. Remember I told you? We used to come here because my grandmother had these two ladies who were married to one man. I guess she would come to see them and we'd just play here. There were a lot of kids, like Alice's aunt, and Rita, and, ahm, Margaret, and myself. And there was a young boy named Listo and my cousin, Juan—Jose Juan, they called him—and Pete, another cousin, and Nelson, and Jose Miguel, that man's father right there [Frances points to a neighbor's house]. There would be a lot of them. We would sit around outside in the dark by the wash behind the feast house and tell stories. This boy was telling us about a story that supposedly happened, but it sounded too good. This man was going to some other village, and he went and stayed. He stayed and he stayed and finally he came home. He was coming home at night, and pretty soon he heard this noise, like somebody was coming up behind him. So he looked back, but there was nobody behind him, so he started going again. And, ahm, and then he turned around and he said, "Where are you? Who are you? Why are you following me?" And pretty soon there was this man standing there, standing there like when you put something in the fire, it gets so hot, it gets red. He was like that. So he turned around and started running his horse so hard, and when he'd look back, he'd still be there with that hot-iron face. [Softly] It went on and on like this until he got home. So he told his parents about this, what happened, so the medicine man who was called in, came, and this medicine man told him that it was the devil. The devil, that's what we tell each other, you know. To me it was a made-up story, but I think what we were trying to do was to see which of us would tell the best made-up story. It was fun at the time. And we'd be scared, we'd be moving closer and closer to each other. We'd sit around and tell all those things. And somebody would tell a really silly story, where you can really tell it's a made-up story, and we'd say "Yah!" and they'd stop. That was a lot of fun. And sometimes we'd try to sing songs, but I guess we couldn't make up the songs. It was lots of fun. And then right in the middle of the really fun parts they'd call us, "Come in, come in, it's late!" So we'd break up and go inside.

One time we went to Baboquivari,[11] just me and my friend, Mary, and we were peeping through there at the graves, you know we used to bury our people in the rocks. And there was a man with a gun and we were saying it must be a soldier, and the next one was a lady, because it had a lot of hair. And I guess there was little kids, because there was those little bones. And we were peeping at all of them, and then we got all the way back to our horse and started going. My friend said, "Are you scared?" and I said, "No, I'm not scared." And we said, "Let's run," and we let the horse run, and it threw us off on the way. Then we got headaches—oh, we felt sick, and we went home and got to bed and I had a nightmare. There was a man coming, had a band on his head with blood, and he was coming, moaning, going "Ugh," and I was trying to yell but I couldn't yell, so that was my nightmare. Okay, turn it [the tape recorder] off.

How we grew up? We were not allowed to talk back to the grown-ups. Whatever they tell you, you just listen, no matter how you feel. My grandmother would preach to me about a lot of things and my grandfather would preach at me, too. Those two people, all they would do is preach. And a lot of times I didn't like it. I used to think they were mad at me. I used to think, "Why are they always getting mad at me?" That was what I thought. Now I know they were preaching to me. My grandfather used to say, "Open your ears, listen. Run. Grind, work, run. Do not be idle! [Ab g 'i-ha-ku:kpi'ok g 'e-na:nk, 'ab 'o ñ-kaihamad, k 'o 'e-melc. cu'iwañ g pilkañ, ha'icu g cikpan, 'e g melcud, pi g'am 'e-paḏmacud!]." We had speeches like that. Sometimes four o'clock in the morning—I used to be mad at him, I wish he'd be quiet so I could sleep. He'd say, "Get up and run, so someday if you need to go fast, it would save your life. Go and run, maybe some bird or powerful thing will give you power. Some thing will give you power [Mat 'ab ha'icu o m-ma: g 'e-gewkdag]." That's what he used to say.

My grandmother would tell me little things, or show me what has to be done. Later, when I was growing up, there was one thing they never told me about—the birds and the bees. I never did hear about the sex life, that was one thing they never did talk about. There must be a reason for that.

I know I may think so good about my grandparents, they are so good. But we had our problems. Oh, when I was growing up, the first time I heard these boys playing guitar, violin, little drum, and big drum, I was so interested. So I went with another girl, we went peeping through a hole where they had a little house with ocotillo walls, you could see in. So we went and we were peeping through, watching them playing, and my grandmother saw me and told me to go home. She spanked me so hard, and I thought, "What had I done?" I was just peeping, watching the boys playing. But I guess that was bad.

Another time, we used to come to the San Xavier Mission to cut wheat for the people, so we can take some wheat home. Whenever we got through husking, they gave us sacks of wheat. I was young, it was San Juan's day, and this lady—she is seventy years old now—she was going to go to a dance. She wanted me to go, and I wanted to go, too. I guess my grandpa and my grandmother went somewhere, they didn't come home and they didn't come home. So I didn't ask them, I just went with her. And we stayed at that and it was in the morning we came home. My grandmother was so mad. She was at least talking to me, but my grandfather wasn't talking. And it was like that—life was like that. Sometimes my grandfather would get mad at my grandmother and wouldn't talk for weeks. When they started talking, I was so glad, I would be so glad, I wished it was like that all of the time. Our life was like that.

My grandmother, she must be a tough woman, because she didn't care if my grandfather talked or not, she just went about her business. Sometimes I wanted to have my grandfather away, because when he was away, we had a nice time, we just did whatever we wanted. We talked, we sang, and did whatever things that were fun for us. But when he came, sometimes he would be mad. We won't be talking so we'd all be quiet, we couldn't even move. We couldn't even sing.

Once I heard my grandfather telling my grandmother, telling her that they were going to go home, that they weren't going to take me with them because I was dirty, I was dirt. My grandmother cried and said to me, "We're going to go, but you follow us on foot. You're not going to stay here, you'll follow us on foot. You are going to get there." And she gave me a sandwich and a canteen of water, so I thought, "Well, I'd rather die of thirst or hunger, but I'll walk." Because I was mad, I hadn't done anything! So they left early in the morning, had a saddle horse, and they tied the horse on the wagon and started going. So every time they went fast, the horse would break the rope and run away, and they'd stop and look for it, and I'd hide. And when they start going, I followed them again. So I didn't go very far and my grandfather . . . I guess he knew I was following them. Finally he said, "Oh, come on and take the horse." I was glad, so I got caught up with them and I took the horse and I went, I was just behind. I don't know why. I don't know why I didn't feel bad at the time they were getting after me for going to the dance,[12] I didn't feel bad. But at that time, after I got on the horse and started going, I felt so bad, I cried. It didn't do any good, but I was crying. So life was like that.

One day we were going to go to town. We were raising chickens and we were going into town to sell some chickens and some baskets my grandmother made. We were coming, and on the way something happened, they were mad [Frances laughs]. We stopped, and one of the hens got away, and we were all chasing it. Finally my grandfather caught up with the hen. [Frances is still laughing] Boy, you should see that hen with the feathers flying. I ran away. He killed the chicken right there and he was spanking us so hard. My grandmother must have told my uncle, and they made fun of that. So that was another life.

My grandfather was real strict. There were times he would get mad at my grandmother. One time we were going. We just had one horse and sometimes he would just stand there, we'd try to make him go and he wouldn't go. One time I was trying to make him go and he was trying to push the wagon. He got the whip and whipped my grandmother, whipped me, and somehow the horse started going. It's kind of funny the way he spanked us and the horse started going! [Frances laughs] My grandparents loved me, but they never did show any affection. I must have loved them. I know I loved my grandmother, I must have loved my grandfather, too.

I told you, Debbie, we used to go to town. They always had four horses. I started doing that when I was eleven, by myself driving four horses. Two wagons because we had wood to sell, each wagon takes a cord. My grandmother knew where to sell it. We would buy groceries to go home, we used to buy at a Chinaman's store in South Tucson. After I got married, we used to buy from him, too. He always had the baby on his back, we used to call him *Ali Cu:kcug* [Chinaman], the baby on his back. And they'd give us candy after we'd shop there, I guess that's why we liked to shop there.

It took all day. If we bed down someplace close, we used to go from that side of that mountain, we used to get the road by the Bug Allen Ranch, this side, going to Three Points. Sometimes we'd sleep there. Or if we started real early in the morning, we might get to town at five. We had to rest the horses midafternoon. We watered them at Robles Ranch, what is now Three Points—just the two of us, me and grandfather. It's not that I really liked going. They went maybe once a month. They'd buy flour, coffee, sugar. We didn't buy any beans because we had our own; no eggs, no bacon, maybe sometimes a steak. Chuck steak cost fifteen cents a pound and a twenty-pound sack of flour was fifty cents. Sometimes we'd get a can of pork and beans, at that time it was real good. And maybe a loaf of bread, like French bread, that we'd just eat. Those days are just gone.

Don't say it's so interesting! As I told you, Debbie, I wasn't gonna tell all good. But I didn't do all bad, I did what any kid would do. We used to go to a village called Akĭ Ciñ. I don't know what they call it in English, but they call it Akĭ Ciñ. My grandfather does work for those people, building corrals and hauling water, and we lived there for maybe two months. And there were kids, and we used to play with them. And one time my grandmother and another friend went away somewhere, and we were playing at the house under the ramada, and we were wrestling, we were doing things. I don't know which one of us pushed against an old big pottery, an old *olla*. We pushed it and down came the water and the pottery, all over the ramada. And we looked at each other and we said, "They're gonna get after us!" And there was an old cow around the back, just eating away, so we thought, we're gonna blame it on that cow. So we started chasing that cow to get it to go through the ramada so it'll have tracks on it, and the cow won't go. And the cow will go this way—there were five of us, two boys and three of us girls. It'll go the other way, and we'll get her back and try to make her go through and just out the other way—no. And finally we're still yelling at the cow, "Ha ha!" and it'll go the other way. [Frances is laughing hard] So this man came along on horseback and he said, "What are you doing?" And we said, "We're just playing!" And he said, "With a cow?" [Laughing] And, ah, so when he came around, the cow saw the horse and the man, and he looked like he was chasing us, and we ran every which way because we were scared.

So later in the afternoon my grandmother and her friend came and she said, [in a high, loud voice] "What happened to my pottery? Who did this?" And I was gonna say, "a cow," and I said, "We did, we did." Oh, boy, they bawled us out. Every time my grandmother would tell somebody, they'd call me "nutso." I don't know what it means, whether it means crazy or stupid or clumsy.

So another time, my grandmother—it was the same place but maybe another year—my grandmother told me to take something to our neighbor. It was far. Maybe as far, farther, than those people on the other side. So it was the rainy season and there are water holes all over. So we went [I went with my friend], and we started playing in the water, and pretty soon we were swimming with our clothes on. And we got up, and we took our clothes off and hung them, and we put the thing that we were supposed to take on the dike, and we forgot about it. I don't remember what it was. And after our clothes got barely dry we went home. And my grandmother said [in a high pitch], "What was she doing?" "Nothing." "What did she say?" "Nothing." And then we said we were hungry, and she said, "Didn't they give you anything to eat? You were there all day!" "No." Then we started eating. And then this man came with that thing, said he found it on the dike. And they found out we didn't go. Oh, she was mad. And then we covered our food, because she might say not to eat, and we were so hungry. Those are the two things that I remember that we did wrong, not really wrong, but wrong for them at that time.

I just thought of something. When I was growing up, we used to go to Ko:m Wawhai, where I was born, and we lived there for several months because my grandmother had some cattle there. Anyway, one year we went at Christmastime. It was the first time I knew Christmas. They had a dinner, they had prayers and sang songs—not that I understood the songs, they were in Spanish. But anyway, there were some little mourning doves, a few apples, and oranges. I wanted to have some, so my grandmother said if I stayed up until three o'clock, I could have some. So I did stay up—I was so sleepy, but I wanted those things, so I stayed up. We waited, and we waited; I thought three o'clock would never come. Then they started praying and singing songs, and after that they passed the fruit and the little mourning dove biscuits, and I ate as much as I could. Well, the next morning they gave out the Christmas presents. One lady gave me a belt. It was an old used belt, but I thought it was something! I had it for a long time, until I couldn't use it anymore. I still remember that first Christmas, so when Christmas comes around, I always think about this. I am sorry that we spoiled our kids. Just because the next-door neighbor bought their children expensive presents, we want to do the same thing! Kids don't know about Christmas, only the presents, how much and how many presents they are going to get. That's no Christmas spirit, I'd say.

My grandmother taught me a lot of things, but she never told me about dressing, so I never knew how to dress. I just wore whatever was brought in to me. So it went on. I never worry about wishing for pretty clothes. Well, I didn't know there was pretty clothes. I never did wish for anything. Then, later on, when I went to school, I went to work, went to work for people and earned my own money. That's when I thought I changed. I liked pretty clothes. I liked combs and barrettes, and beads and pins. I thought I liked that, but it didn't last long—it wasn't me! It was just somebody else. So I went back to simple things, the way I grew up. Well, I learned to wear the right color clothes. I have dark skin and I can't wear just anything. This I kept, I worry about what matches my skin. But the other, I let go about pretty things. Rhinestones, I don't wear. Well, I like them, but I don't want to be wearing them. When I worked with white people, I used to dress up in pretty clothes. I would go to my people's dances, and the people maybe looked up to me, maybe that's what I liked, why I wanted them. That was when, ya know, I had a little looks on it! [Frances laughs!] But I knew it wasn't me so I [softly] changed back to simple things, the way I was raised.

Frances's old homesite is marked only by a dead cactus pointing to a pair of crosses in the desert. "That's my grandmother's grave," Frances said quietly.

"Somebody by the name of Louise was also buried there, my uncle's wife's sister." After spending some time there, I asked Frances if we could see her grandfather's fields. They were nearby, behind that little hill, she said, pointing. They drove and I walked, arriving a few minutes before the others.

I had never imagined S-koksonagk to be so spread out, so beautiful. The fields were overgrown—they had been abandoned since 1930, but you could see that they had been vast and flourishing, covering the whole valley. Alone while I waited, I imagined the monsoons watering the corn, the horses coming in from the fields to the corral, and Frances hauling water up to the house.

Frances arrived within a few minutes with our two friends, and she showed us where the house was, in ruins—it had burned down several years before. All that was left were some of the old wood beams, broken pieces of pottery, an old tin bucket, and part of a child's wagon. As we walked, we found some old pottery, indicating earlier settlements in the area.

We put a plastic bouquet of flowers on Frances's grandmother's grave as we left. It was a thoughtful and difficult time for Frances, so we didn't talk much about it. Her life was forged here! This is what Frances wanted to talk about first: living simply in the world, the way she was raised.

2 ◇ Spring Spinach

We had a BIG farm
a field, we grew CORN
squash
four kinds of BEANS
four kinds of squash
we had just ACRES and ACRES of corn
and beans too
and WATERMELON . . .

Watermelon was my favorite

. . . And when the season comes
    we'd eat
    SPRING SPINACH.[1]

*For untold hundreds, perhaps thousands, of years, Frances's people gathered
wild plants from the desert, farmed the desert soil, and hunted rabbit and deer.
Their main food was a gruel made from seeds and beans, parched after harvest, and then ground before eating. Wild spinach is often fried with some
beans and eggs, or meat. Other plant foods were sun-dried or baked before
storing, and then eaten with water and salt, or baked in ashes when water was
scarce. Sweet dried fruit, honey, and jam were made from saguaro and prickly
pear cactus.[2] These varied foods were still available during the drought years,
years with too little rain, and were very nutritious.[3] Frances is fond of saying
that when her grandmother said they had nothing to eat, she'd put together
something from their storage. That's when they really ate well.*

    *Talking about spinach, Frances breaks into a story. Here we enter the realm
of the sacred beings, Cloud and Wind, mingling with humans as the people
work and pray for rain. This is one of the collective legends of Frances's people,
told here in summary form, as a "little story."*

This is a little story, the real story is real long. This is what they tell us when
we are really little and they don't want to go into these long stories, this is
what they tell us. This is about the chief's daughter. The chief's daughter
was a beautiful girl. Boy, she was beautiful. There was nothing too good for

her, nobody was good enough for her. So one day there were men at the well, there were a lot of men gathered there, and the Wind and the Cloud were there, too. The Cloud was blind and the Wind was crippled; they were brothers. Anyway, they go there and talk to the men, and finally the men ask the Wind, the twister, "Say, why don't you do something so we can see what the lady, what the girl looks like?" I guess the Wind is a follower, so he'll do whatever anybody asks him. So he went under her and twisted her skirt above her head, and the men saw her, saw what she's like under there. I don't know if they see any good, but they saw her. So she went back and told her father what the Wind did. He came and spanked the Cloud and the Wind and told them to get out of the village and never come back, to go as far away as they can. They didn't want to ever see them again. So the next morning the Wind got up early and swept up the flour in the metates to make some gruel, and they ate that and left. They went back east, so pretty soon the desert ground got drier and drier. The moisture was gone, there was no breeze, there was nothin'; they almost smothered to death. So the chief told the people to go look for the Wind and the Cloud. So they looked, and they looked, and they looked, and couldn't find them. So one of the little birds . . . it's a little bird — not a hummingbird, but a little bird — anyway, he took off one of his feathers and started his journey to the east.

He kept going and going and holding up the feather; it was so still. He was looking at his feather and it didn't move. And he was so cold because he was close by them. And he went and he went, and finally the feather moved a lot, and he kept going, kept going, holding the feather, and finally it moved more, and more, and more. He was close to the home of the Cloud and the Wind. Everything was green, the fields were green, planted with corn, everything that these people should have. So he went to the home of the Wind and said, "The chief wants you back." So he said, "He never wants to see us again, so we are not going." So he pleaded with them, he pleaded with him, but he said they weren't coming. So he went home and told the chief. So somebody else did the same thing, went and pleaded with him, but he said they weren't going. That was the second. The third time somebody else went and also pleaded with him, pleaded with him, and he said they weren't going. So, ah, the fourth time somebody else went, and he said, "Go back and tell the chief to send us something of his daughter's. So he went back and got something and took it, but they told him that they didn't mean *that*, but something else. So a second person went back, took something else, and they told him the same thing. Now the third person took some of the chief's daughter's hair, because the Wind said, "The things we tie our braid with are worn out, so we want something of hers." He got there, and the Wind and the Cloud said, "No, we don't mean that, we mean hers, hers," and so he [Frances laughs] went back and told them they didn't need that, they wanted something else. So finally somebody else said he means the daughter's hair, and he says, "I guess they mean *mu:spa* [her pubic hair]." So I guess the chief got his daughter's hair and sent it over. So when he got there, the Cloud and the Wind said, "Yeah, this is what we mean." So they tied their braids, and there was some left over and they tied them around their wrist, and they started coming. And they went. The Cloud's blind and the Wind's crippled, but he always leads the Cloud, because the Cloud is blind. As you see, whenever it rains, the storm comes in first and then the rain, that's how it went. So they have some of that on the wrist while they are going, and some of the hair got loose when they shook their wrists, ya know, with the gourd rattle, and that spinach landed on the ground. So each time, the first wild spinach we cook we have to look for the chief's daughter's hair in our spinach. That was the tradition we were supposed to do when we first eat the wild spinach.

It was February 1987, and I had just taken the qualifying exams for my doctorate, a grueling three-day ordeal. Ready for a break from academe, I drove from Wisconsin to San Pedro to stay with Frances through the spring, with the hopes of working on her book. I borrowed a small camper to sleep in, and installed it in the back by the clothesline.

The doctor told Frances to walk for her arthritis, so every evening we would walk from the house to the old house, and then back again, following an old road that led up to the two-room adobe house where Jose and Frances had raised their family. We'd walk almost every evening, circling the Blessed Mother shrine, where we'd clean things up a bit, and then venture down the hill, arm in arm.

Some years are better, some years are not, it depends on the rain. Everything depends on the rain. Like I told you, Debbie, everything on this Earth is good for something, they're not just here. This is a little story, it's not really a legend. It's just a story. We were getting ready to go to war. A leader of the clan said to make moccasins, real strong moccasins so they can travel. So they went and started making them. So there's something that comes out when it rains, it's about this long [Frances gestures, as long as her hand], and the Indians call it *kommol* [centipede]. But anyway, it's got a lot of legs! And he told the people, and he went to the leader and said, "Well, I can't go to war with you. Because not even half of my legs have moccasins, I can't make any more. But I'll tell you what I'll be good for. When I die and I'm somewhere in the open spaces and the sun shines upon me and fades me, you get it and grind it and use it when a baby gets blisters, you use that one." And I remember my grandmother used to use it when the child gets blisters.

That one's for stomach [pointing]. We call it *s-siw 'u:s*, "bitter stick."[4] Sometimes we take what they call blood plants [greasewood],[5] or, um, something like for diarrhea, and for cramps and for sores, and a liniment for when you have a sore muscle. And there's little white flowers they used to say is good for headaches. I tried that once and it didn't cure my headache. A lot of things like that. I had a strange talk with a lady. She was telling me her husband got so sick, she had cramps inside and she thought she was gonna die. [Frances straightens a votive candle in the Blessed Mother shrine.] Then she ran over to the neighbor, and he said, "Well, why don't you boil some water and get some salt, and put a lot of that chile, red chile?" So she had to make the fire, boil the water in a pan, and put a lot of salt, and he couldn't lay down, he was just walking like this [Frances hunches over]. And she said, if you can sit down and if you can stand it, drink this, and in about an hour he was all right and the sweat came over, he got all right! That's what she told me. And sometimes I have cramps right here [Frances points to her abdomen], and it hurts! I think about that, but I get all right. How strange! When we used to eat chile, we get burn and it hurts! I guess whatever he had was more painful than the chile [laughing]. That's a plant for diarrhea [pointing]. It's called *a'ud*,[6] "century plant." That's one time my horse got into, got scared and went sideways, and I fell down. It's so sticky, just like glue. You get it and break it and it's sticky. Look, the bulbs are coming [pointing to the saguaro]. And the red flowers on top of the Indian kitchen, on the ocotillo.[7] And my plants are in bloom, too. I used to have a lot of them but the horses got into them.

When I got here [to San Pedro], my in-laws used to camp way out on that side of the mountain [pointing to a mountain called Komalk]. That's to harvest saguaro fruit. I would go with them because that's the only time I got out. Well it was hard, hard work, because we had to get up at four o'clock in the morning, and come back and cook breakfast and eat and cook the saguaro, and then start boiling it. Maybe by two o'clock the syrup will be ready and then we'll go after some more. We'd leave it for the night, and the next day we'd go for some more. We'd do it for five days. But boy, everything was good to eat, we'd be so hungry. That's about all we'd do, we'd go to bed early on the earth. When I was growing up, my grandmother taught me a lot of things about cooking. She taught me how to grind wheat and roasted corn on the metate. She taught me what is edible in the desert, how to pick cholla buds, prickly pear, saguaro fruit, and mesquite beans. She taught me how to roast, and at harvest time, how to roast corn and to store the young winter squash. We cut them up and we dried string beans, we'd snap them and dry them, too, for the winter. All those things I was taught, and I know them up to today, I remember all of them. I know how to roast the wheat and make it into *pinole*. We have to be fast to roast the wheat in the basket, and after it's roasted, we grind it up in there and use it for cereal, or a snack sometimes.

We like to eat beans, a lot of beans—pinto or tepary, sometimes potatoes. Once in a while beef, dried beef, chile, corn, tamales once in awhile, because it's hard work. We used to eat rabbit and we used to eat deer. One thing we never ate is snake, frog, and turtle. Some places, some Indians do, but we don't. We're superstitious. But later on, my father was working for white people, he used to kill squirrels. So I ate that, I thought it was good. But nothing else, not any other of those things. I never did eat fish or something else, we're superstitious about it. But now I can eat . . . once in a while I'll eat a tuna sandwich. Well, we better go feed the dogs! It's time for my show!

3 ◇ Met My Womanhood

Met my womanhood . . .
And for sixteen days
I stay away from beef
lard
and salt
.
Didn't eat salt and I stayed away from the fire.
So the sixteenth day we got up early
and we traveled on horseback.
We had a horse even whiter than that wall there [pointing]
.
We traveled with my grandmother.
My grandmother was big as I am,
but she rode that horse and I was sitting in the back
.
We traveled through Kwin's Well
and we traveled through San Ignacio
and we traveled through Santa Rosa and we got to that in the evening.
It must be March because I remember
the sun was still way up [pointing to the sky].
   (1970s)

When I met my womanhood, my grandfather was going to a dance. My grandmother told him I got my period, so one evening he started singing, going back and forth and back and forth. And this is what he was singing:

K-kaicu yuwhiñe
cewaiwe donowhaŋe kukug ʻab ʻo molsuna
s-ap ʻo kakaidam ʻo pici-pikime
[Quail birds
At the end of Long Mountain you all walk close together
"Pici-pikime" sounds good][1]

So I thought to myself, who would go out there and sing with him? So he laid down and made some ugly remark. I really did get mad at him. That was it! I never did really the purification dance like my grandmother did.

She danced for eight nights straight until morning.[2] We went to Waw Ke:k, Stone Stand—it's deserted now. I guess when we got there my grandmother told the man why we came. I was going to have the clay—be purified—so he said, "Well, I usually do it before the sunset, and I usually do it at sunrise." So my grandmother told me that she wanted to have him purify me in the morning. The two of us slept there in the desert in the open space, waiting for morning to come.

So when morning came, we went to a place, just like about here to that open space over there [pointing]. It was just the medicine man, the lady, and my grandmother and me in that open space in the desert. We put a rock, a big rock, [slowly, softly] to sit on it. I sat there with my hair down. He did all these ceremonial things, and the lady, the middle wife—that was the second wife—got a brand new olla and put water in there. I thought we were going to drink it. I thought we were going to be through and I'll eat salt.

And so we got through and we stayed there. It must be because it was still dark. It was coming to light but it was real dark. They got me up again and told this lady to wash me off. We used to do that, have someone wash off the clay, because I ate the clay. So at the time I got up and sat on the rock. They poured water on me. Oh, it was cold! They washed me off with that cold water. It was really cold. They told me not to [Frances inhales quickly], not to say like this [shivers and inhales as if from the cold], but that's what it's supposed to be to grow up tough and smart. [Laughing] I don't know how come I'm not smart!

After they dried me off, they gave me a blanket. It wasn't cold after that. And I started eating salt at that time, but the salt didn't taste the same, it was bitter. They said that the reason they did all this is because I was going to be tough and ready to meet up with whatever would come. So we went back to the village. There was no other people but us. We went back and we started living again. We farmed, we raised four kinds of beans. . . .

We went to the same medicine man with the first child, Juanita. But then after he died, we used to go to another medicine man farther up in the mountains; he died, too. So there's one, one medicine man that's still living. He did a ceremony for Christy and Linda. That's how I remember the ceremony. They do a circle like this, I think it's counterclockwise, four directions, and they walk through that. When they did the ceremony for me, they walked through and brushed me off with that feather, the long eagle feather. Then the medicine man went that way, then he came back. Then he went around and went that way, came back, and went around and went that way. He went in a circle with me in the middle. And he sat down on his knees. He sat on his knees and put the tip of that feather in the clay and made marks right here, on my chest, shoulders, back, and head. Then after he was through, he gave me the top of that cup to drink it. It tasted good! And then after I drank that, he put water on it and told me to drink, so I drank it again. Then I was through! You wash off whatever you have. You start a new life growing up, ready to face the world. The sun was halfway down on the horizon, and I went to bed. I slept on the floor with the other women; in the morning they washed me off. I thought I was going to eat something, but they only gave me a boiled potato. You know how potatoes taste with no salt [Frances laughs]. The rocks were still there but not the marks. The lady got some sort of branch and erased them.

After that, when I got my period, I just stayed away from whatever. I wouldn't eat at the table, I wouldn't eat from the same dish — I had my own dishes, that's all. I wouldn't cook for them. And I couldn't drink from the same pottery. We didn't have a hut, there were no other girls where we lived, and my grandmother was too old to go. Twice I went to segregation hut; I made three baskets when I was in there. I was just there at somebody's house, they do that so my grandmother sent me there. I did it twice. I went here, because my two aunts had a hut. I had cramps so I just slept.

Ahm. This is about long, long time ago, my great-great, my grand-mother's great-grandmother was in this war. The Apaches and the Papago had this war against each other.[3] It was one night, the women usually go out, at the monthly period, they go live in a little hut, a little ways from the house. But this was earlier, the thing we have in every walk of life, ya know. Something happens that's supposed to be warning you that something else's gonna happen.

There's a hut that's way out there in the middle of nowhere, where they keep their whatever they harvest, like wheat, corn, seeds of the saguaro, or syrup, and they have no road to it. Each time they come, they come from different directions to the house. So one time this man goes to get some wheat. And he had an old horse. He got off the horse and put a blanket by the door, so he goes in there and gets the wheat and brings it out, puts it in the blanket and goes back again. When he went back, when he came out again, the blanket was all covered up, you know, like if somebody gathered the blanket and covered it. But he didn't know, and he thought, "Who could have done this?" And he looks at the horse, he was standing there asleep. He went back again and he came back out again, I don't know how many times. Finally he saw the footprints in the wheat. Because we wear sandals and the Apache wears moccasins, he knew the footprint — whoever it is, was wearing moccasins. So he went back home. He went back home and told the people, and they said, "Well, it's just something that happened." I don't think they even believed it.

Well, that night there was a woman, she had a dog by the house and it was barking and barking. Finally she peeked out and she saw these two men standing there by the *ramada* with feathers sticking up, and they went to the next house and to the next, and finally they got farther away. Finally her father-in-law came out, and she told him that she saw some Apaches. They wear their feathers this way [gestures], we wear our feathers hanging down. And the old man said, "Well, it was just a dream or something." She went, and in the morning they attacked just before sunup.

And, ah, the ladies gathered all the women and put them in the hut, the menstrual hut, and let the men try to fight — run, you know, around there. And pretty soon some of them wanted to go out there and run. But the others wouldn't let them. So, finally, they made a hole at the corner and ran out. This lady that was telling about that, she saw them that night. She was a good runner and she had a black blanket, and it was so heavy so she threw her blanket and ran. She could hear the noise of the arrows — they were trying to shoot her, but she was too fast. And she ran, she got away, you know, far away, and she came to a place where some people were camped. There were some men getting their tools ready to go, and she said she heard this man tell them, "If I get hit, don't stop, keep on running until you get to the mountains and hide around the big stones and just lay there. Don't get up for anything." She told them that about half of the people were gone, so they start running. And she ran the other way, and I guess this other man . . . When she got up on the mountain, she saw this man running. Two little boys were in front of him and he was in back of them, jumping back and forth, you know, in back of them so the little boys won't be hit.

Night came, so she came down and went to another village, and walked and walked. And finally she got tired. She found a big wash and buried herself in sand to keep warm. And the next day she walked again and she got to the village and told them how the Apache attacked them and killed all of them, the women were killed, too. So they gathered up some men. They used to do that when somebody like that comes to the village, they'd go out and yell, the people would come over and find out what it is. So that's what happened. They tried to gather some men, and . . . but they were already gone. They just saw the dead people. They call it "Kui Tatk," Mesquite Roots. But there's no village anymore, that was the end of the village. That's what my grandmother told me.

Sometimes I used to get little bugs [lice], I don't know where I got them but there was a reason for the little bugs. You know, sometimes we'd be fast asleep and our heads would itch, and then we'd wake up and hear something coming, like Apaches. Or, um, things will be happening, like, um, something that's wild will come close to the house. That's supposed to be a warning, too.

A lady was asking me how was it when the Papagos and Apaches fought, and I said, "I won't tell you because you won't buy the book!" When the Papagos went to war, they killed, so when they came back, they stayed away for sixteen days. Somebody would go ahead of them with the scalp, and would say they had killed, and right away the ladies would go and get the wives and take them to some home and keep them there, and they would have camp, the ones who went to war and their wives. Her mother-in-law was one of those wives who made holes when it was time to have the ceremonies, and set the wives in there. She said those little ants were in there biting her, and she couldn't move or scratch, because the ladies taking care of them told them to be still. When the men came in, somebody had to lead them, and they started yelling and crying, the people who lost relatives, and they danced and danced. When the husbands came, they went out to meet them. That's the way she told me.

That's all about the Apache stories. I want to tell now of my own experience.

It's 1990, and I'm still talking about things that happened a long time ago, in 1912, or 1916 or 1920, somewhere along there. I'm still talking about it.

The other night I was sitting outside [at San Pedro]. Somehow Lorenzo got tired and went to bed at eight o'clock, so I was sitting out there and, um, and the night was quiet. And pretty soon I hear this lonely sound — an owl hooting. Then I thought about it, I wonder who could that be hooting, why is he hooting so close to the house?[4] I think he'll fly over to the well and to the old house and stay right there. And I thought about my grandmother, she used to say you could hear a lot of things when the night is quiet. I cannot say this word in English, but it's a very, very interesting word my grandmother uses. "When the night is quiet, the only thing you can hear . . ." I can't say this, but I'll say it in Indian. "The only thing you can hear is *sisk*, that's when the night is real quiet. What little noise comes up, you can hear it. And you can hear the faraway things passing by above us or around by us." Then I thought about my grandmother when she was very sick.

My grandfather would go to the wine ceremonial, he'd stay for days. And one night my grandmother didn't sleep at all, she kept on moaning and getting up, and getting down. And so I stayed up for a while, and then I'd go to sleep again and I'd hear her moaning again, and I'd get up. I tried to do something for her to make her comfortable. So in the morning, as we were eating, eating breakfast, and, ah, and I looked up at a fence, there was the horses on the other side of the fence, the horses that would pull the wagon. So I told my grandmother, well, just stay here. Of course there were two little kids, Elizabeth and Raymond, my grandmother's grandchildren, so I said, "You stay with her and we'll see if I can get those horses in, and we'll take her to a medicine man." Some kind of medicine man, medicine woman, would come to San Pedro, because her son in-law had a truck, and he's married to two sisters, my aunts. So we'd come over and see if they can do something, or can take her to a medicine man. At that time we didn't have any doctors around. So I went around, the horses were so good they just ran to the little corral and got in. So I told the kids to get ready, we were gonna travel. So I quickly made some dough and made some tortillas, and of course beans was there, so we made some sandwiches and we got water. And then the next thing, we thought about it, how are we going to get my grandmother in the wagon? I asked her if she was strong enough to crawl if we lift her up, close enough to crawl into the wagon. She said she would try. So we got her in a wheelbarrow and took her in the wagon. And those little kids were in the wagon, and so we finally put her in the wagon somehow.

And then I put the horses, and I put everything that they have to have in order to pull the wagon.

Then we start traveling. We traveled all morning until we get halfway to San Pedro. And then she was tired and she was moaning and she was thirsty. So we stopped under a big tree because she can't get off the wagon. I got off the horses to give them a little rest. Then we ate our sandwiches and we kind of rested, too. The kids could play around. Then it's time to go, so we put the horses back to pull the wagon and we traveled on. It must be about four o'clock when we got to San Pedro. And the two ladies were sitting under the ramada and the old man was sitting across from them. I never felt so mad, I don't know what it is, I was so mad and I felt so bad. Because the two daughters of hers were sitting looking at their old man, so we stopped, they just looked at us and all smiled at us.

We just got the horses off the wagon and we tied them up. And I told my grandmother, "We're here." And she started moaning again. And finally, the two ladies helped us and took her down, got her in bed, and did whatever they can to make her comfortable. I didn't feel sorry for them because one of them was crying, ya know. So that night, she suffered again. The next morning we traveled to some village where there was a medicine woman. They did something to her and she felt a little better. We went again to San Pedro and we spent another night there. The next morning we traveled again. At that time she was able to get in the wagon. We traveled again and we got there in the evening. My grandfather was there. I'd never been so disgusted in my whole life. I thought to myself, "If she dies, what am I gonna do?" And I thought, "I'll find myself getting her whatever has to be done. I'll do it," I told myself.

Today we'll talk about my health. I was a very healthy person, ever since I was a baby. I was about thirteen when I got smallpox, the O'odham call it *hiwkalig*. I had pimples all over my neck, I was so sick because I was overheated with fever. I had my period then, and something happened with that. I didn't know what I was doing or what I was saying, or how long I had been delirious. But that night I woke up and I saw this [medicine] man sitting and singing with rattle and feathers. They were doing it all. Then I came to, and knew I had been sick. In the morning the medicine man was telling my grandfather that I was a very sick person. But he tried something that would help me. He said, "If you look for those ants, red ants, the one that has the anthills, get some dirt from those anthills, and soak it. Give it to her to drink. If all of those pimples come out, you know she's going to be all right. But if not, look for someone else to try to save her." That's what he was told, so I drank that. That night I couldn't see because all of those pimples came out and my eyes were so swollen. My mouth was swollen and I couldn't breathe because stuff came out of my nose. I was real sick for a while, but after that I got well and I was healthy again.

Sometimes people say when you're real sick that you dream something about dying or going to heaven, or going someplace where the dead people go. I never did dream anything. I never saw anything during the time when I was delirious. But when I am well, sometimes I dream that we'll be flying across a river, trying to cross the river, and the river would get wide and we can't cross it. And we'd always go back. Then the river will be more narrow and we'll start to cross, but it will get wider again. It will be so wide, just like the ocean. That's what I dream, but nothing when I was sick. This is just dreams. So I guess it's not for me to dream something like that. Then, when I was in school I got TB, so they sent me to East Farm Sanatorium. That's where the Indian Medical Center is now, where I go for my eyes.

You see, I went to school in 1924, and in 1928 I went to the sanatorium. I had big hemorrhages at that time, I remember it was in March. I was look-ing forward to coming home, then I had this hemorrhage—it just poured out of my mouth. I was in bed for three months, just in bed! The only thing I could do was go to the bathroom, that's all! And after I got up, I went around, I would walk around and I'd go to this nurse and I would sit there. Kids would come in but I'd be in the back, sitting in her office, and we'd talk. She'd read me things. We talked about a lot of things. I was there for about a year. I never did finish high school. When I came home, I thought I'd go back to school, Phoenix Indian School, but I was too old, I had to make room for the younger people. I went to school when I was twelve, I was eighteen or nineteen then. I went to Phoenix Indian School at twelve years.[5] I wanted to go to school, so I was sent there. From the last part of August until summer we didn't come home.

[Frances laughs] I don't know why, but I always get into trouble at school. We used to go to bed at nine, and we were supposed to be in bed at nine, but sometimes we used to go to somebody's bed and talk and talk. So one time I was in somebody else's bed talking, and there was a lady that we call Lieutenant, so I used to tease this Lieutenant, and I thought it was her, but here it was the Second Major. I went under the bed and here she was standing there, and I pinched her leg, like this [Frances pinches herself]. And she kicked. We were punished, the three of us, because there were three of us in that room. So we were standing in the office at night, and one of the girls would get my hand and touch her on the head! And she was typing and she'd say, "Who did this?" We didn't say anything. We were punished. And Saturday nights they have a show and Saturday afternoons they have a game, so we sat home darning boys' socks. I didn't care because I didn't like the game anyway. And one time they had a roll call, somebody did something, and I was standing in the line with my company. And somebody looked back at me and I was winking at her, and my name was Blaine at that time and she said, [laughing] "Frances Blaine, you stop winking!" I was so embarrassed because everybody looked. A lot of times I'd get into trouble! One time I was talking Indian—they didn't want us to talk Indian—and we were talking Indian, and I heard somebody standing here. But I thought it was one of the girls, and I said, "Here goes!" in Indian [O'odham], [laughing] and I turned around and it was the Major!

And a lot of the girls didn't like me, because something would happen and I'd just make a joke and laugh about it, like I am now, ya know. The girls don't like me for that. And another thing, I used to play with their boyfriends. And I was wondering, [in a high pitch] how did we look? We used to wear bloomers. And I used to wrestle with boys! How did I look? Upside down, kicking and everything! How did I look? Yeah, I was always getting into trouble. Not real trouble, but I always get caught doing something. I still do! [Frances laughs] Little things. I think that is just life. It's just there! It's not really that I'm bad, I don't think so, but maybe I am! [Frances laughs]

Frances's little granddaughters, Amelia and Sonya, who had been listening, ask Frances to tell "that funny story."

Once upon a time there was these two people, a husband and wife, and the husband talks . . . [Frances curls up her face, feigning a garbled speech] this way, and the wife talks this way. . . .

We laughed! Frances speaks in a more somber tone, to the girls:

I was a little different than any other little kid. I don't know why, but I always felt that I am different. I can't understand that, but that's the way I feel. We used to go to a place called Ko:m Wawhai—it's farther down, and we used to live there for three or four or six months. I never did know why we went over there. You see, I never did play with kids, and I don't know how to play with kids. I play with kids, and they play, I don't know how to play [Frances inhales, her voice fading] with them. I don't really know how. So one day I was playing with them, they were a little bit older than I was, so I don't know why I remember this, but I remember it very clear. We were playing something, then they were going to play something different, so they were going to play couple. Because we were playing with boys. So they said, "This is going to be your husband, this is going to be your husband!" But I didn't know about it. I didn't know what they were talking about, because I never was told about husband and wife. I was never told!

And, um, and so [somberly, slowly] supposedly the night came that we were supposed to go to bed, and they went to bed with the little boys. And I couldn't! I couldn't! They were calling me names, and I was backing up—going backward, going backward, they were calling me names. And, finally, I cried. I couldn't stop crying because I was so shocked! Me? Laying with a boy! I was eight years old, I was young! And so finally, I couldn't stop crying and my grandmother asked why, and I was too embarrassed to tell her. And finally I told her, and she got mad at the kids. That's what I said, I'm different! I don't think they were doing anything. But they were laying together, boy and girl. That's why, when I grow up, I was always scared of that. And another thing. I told you I used to play around with boys [with feeling]—oh, I like to play around with boys! That's all! We went to a dance, and this lady—she's still alive, she's in a wheelchair now. This lady, her boyfriend, and a friend were dancing, and dancing, and dancing. And finally she came over and she said that [very slowly], "These boys want us to go over there in the dark." Right away something like electricity went through my head and clear down to my feet, and I said [laughing], "I can't go," I said. "Come on! Come on, let's go!" So I slowly went with them. The two boys ran back to the dance! That's what I like, dance, just dance! I have a good time, tease the boys, playing with the boys. And I could tell, when you play with the boys, you could see in their eyes the sex action coming on. I had nothing to do with it after that. No, nothing. That's why I said I am different. Don't you think I am different? It's because I was never told. Do you think I was weird?"

"No, Hu'uli [grandmother]," the girls said, "not at all." Her grown grandsons, watching television in the other room, laughed!

Frances taped the following segment alone, sitting on her bed one night in the fall of 1981.

[Thoughtfully] Well, Debbie, yesterday's gone and tomorrow's already here. If you want to hear about my life, I think I'll start it from the time I was about fourteen. I grew up in the middle of nowhere. I had just two uncles and a cousin, never did have any children around. And I played with, you know, teased my two uncles and cousin. My grandmother told me not to play with them, you know, really play, because . . . It's not their fault, it's their nature, because they might get the wrong idea. What my grandparents wanted me to do is to stay home, and then pretty soon they will marry me off. But I wanted to go to school, and I went to school. I was getting into my womanhood, but I never thought of becoming some kind of higher person. I wasn't thinking of becoming a chairman or a chief, and marriage didn't even enter my mind. So I went to school. But to tell you the truth, I did like men, because I grew up with men.

Once a month we would have a social, boys and girls, and we played around. Because I didn't feel close to anybody, like a boyfriend or anything, I didn't have that feeling. Like the girls would be sitting around with their boyfriends holding hands, but I would just be playing, wrestling with the boys.

I think I was about sixteen when I started thinking about being a singer [of traditional songs], but it never came out—my voice sounded like a train coming [Frances laughs]. I was in school, I passed every grade from first grade to fifth grade. Then I got the TB, so I was sent to a sanatorium. I was in bed for three months, and I was there for two years. And after a year I went back to school, but they sent me right back to the TB hospital, so I stayed there until I got out. By then my grandmother was sick, so I had to come home. She got better, so I went to work in town. I was working for some people and there was a girl working nearby. We used to go to her aunt's place and stay.

One evening I met her uncle. We just got closer together. This scared me because I felt different than when I was real young. I was scared I could be in love with him. Love was very strange to me, so I was scared. Well, anyway, it went on for [slowly] months and months and months. Finally, I think I knew I was in love with him and somehow felt that he was in love with me. He used to work out of town. Then one day he didn't call, he didn't come over. We'd go over there and he wouldn't be there. And it, you know, I felt bad because I never knew what happened.

Then one afternoon he called and he said, "Are you coming Saturday?" And I said, "Yes, I'm coming." So I went over and he was so distant, so he told me, "Well, I want you to go home. I want you to go home because I am going home. [Softly, sadly, slowly] I got some kind of sickness, so I have to go home and get some kind of treatment. But when I get well, I want you to be home so I can go after you, go pick you up and we'll be married." And I thought, "Me? Married?!" That scared me because I never thought of marriage. So . . . it went on and so he left, and I left. I never thought about leaving my job and coming home. I stayed on the job, and then it was in the summertime so the people I work for, they had a little baby, they went to Prescott. I went with them for two weeks. Before I left, I had word that he wanted me to go see him. That he was getting sicker, you know. I didn't know how to get there and I didn't even try. So for two weeks we went to Prescott, and when we came back, I called my girlfriend. She came over and she told me [in an ascending pitch, softly] he was gone. You know, I felt bad. And I thought, well, it wasn't for me. Somehow the word came [in a high pitch] "Now I'm alone."

I felt the word always coming, "Alone." I was alone. And sometimes, like today, I still wonder why. So it went on and on. And then my grandmother died. I had a girlfriend—she died, I was alone. [This is followed by a long silence.]

After my grandmother died, we moved to the ranch. Santa Rosa Ranch. We lived there, and there was always these people coming and coming. I was cooking, and, you know, I like to tease the men, I like to tease them and my grandfather didn't like it. I couldn't stand my grandfather because he was jealous when these men would come over and tease me. I felt dirty. But he was just an old man, and he knew I would leave someday. He hated the idea that I would go off and leave him there, couldn't stand it. But at that time I didn't understand it.

I used to come over to San Pedro village when I was a child. My two aunts were living here, they were living, you know, over by the community house. They were living there and, you know, two of them were living with one man. So we used to come with my grandmother and we used to stay and I used to see Jose. He was a little boy, an ugly little boy. Later he was sent to school in California, you know, Sherman Institute. Seven years later he came back a man, a great big man—broad shoulders, handsome. I don't even remember what I thought when I saw him, but anyway, we met up, and we just decided to get married. We got married on May 6, 1930. He was a young man, I was older than him. And we started a life from there. From that place where you see the little house, and it went on and on, and then he died. I was alone. The word came back again, I was alone.

So with Lorenzo I never did think of that word "alone." I never did think he was going to die. I wonder why those words? It's very strange, isn't it? I never did figure it out, even when I was getting old. And I thought, "I am alone again, the word's still there."[6]

Frances had her puberty ceremony in the old way, but without the dance that her female ancestors performed in honor of the transition to womanhood. But although the longer ceremony had already begun to die out, among Frances's descendants the same core rituals remain to mark the sacred transition today.

Knowing that there is currently no menstrual hut at San Pedro, I asked Frances if she practiced menstrual seclusion back then. Frances readily digressed into a series of stories about the Apache wars, passed down from her foremothers, stories whose heroines contribute significantly to the people's survival in war. It is here, in talk about the formation of her identity as a woman, that Frances's concern to write from her experience becomes explicit: "That's all about the Apache stories. I want to tell now of my own experience." Here that experience concerns her disappointment and heartache, and her loneliness, thirty-three years later, after the death of her husband and, later, Lorenzo.

Frances switches to the story of her grandmother's illness in order to illustrate how heartless people can be, even to their own relatives, illuminating a major shift in values taking place in a world where a people's survival depends heavily on mutual support and assistance.[7] We get a glimpse of the effects of white man's diseases—smallpox and tuberculosis—and what boarding school was like for Frances. Thrown into a military-style environment with girls from other tribes and forbidden to speak her native language, Frances demonstrates her resilience and sense of humor against a backdrop of drastic, forced change. The emotive force of these changes is captured in Frances's dream, in which she is unable to cross a river, as it gets wider, and wider.

Part II ◇ San Pedro to Tucson

Marriage and Family, 1941–1981

I still like Tucson because of my friends. Right now I have those basket weavers, they are learning to make baskets; I teach them how to make baskets. I don't feel like they are my students, they are my friends. Most of them are retired, some are widows, but others are young, too. But the village always feels like my home. In Tucson I was just a resident.

"For thirty-nine years?" I asked. "Was it thirty-nine?" "Yeah, thirty-nine years," Frances answered. (1987)

4 ⟨·⟩ San Pedro, 1931–1941

My grandmother told me one night my father came home with
this
with this young LADY
.
They came home
and they came home on horseback
.
Now I was wondering how is she
carrying her suitcase,
her makeup bag or something
.
Well at that time
they didn't have anything
So I guess she started living there.
   (1987)

Well, what do you think you want to know? Do you want to know about my grandfather's marriage? Of course there are typical ways of getting married. The young man should go to the young woman's home and sleep there for four nights before he can bring her home. So my grandfather went to go sleep with my grandmother the first night, and he's always scared of the dogs. So the dogs chased him, so he never did go. The next night his father took him. So on the fourth night my grandmother went to him, and he took off. She took all of her belongings in that burden basket and she came to my grandfather's village, and my grandfather's mother told them where they are going to sleep. The house is round, so you have to lay on the ground, you have to sit down and then crawl in. My grandmother tried to crawl in and then she hit her head, and the dust that had settled and whatever was on the roof came down, cobwebs and everything. That's my grandfather's wedding.

I just got through with the morning chores. I was talking about my grandfather's marriage; now I'll talk about my marriage. When my grandmother died in 1927—March 29th—a few weeks later, Santa Rosa ranch was released—there was a man that was leasing the ranch and his lease was up.

So he turned it over to the Indians, and my uncle was going to take it over. So we moved to the ranch. I guess it was in the middle of April. My life changed then. There were men there every day—young men, old men—because they were ranchers. I liked to tease men, and they liked to tease me. My grandfather didn't like it. He always embarrassed me in front of the men when it was time for lunch or dinner. I didn't like that. By that time I was a grown woman, so I thought I could make my own decisions. And I had this young man, he was a friend of mine, I'd known him all my life. There was nobody to talk to but him. Sometimes I wanted to talk, but my uncle's wife wasn't sympathetic, so I couldn't talk to her. So I talked to this man all of the time. I never had a father. Not that he says anything to encourage me, but he listened. So one day I was fed up with things, the way things were going. I was fed up with it, so I decided to run away.

There was a truck that used to come to the ranch, so I planned to go with it, go on that truck to the road and then to town to find a job. And then to move on to wherever I can. So I told this man that I was going to go away, and my grandfather said, in front of all those men, "I'm embarrassed and I don't like it." You know, about me talking to the men. So this man, he didn't so much say, "Will you marry me?" He just listened and he went home. So the next day he came with his father, the next evening. His father talked to my uncle and my other uncle—of course my father wasn't there. He couldn't talk to my grandfather because . . . I didn't want that. And he asked me, and I thought, why not? As long as I can get away from this place, I'll be glad to marry him! I didn't tell him that, though. So we decided to get married and my father put up a big wedding, he put up a dance, food, and all the works. We got married May 6, 1930. I didn't love my husband then, but then I fell in love with him afterward. He was a good man. He was the only man who really loves me! I couldn't find another man like him. Anyway, the children came almost a year later, and they came every two years.

The following segment was recorded in 1980 as we were driving into town for a basket-weaving demonstration. We had gone out to the road, and on the way Frances had shown me the "dancing cactus," two saguaros standing tall, arm

in arm, dancing the chicken-scratch. Twenty minutes later we passed Three Points and Wing's Field, and were headed over the pass to Tucson. "Did I ever show you the lady lying down?" I asked, pointing to the contours of a mountain range in the distance. One of my Yaqui friends had pointed her out to me. To me, she seemed elegant and mysterious, her hair outstretched upon the earth. She was strong, with prominent nose and breasts, even knees, although toward her legs one had to work harder to imagine her. "Oh, yeah, there's the lady lying down!"

It's March, and it's my daughter's birthday — Mildred. So I'm talking to you now about the life of San Pedro. I came to San Pedro when I got married, on May 6, 1930. We lived in a one-room house, slept on the earth floor. And my mother-in-law and my father in-law were there. I got married Saturday morning and Tuesday morning my husband drove the cattle to Marana, so I had my honeymoon alone. And during that time I watched my mother-in-law do the cooking and tried to follow her, doing the same things she did. Later on, I found out that I wasn't really at home, I was just there. My husband was always gone [inhales], either at the well watering the cattle or the horses, or somewhere in the open range riding the horse at night. Sometimes they would play what they call *gins*, the stick game, and they'll play it all hours of the night and they'll come home late.

I don't know what to call how I felt. When my father- and mother-in-law would be talking, I would walk over there and sit down with them, and they would quit talking. They didn't want me to hear what they were saying, so I got smart and stayed away from them. I was alone, alone in the house trying to do things that would keep my mind from worrying. I felt I wasn't welcome there.

Years went on like that, and then I got pregnant. They were making fun of me when I got pregnant. I would carry water late in the evening or early in the morning so I would have enough water for washing and rinsing our clothes. My first child was very, very hard, and the people talked about it. My sister-in-law didn't like me either, I did whatever I could to try to make her like me. But one day I quit doing that and tried to avoid her. It occurred to me later that they probably thought Jose should have married somebody from Ban Da:k, Ge Aji, or Si:l Naggia, because they are in a group together, a circle with San Pedro.[1] So I guess they thought that Jose should marry somebody in that circle, but he married me, from outside. So that just went on like that.

And then one time I overheard somebody saying I was getting fat! And my mother-in-law said, "Well, the way she eats, she should get fat." That really hurt, and so from that day on, I ate just a little bit. Then she told people I didn't eat her cooking. And we used to milk the cow, we'd get up early in the morning and milk the cow, but sometimes some of the cows won't come in, so we'd sit and wait. I guess my mother-in-law said something to an old man, and one day when he was drunk, he came over and bawled me out for that. He said that I don't do anything but go sit at the corral, while my mother-in-law has so much work to do. Why couldn't she just say that to me? Whatever I did, it was never right. But one day, I remember one day a man said to his sisters and his wife, "You know, you always talk about Frances as being lazy, but when I go over there, she's always working. She's always doing something." I always did something.

So after some time it came to me that I wasn't going to be walked over—I was going to stand up for myself! Because sometimes I'd feel so low, and the only thing my husband would say was, "Oh, did they say that?" That's the only encouragement he gave me. During that time I was working with a lady at church, we did everything for the church, and they even blamed me for stealing money from the church. When Juanita was born, it made it easier for me because I could take care of the baby and be away from them.

We didn't have anything because we didn't have any money [matter-of-factly]. A rancher doesn't always have money, sometimes they're broke, too. The way the ranch life is, you can have money and you can have none, because it takes time for the calves to grow up. They start sending them to the market when they are eight or nine months old. Because after a year the weight goes up and they are heavy. If someone came and said, "How old is the calf?" and you say nine months, they put the price up, you know. But if it's over a year, the price goes down.

I can hear them crying now. Last night I kept waking up; I kept coughing and waking up. Like this lady. . . . At Santa Rosa Ranch there was a roundup and I guess people got drunk, and this lady ran off with another man, and her husband was gone somewhere else. She ran off with another man and left her little one, her little boy. He was a little baby, not more than a year old or a little over a year old. He was still nursing. The two ladies got him.

The word got out. There were some Mexicans with them, rounding up. And one old Mexican said, "Well, the humans are worse than cows. If the calf is corralled, the mother will be there all night until the next day." And here the lady ran away with that man [Frances laughs].

We have had cows since I was a little girl. My father in-law had a lot; when he died, my husband got it. But we needed money that year, so my husband got a job at the CCC [the Civilian Conservation Corps's Indian Division] making water holes for the livestock.[2] We would travel around the reservation making water holes, building fences and dams, because my husband was a stone mason. We lived in a tent then, camping wherever they camped, changing camp every two months or so. When winter came and we didn't have enough blankets, I took those barley gunny sacks and some yucca fibers and dried the yucca and stuffed the gunny sacks with yucca fibers and alfalfa for our mattress and blanket; we weren't cold anymore. I went home to have my second daughter, and then had another child two years later. We had the wagon and the horses, so we just piled up our stuff and we'd go. It was easier for me to talk to the ladies there.

Later Jose got hired in Sells to make the schoolhouse, so we stayed there.[3] Mildred was born there, she'd be sucking on a tortilla, and we'd be eating beans and potatoes, and sometimes rabbit. Then we went back to San Pedro again. I had the two children, the two little girls. I made their clothes and fixed their hair, but we were on the other side of the wall. My father- and mother-in-law enjoyed the children, but I guess they wished I wasn't their mother. My father-in-law was sick; Mildred was a year old when he died. I'm sorry to say this, but when he died, things started changing. We had our own money and decided to build a house. We got some Yaquis from Tucson to make the adobes, about five thousand adobes. It was a great [Frances gestures with arms spread wide] big house, a one room house, and in the middle was the kitchen and dining room. That was the first time I had my own home. We bought a stove, a dish cupboard, a table, and dishes, and I started to live like I dreamed. I had a dream house in my mind, that's what I want! Like a dream, I'm just dreaming that I'm gonna have this, but we never had it because my father-in-law was so stingy with money. It was very important to me, that was the first house that looked modern, a little bit a modern house. I never thought it would be possible, because I grew up in a mud and ocotillo house, saguaro rib, and all that.

It went on and on, and then the third baby was coming. At that time we had two homes, we farmed farther down in the rainy season, and in the plowing season, and go back and forth to pull the weeds and harvest. It's near Santa Rosa Ranch. In October we went over there for the harvest. The beans were ready to be pulled, the squash were ready to be pulled, along with the watermelon and corn.

One day when we ran out of rations, my husband went to town. He didn't come home and he didn't come home, and I got sick right from the second night he was gone. A lady came and stayed with me, so when the time for the baby to come, she ran to get the midwife. When the midwife came, Floyd was already born. Two days later my husband came home. He had a son! So we stayed there, and came back to San Pedro after the harvesting. We started living again. My mother-in-law was there, but she wasn't the same mother-in-law that she was when my father-in-law was living; she was nicer, and the kids loved her. They thought she was their real grandmother, until they were older. She was their stepgrandmother, because my father's mother died a long time ago.

A year or so after that, my husband got a job at Silverbell mine, so we moved over there.[4] But he got laid off, so we went home, that's when Florence was coming. One day in November . . . It was All Souls' Day, and we went to decorate the graves. I felt so cold! So I had some coal, and a pan, what we call *kommol*, and I put some blankets on it. I was sitting on it because I was so cold [Frances laughs], and that night I went into labor! But the labor pains went away in the morning and I made some dough for the bread. I baked the bread, and in the evening my pains were getting worse and worse [she says softly, inhaling, fading]. That night they were going to light the candles. I said I wasn't going to go because I didn't feel good. So they went and we stayed home. And pretty soon it got worse and worse. There's a little house that's big enough for a double bed. We took the bed out and put a single bed and put the things we need for the baby in preparation. It was getting worse, and my husband was sitting on the bed looking at me like I was going to burst. So I told him, [in a high pitch], "Why don't you go and sit outside, until I call you?" So he went out, and a few minutes later Florence was born. I called him and told him to come in and cut the cord. He took his knife out, it was shaking, so I took the knife and cut it off, and I guess I fell sleep. He came back in a while later and said the kids were coming from the graveyard. So I told him it was okay, and they all came in to see the baby. The next day the nurse came and washed her off and weighed her, a field nurse. That was Florence; she had curly hair. So we'll stop here.

I had six children: Juanita, Mildred, Floyd, Florence, and I lost two in between. And seven years later two more came. After having those babies at home, I started to learn . . . Well, my grandmother was a midwife, so I used to deliver babies. I delivered a Mexican little boy, but I don't know where he is. But lately, some years ago, I had a problem—the law came after me.

We'll talk about the midwives. Like I told you, Debbie, my grandmother was a midwife. I don't know how I learned, but I guess I learned from her. But anyway, there was a lady. A lady was having a baby and there was nobody there. I was just a young girl then. She was really having a hard time and her husband didn't know what to do. How did we get over there? We were just curious, I guess. I couldn't stand blood. But anyway, she was sitting up, and she said [softly], "Can you do something?" There was a certain thing, you know, you hold her and press her in the back, where the cheeks are. I did, and, ahm, I guess I was really shocked when the baby came. The blood didn't make me faint—it usually did—and I got the baby out, and then the cord. I had heard my grandmother say that as soon as the baby is out, you hold onto the cord and don't let go until it's out. So I did that, and the cord came out. From that time on, I knew what to do.

So when Susie was going to be born, they called me over there to that little house where we give birth—it's still over there [pointing toward the east]. The midwife and I stayed with the lady, who had been in labor for a long time. It was a cold, cold night, and we got sick. Florence was a little baby and I couldn't carry her home, I was so dizzy. The next day her husband came over and wanted me to go check on her, and, oh, I had a headache! I got there and did what I had to do, and I forgot my headache! The cord was twisted around her neck, [inhales] around her neck. And I don't know, somehow, the midwife knew what to do. The little girl was born. And then one night, Lorissa's sister came over with those two little boys, it was late at night! They wanted me to go and see that the baby was coming! That was Lorissa—I delivered her. I delivered one of my sister's babies, too.

Some years ago I got a letter from the tribe saying that I was supposed to go to court. So I went, and they told me they had canceled the court. And, another time, they sent me a letter again, that I was to go to court. Here my sisters were asked which doctor delivered the baby, and they couldn't put a doctor's name. They couldn't find any record of a doctor, so they had to trace it back that she was born at home by a midwife. So we went to court, and they told me not to deliver any more babies. They said that the person that I delivered was healthy, but if I try again, something might happen, I might get myself into trouble. So he said, "Well, just quit now."

Another thing, the midwife will know if the baby's not right. A midwife knows how to deliver a breech. I had my own breech, I couldn't deliver it because it was facing the wrong way, so just the hand came out, and it broke the sac. We had to call the doctor. Oh, we called the doctor, but the doctor didn't come. And here my husband was working at Davis-Monthan [Air Force Base], so they called the service doctor and he came. The baby died, choked herself. I lost that baby, choked herself. That was the fifth one. And then seven years later I had those two, Linda and Christy, so I had two sets of families.

We worked hard. From the very beginning, when you get married, you have to go with what your husband wants, but you have to meet your husband halfway, and your wife halfway. You have to do what the man wants you to do, and the man has to do what you want him to do. That doesn't mean it's easy. But he really liked horses. That's why I really understood him, because I like horses as much as he did.

And a woman should let a man be with his own kind. We cannot separate a man from his ways. Like if some women when they are first married, they want to be with the man, but that's not right, because men get tired of women. Sometimes I just want to be with women and I just hate having a man around. I'm sure the man sometimes feels that way. When I got married, my husband left me a lot. I'm not saying he doesn't love me, but he drinks! He loves his drinking!

These segments concerning marriage and family were recorded with me in the fall of 1981 and spring of 1987, and with Hazel in the 1970s. Here we get a sense of the hardship, reminiscent of the rainbow story, that Frances experienced

with her in-laws while living in her husband's village. From a woman's point of view, we learn of her husband's efforts to find wage work at the mines, ranches, and barrios while Frances bears and raises her children.

In early October 1981, Frances and I went to Mexico for the fiesta of St. Francis in Magdalena, Sonora, a curing festival.[5] Frances's family had been going there for years, and her people for many years before that. I was twenty-seven and Frances was almost seventy. After a beastly hot day among the crowds, I suggested that we could easily travel to the ocean, only sixty miles west as the crow flies, I thought. When I suggested the idea, Frances shrugged her shoulders and said, "Why not?" keen for the adventure. It turned out that the ocean was over three hours away, via a long and dusty road heading into ever-receding mountains. Finally reaching the coast at sunset, we discovered a small fishing village, where we camped on the beach under a wide-open sky. After an almost sleepless night, we cooked breakfast on the outdoor stove at the home of a fisherman.

Unfortunately we had car trouble on the way back, which made Frances late for an important family gathering. This gave one of her daughters good reason to lecture me on the care of her mother. It was my first and, luckily, only small rift with the family—I had been having much too much fun. Hanging out with Frances had become my favorite pastime. But when we couldn't get home, Frances and I had our first good cry together.

5 ◈ The Bad Year: Tucson, 1941

Well ah
[slowly] when we were leaving
my two little girls

No
there was just one
because the others were in school when we left
.
She was just standing there when we left
looking
watching us go
.
And I cried
  and cried
    and cried.
      (1981)

The story about "the Bad Year" lies at the core of the family's oral tradition. It represents a major turning point in Frances's life and the life of her family, symbolized in the image of the carnivorous buzzard flying down to eat the dead cows and horses. Set during the worst of many drought years caused by overgrazing and erosion, the story documents the family's migration to the barrios *of Tucson and the disappearance of a way of life. It was here that Frances and her husband, Jose, began a life as urban Indians, working for the Milga:n.[1]*

In 1941 a bad year came, it was like now, 1981. There was no rain, everything was dry, the cattle were dying, and so we sold most of our cattle and we had to move into town to find work. We had to do something because we had four kids. We had to go, they had to eat. I was sad leaving, but there was no other way. You see, the sickness came and killed most of our cattle. And the calves will come . . . it'll take about a year before we can sell them [Frances inhales deeply]. You could see the dead cows. My husband was so sad, because that's all he knows. You see, his mother died and he was raised by his father. She started throwing up blood. So he was raised by his father and later on, we married. And that's all he knows—cattle! He never worked anywhere until we went to town and had to learn to work. It was nineteen, ah, forty-one. It was on a Tuesday we came — that's when we moved to town. We thought we couldn't feed the kids — four kids — on so few cattle, so we left.

We came, it was on a Tuesday we came. My half sister was in Tucson. And there were other people [Tohono O'odham] living around there. We moved into our one-room house with some Indian people there and we just had one chair and a bed. We didn't have a stove, we had to cook outside. We didn't have a table; we had a box. He'd sit on the floor and eat, and I'd sit on the bed. And then, later on, we moved to Osborne; [softly] that's where we lived when he died.

I came back to the village every weekend, then pretty soon we went every two weeks, or . . . unless the kids were sick, we came back to town. I had my house there on the reservation; [in a high pitch] everything was the same because we had my mother in-law there, and the beds were made. Nobody would ever go in there unless the kids would get something, and the beds would be always fresh — will be just made [Frances inhales], yeah.

The second day we moved into town, Jose was washing dishes at El Presidio, and two days later I worked at the Pioneer Hotel as a chambermaid. I started off with forty cents an hour at the hotel, but at that time forty cents an hour was something.

So it went on, then finally he got a job at the railroad. It was a good job. When I got pregnant, I quit working. That was Linda. I did domestic work after the baby was born, a lady by the name of Folger. I got — it was fifty cents an hour. That lady, she gave me her friends so I worked different places, full-time every day. Pretty soon seventy-five cents, and a dollar and a dollar-fifty and then two dollars — they say it's six dollars an hour now. I think I'll go back to work [Frances laughs].

We would go to the reservation on weekends to see our children. We sent fine things to take home, whatever we think they'd like, what would make them happy. Every week we'd go out there and take them things. Knowing the kids like sweets, we'd take them fruit, candy, eggs, bacon, whatever. Every weekend. And then later on, it was every two weeks. So pretty soon the oldest child moved into town because she was ready for high school. So we lived in town — that was 1941. Then later on, the other children went to school — Drachman, to Safford, Tucson High School. And my oldest girl attended the university for two years. And she met a man, a German man, and she married and she is now in Ohio. So that was why we moved into town and we lived there, why I came to like Tucson. And I'll sing you a song. That's what the song was about—the bad year. Whenever animals die, the first thing we see is buzzard flying over, maybe two or three, circling around, then we know that something is dead there. So this is the song about the buzzards and death of the cows and horses.

'Ali wa si cu:cuki nuwĭ ta-we:me-ga
'ia wa t-da:mai sisikola hime k-amo ṣa:kali kekiwupime
mumkidage 'o 'a:gaime
[The little black buzzard, our brother
It circles over us and flies sideways
It warns us of the sickness]

There's another song we used to sing, an old song:

Jeweḍa meihim, jeweḍa meihim
wa ṣa 'al kukuñuikime we:s haicu duakam we:s 'al kukuñuikime
kunṣ heg yoime k-am-o 'al hime k-am-o ñeina ṣoig 'al ñ-i:muina wa:ṣ
*   'al kukuñuikime*
[The earth is burning, the earth is burning
Over it is reflecting, every living thing is reflecting
In that I walk and see, my poor heart, everything is burning]

Later on, we went home once a month; we still had a few cattle. We had a few cattle and we'd come home and find out, because there was a man taking care of them and we'd bring groceries to him and pay him, or hay or rope or whatever he asked us to buy for him. We would go home to see how was it going.

It was 1941 when I started working for white people, but I've been working for them since I got out of school. When I was eighteen, I had a job. This was before I got married. Well there was a place where you go to hunt for a job and they place you with people, and [softly] so you work for them. I was working for them until my grandmother got sick. I worked for them and then came home and took care of her [more softly] until she [inhales] died.

So these people got me, I was with them. They had two little kids and that one little kid, one time they were away so I sponsored the baptism with that little baby. So I worked before. I did domestic work. Now [basket-weaving] demonstration is my job, remember? Well, I stayed. It's been ten years since I really started doing demonstrations—in the schools, at functions and festivals. I don't know when I started, but—ten years, I think. But I started before that, too, in the sixties, after my husband died.

One time at home in Tucson, I lived there and I went to work, and came home and my house had been vandalized. Everything was broken—the wall, only the saints weren't broken. And they got tomato sauce and watermelon out of the refrigerator and threw it on the wall—they broke the lights. So later on, I had talked to a lady detective and I was saying that I'll find out somehow. She said, "Don't bother, you might get hurt." So I just let it go, and it went on and on. Then one time I was making tortillas outside and these little kids walked by and asked, "Can I have one, please?" Of course, if it was a different day, I'd probably give them one free, but that day I was kind of on the hard side. So I said, "Why should I give you a free tortilla the way you treated my house, and what you did to me?" So the little boy said, "No, we didn't, David did it." See, that's the way I find out things—slowly.

So when we had that family meeting in the neighborhood, I brought it up and I said, "If my child brings something home like that, I'd surely ask him about it, and I'd make him bring it back." That child must be worse off than I am. Later on, this lady was telling me who David's mother was, that she was sitting next to me, sweating. They talked about cockroaches, too, at that meeting. They're supposed to take it to the higher person about what we talk about, you know.

One time I was doing something with the hammer, and then the hammer was gone. And another time I was washing my hair and I had to hang some laundry, so I put the shampoo by the clothesline and forgot to take it, and that was gone. That was long before. So I just made up this thing, I said, "Whoever took my hammer, they will never have a hammer, it will always be gone." I just made that up, because once I put a curse on somebody that gets my stuff, they'll never have anything. One time I opened my door and there was my hammer. One little boy threw rocks and eggs at my window, and I scared him. You know, being an Indian among those Mexicans, black and white people, I was the black sheep. They'll do it until they can't do anything more. Now they don't bother me anymore.

Once a little girl—oh, she had a dirty mouth, so I said, "Okay, you may think you have a mouth dirtier than that black cloth over there, there is somebody around the corner who has the dirtiest, and someday you're gonna run into her." I said, "You told me to go back to my tepee, and you're mistaken, because the Papago Indians don't use tepees. I'm glad you told me, because I can go back to the reservation. I am proud to have a reservation, and where would you say you'd go if I chase you out of here? You don't even have a tepee or a reservation!" And I said, "You may think, because they said 'dirty Indians,' you may think we are dirty Indians, but we can do whatever we feel like to you. It's not gonna happen right now, but it'll happen" [Frances laughs]. Oh, that little girl started running and then she tripped, and just fell on the cement, and she was crying. So I was through washing and I was cleaning the washing machine, and I said, "Well, I guess you were never taught at home how life is and how you are supposed to treat people, and that means your parents don't care whether you are alive or not." So that afternoon they came back and apologized, and the girl said, "My mother loves me." I felt like saying, "Who cares?" So they never said anything.

And then when I first started demonstrating baskets in schools, some kids would act like, "Oh, what is she doing there?" You can feel it. One time I told one little boy who was laughing and laughing, I said, "Hey, little boy, why don't you come over here and tell us the joke so we can all laugh?" And he got scared. So that's what I do.

Here's a joke I heard somewhere. The American said to the Indian, "You are dirty." And the Indian man said, "You are just as dirty," back and forth. And the man said, "You go to the bathroom in your house, and it's dirty, the smell goes all over," and the white man said, "You don't take a bath for six months." And he said, "We're not dirty, that's why we don't take a bath." And another thing the white man said is that the people are dirty because they have bugs in their hair, and the Indian man said, "You are dirty, too, because you always have something under your bugs. And you put something over your body, we don't put something over our body, our bodies breathe the clean air."

What else did I want to talk about? I was thinking of something that's good to talk about, now I can't even think. . . . Oh, about Tucson, how small it was when I was a little girl. I know Steinfeld's was there, and Ronstadt's. I couldn't read, then, but that's what they say was there. Green Horse—has a horse in front, a grocery store, a Chinaman's store on Broadway, and later, Sears. Then years went by—Jacome, a Mexican store. Then J. C. Penney's, the latest was Levy's. I liked to buy things in Jacome because they carry a good quality. And I bought my furniture at Reuben Gold's. I never did care for Montgomery Ward, the quality wasn't very good. Oh, there's Porter's. My husband bought his hats there.

Winding down our session, we'd talk:

"I went to Porter's with Lorenzo once," I said, "We looked around, he showed me things, saddles. . . ."

"Lorenzo's still talking about how he's gonna overhaul his saddle. I wish he'd do that," Frances added.

"I wish he would, too. Maybe he'll feel a little better and he'll do that."

"Yeah, I think so. . . . So that's how small the town was when we first started coming to town. And it got bigger and bigger, and now it's real big. Town . . . and hardly anything downtown, but a lot of shopping centers around town. It's kind of sad, because Tucson's like a ghost town."

"I bet it's changed a lot. . . ."

"Yeah," she said, sitting back down. "I think I remember, in the 1920s, I really remember those stores."

"And the dirt roads," I added.

"Yeah, there were sidewalks, but not much like now. And there were no meters for the parking. Now it's all paved. And we had a streetcar. That was in the 1930s. So it changed," Frances said, with little sense of nostalgia.

"How was it when you came to town?" I asked, hoping she'd tell a story.

"There's a stable where we'd go. We'd just cook on the open fire. Later on, when I came with my husband, we'd stay at the stable, but sometimes we'll eat breakfast or dinner out. But it was on Mars Street. I remember very clear.

Sometimes there would be a bunch of people, wagons and horses, and people drinking—they always drank. One time, there was another woman who was kind of shy or something. I guess they sold cows or something, so they came in. And this man gave me a handkerchief with a bundle of money and told me to keep it, so I kept it. He was still . . ." [The phone rings.]

After Frances got off the phone, I asked, "What happened with that money?" I was looking forward to the end of the story.

"They were still drinking, and we were going to leave for home. He wasn't drunk, but he was drinking, and so I asked him if he wanted the money, and his eyes got real big, and he said, 'I thought I lost all that money!' He could have given me five dollars, but he gave me a dollar-fifty [Frances chuckles]. But I guess at that time it was a lot of money. So we left. I don't know what happened to that money after that [laughing]."

"Where's Lorenzo?" I asked, still laughing. "Dinner's ready."

"I don't know, I guess he's out there looking for his star."

6 ◈ Alone

Jose was a young man
I was older than him
and we started a life from there
.
From that place where you see
and it went on
 and on and on
and then
he died
.
I was alone
.
The word came back again

I was ALONE
.
It's very strange
Isn't it?
I never did figure it out
when my husband died
.
Of course I didn't think of anything like that until later on
When I was getting old
And I thought
[softly] just think
I am alone again
and the word's still there
IT'S THERE
.
And I WONDER
is it going to come back
Come back to refresh the word
"alone"?
    (1987)

Living at San Pedro in 1987, I came to a greater awareness of the amount of hardship Frances's people were forced to endure. I had seen it in the violent death, incarceration, alcoholism, and diabetes. But it wasn't until that spring that I began to understand why Frances worried so much about her grandsons, and why she would get so tired when we talked, for her time and her moods were often not her own.

The hardest part of my life was when my husband died, and I was left with a little baby, and then she got sick. That was hard because usually when the husband's there, we sit up nights to take care of the baby. The nights were long, the baby's sick and you don't know what to do, you have medicine but it doesn't help. . . . That time of my life was very hard, when Christy got sick. She didn't get sick that often, but when she did, she got sick.

I'd hold the child when I eat, if it was crying; I hold it when I do things; I'd hold it when I went to bed. A lot of people don't do that now. We are really different kinds of people here. And I'm glad that the kids come back to their home. It's because I'm their mother, that's how I feel. When I see people sometimes, they say, "Oh, let me hold him," but where were they when I was alone? And if I had to go someplace, I always took my kids.

They are all two years apart, the four of them, Linda was five when he died. It was Sunday about nine o'clock, and those missionaries came and they were singing, and the leader was talking. And she brought the baby, and I looked at her and I said, "That little baby's never gonna know her father," and I started crying. And the missionary said, "See, this lady met Jesus!" But I was crying for that [Frances laughs].

Raised six kids. I'd call myself a strong woman, even if nobody thinks I'm a strong woman. [Softly, thoughtfully] I went through a lot sometimes. My husband would be gone, he'd get off work Saturday night, and then he'd come home and take a shower, meet somebody, and then he'd be back Sunday night. No matter how he feels, he'd go to work. He'd give me the money, but we'd pay for the kids, the rent, and the groceries, and there'd be nothing left for me! I thought we were bad off, but when he died and I heard all these little kids hungry, with no shoes—I wasn't bad off, I was wealthy. But that's all. . . . When I go, I don't know why I'd go to the fiestas. I'd have one on one arm, one on one hand, and the other one would be holding the other's hand, and I'd think, "Why did I go to the dance, with all these kids?" Now what shall I eat?

It was May 5, 1990. Frances and I had been friends for twelve years. Frances looked at me hard, and her voice took on a somber tone.

We moved to town in 1941, and in 1953 my husband was killed. It was a hit-and-run. On Congress. We were living on Osborne, close to where I am living now. I was so lonely. Nothing mattered to me, whether I went to work or whether I cleaned house. The only thing I did was to get up and feed my kids. And send them to school—Drachman. By that time Juanita was in school—Phoenix Indian School.

Is it [the tape recorder] on? My husband was a really young man then, good to me, good to the kids. And he thinks it's fun to have kids, that's why we had all those kids. He really loved Linda, because he was a really grown man then. Of course he'd go off and get drunk and take her. When you come home from work they won't be there. One time I came home and it was real cold. And I asked the lady next door, did you see where Jose went? "Yeah, I saw. It was about ten o'clock when they went with this other man who had a car. They came and went with that car. The other man had the diaper bag and Jose had Linda all wrapped up." My brother came and helped me look for them. We found them in the car, the other man sitting in the back with Linda with the bottle [Frances chuckles], and Jose was driving. Oh, my goodness! That's why Linda drinks now. She's a very strong woman. That's when Pancho got mad and left, he went to his father, who said, "If you leave a good woman, don't come here." They got back together.

I feel like telling you, I've never told anybody, never really talked about it. I've never really talked about the day of my husband's death. It was Saturday and I was working and he was working. So we got off at four o'clock. That's when Sears was on Sixth Avenue. He was waiting for me up there, so I got off and went in. He bought me some shoes and he bought some shoestrings. It was Saturday, so we went home and there was gonna be a dance down at Fresnal [Jiawul Dak], between here and Sells, and we were gonna go and we got ready. Linda was a little girl, she must have been about five years old. So she got ready and we got in the truck. There were some people, there were some men standing there, we got in the back of the truck. He came, he said, "I'm not going." First he said, "You got eight dollars?" I said, "I don't have eight dollars, I got ten dollars." He said, "Okay, give me that."

So I gave him the ten dollars. When he came that evening, he said he wasn't going to the dance. He said, "Let Linda down so I can stay with her and we can go to the carnival tomorrow." So I said, um, "No, Linda wants to go with me," because she was already in the truck standing up with me. That was the last time I saw him alive.

And we went to the dance, all night. I don't know why, I kept asking my sister, "What time is it?" So in the morning when it was over, when we came home, and I told the other kids, "Well, she's hungry, so you can fry some eggs for her," and I went to sleep. And I went to sleep and I woke up and it was Sunday. And he wasn't home, he wasn't home. Monday I was gonna go to work, I got up early and took a shower and went to the stove and was gonna build a fire, and I was cleaning the stove, and I started crying. And here that night I was feeling he was coming home, that he was coming. So I went to work. His boss called me and asked if I knew where he was, because if he gets drunk, he goes to the jail and bails him out. I said, "He's probably in jail." He said, "I already tried over there. He's not there!" Another one called, and his [the boss's] wife got the call and said, "Well, we haven't heard from him. His wife's here." She said they just found a body and it's at the morgue. Answering to his description. And I said, "It couldn't be him." And I thought about, about, how we never did anything wrong for that to happen to us. We tried to be good people . . . everything came back. So the next call was my brother. He said that they think it's him. I said it just couldn't be him. So his boss went up there and came to the place where I was working. I knew right then it was him. He came, and then he said they wanted to take me to the morgue.

All the way to the morgue, I was telling the man it can't be him, it's somebody else. I kept telling him. I was very anxious to see him, so I went. I guess I blacked out. When I came to, it was windy, and dark. And then we got out, they were gonna take me home, and the truck came and there were a lot of men, Indian men, and the one that brought them said, "Is he identified yet?" I guess they just brought the men to identify him. They turned back. Because when we found his wallet over there, seven dollars was there — he always took three dollars — and his good hat was there. . . . [Slowly, with great feeling] So it was dark, it was windy, everything was *wrong*. Seemed like everything was upside down. And it went on. And then the kids were picked up at school and they came home. . . . That was the hardest thing, to face the kids—no father. The lady, her name is Betsy, she stood by me all the time, and it went on until the next day. The night was long, I don't know about the day, but the night was long. The tears were coming. . . . Finally Emma came. You know Emma? She was the first one that came. Because I would just sit there, I couldn't do anything but just sit there. Look at the wall. I guess I wasn't seeing anything. The only thing I could remember was the day we met in Sears and the evening he went back into the house alive. Those are the two things I kept remembering over and over and over. So his boss came over and made the arrangements, and Frances, his wife, and my brother came and arranged for men to come and dig the hole. Everything was arranged . . . and the horses were there, to round up the horses, ya know. And, ah, I just left everything up to them, and up to my brother.

The lady that I worked for, Frances, she had five children and she offered to take the children. She said, "Well, it won't matter, I can just add some more." And I said, "I'll manage it, somehow I'll be all right." Especially Linda, Linda kept running around saying that her father would come home in the afternoon. She kept saying—I don't know why—"My papa's gonna come home in the afternoon." Even after he was buried, she said, "My papa is taking so long! I thought he'd be home in the afternoon." Christy was only two months grown, I was pregnant with her. No, I was three months. It was really hard. But he left that behind for me.

So it went on and on and on. I came back to face the people. And we butchered the cow and fed the people, and then we brought him home and buried him. They had the wake in town, and we brought him to the village in the morning. When we came, there were already people here. It was just like a feast, we kept feeding people and feeding people. So the next day we went back to gather up the stuff he left behind to bring home. That was another thing. We brought his things. Seemed like it was just a dream. When we brought him, the horse was already saddled. It seems like the horse understood when they were getting him down from the truck, he was looking up just like he was getting ready for his master—that was really hard. We saddle the horse and tie up four nights when the man dies. Nowadays when the [death] anniversary comes, we do the same thing. His horse's name was Tony. So they did whatever has to be done. We buried his shaving things, his wallet and things. Then later on, somebody said, because he had wedding clothes . . . , so we just buried that [the wedding clothes] on top in a box. I don't know if we do the right thing, we just did it. I was so lost that I couldn't even think. Somebody else had the idea.

I was there, but I couldn't do anything. And, um, so the fourth day we went back to live in town again. My house was worse. I'd get up and make the children lunch and send them to school. It took me a month to really get up and do something. Seems like when I open my eyes, there is a book that keeps going and going, and then it comes back. It was really hard.

One morning I was cooking breakfast and the radio was going. I don't ever listen to the radio in the morning, but it said, but this morning there are ten fatherless children, the plane crashed, eight men and each of them have children. And I thought to myself, that's even worse! Burned, and the children didn't know why their father died! Of course, that's what the children are thinking, "Why did my father die?" In this world, it happens every day. And here it seemed like I was the only one going through this, seems like I was feeling sorry for myself. So that woke me up. So I knew what to do. I cleaned the house, I took a bath, and got dressed [Frances inhales deeply]. So the next week my people kept on coming, asking me to go back to work. That was the best medicine. So the next week I went to work, I got dressed and went to work.

Of course it was sad to come home to nobody but the kids. It was really sad when the kids would be waiting at the door, that was really sad. It went on for months. The children's pension didn't come in for about six months, so we were really going down. [Slowly] And, ah, I had an uncle, I had a real well-[to]-do uncle, a rich man, he was a ladies' man, too. The ladies come across the street where I am living, and sometimes I see his truck. And in the back of my mind I think, uncle will come over and see the kids and maybe give them a dollar or maybe buy them a loaf of bread. Of course, I never asked him. No. It went on. . . . So that's what happened. And of course, years, I think of him. Sometimes I cry, even months after that. I think how just one day it happened, he's gone. Crying won't bring him back. Maybe he's happy somewhere.

It was five years later that this man used to come to visit me. And my uncle, then he came over and said he was no good, to leave me alone. Why didn't he come when I needed him? [Frances laughs.] I just told him I think I am a grown woman, I know what I am doing. What I want to say is to have whoever reads the book to know that Frances—Jose's boss's wife—wasn't even my relative. I worked for her, but she stood by me from the time he died, eight days after that. And I felt bad that he died, and I didn't even know why he died, right here in Tucson.

I've been thinking about this. Clara got sick, I thought she just had arthritis like me. Clara from Ge Oidag, too—Danny's mother [Danny Lopez, Frances's son-in-law]. We used to joke about our arthritis. One time she said, "I don't think I am able to walk now." So the girls got her a wheelchair, and then she started walking a little bit again. Whenever they have anything, she'd come and we'd talk and talk, and Florence said, "I don't know if she doesn't feel good, she always sleeps!" One time we went again, and she was sleeping all the time. And I said, "It's too much sleep for you." And she said, "I don't know, but I'm sleepy!" Then again she had a birthday, and we went over there, and she said, "I didn't know you were here." "We just came," I said. She said she was going to go to sleep. And the next week I heard she was having an operation, I guess they found out she had cancer. So they sent her back on a Monday, and she died on Saturday morning. I've known her a long time, it was Danny's mother. She was born in 1900. We went to mass at five o' clock and buried her—must have been seven-thirty. It was a nice funeral, nice flowers. I was telling a man one time, we were at a funeral, I said, "I bet when I die no one will even put any flowers!" He said, "We'll just put the greasewood flowers." [Laughing] It was so funny. What happens if they don't have any flowers?

I don't know why he said that. Jose said he was gonna go home and just lay around. He came home in a pine box. I guess that's what he meant. One day he was telling me that he dreamed that he died, and he was walking, there were trees, tall trees, and he was walking. It was dark and windy and he was walking between four candles, four candles were lit. And he was walking and pretty soon the candle went out. He was walking in circles, and then he finally came back to his body that was laying. He dreamed that, so he said, "When I die, be sure to put four candles." I know it's important. I never thought anything about it.

And another time, it was years before he died, he said, "Whenever I die, be sure to put water, because whenever we die, I don't think we go straight to the water hole and drink." This man that died a long time ago said he wanted a cup to drink water out of the well. And he finally found a rusty can, and he said, "That's all right." And he drank from that rusty can. And he said, "I'll show you why I can't drink." So they went. There's a wash right next to the corral. And there's a water hole with sand and water in it. And then there were owl feathers. And people would come and kind of push the owl feathers with their hand and drink. So he said, "When I die, be sure to put water." So we put candles and water every day for a year.

I dreamed he was eating beans from an olla. He never really did stand by me and talk. But I hear him—he was talking to me out of our sinks. We didn't have any running water then. He said he didn't mean to leave his children, he didn't *mean* to leave me, but, he told the children, "Your mother is strong, she will take care of you." And another time I dreamed he had a red or white jacket, he was talking to me, he said the same thing. To me it's real, but it's just a dream. Like one time I dreamed he was lying under a big tree and the horses were there saddled, and he got up and he turned around, and he got up and ran. He was crying. The next day his cousin was hit by a car, she died two days later. And I thought maybe that's why he cried. They say there's no sadness in the next world, there's no sickness or anything. But that's what I dreamed about. Sometimes you think about your dream but it's just a dream. Other times it's real! That's how I feel about it. I don't really believe in dreams. But sometimes something happens. Sometimes it happens similar to the dream, on this Earth, so sometimes I think that dreams are true.

I have had a lot of funerals lately. One was my cousin who died on the road. And one lady was from my basket-weaving class, she died. I guess she was cremated. It was a pretty funeral. They had her little stuffed puppy dog and bear there, and the horsehair baskets and a basket she had made in class. Lil. Also one of my godchildren's daughters. It's true—Joe said, someone was asking where I went, and Joe said, "I think she went to that wake they are having tonight, you know how grandma likes dead people!" [Laughing] One time I was talking to a lady, she died, too, not too long ago—it's my fault, I shouldn't have been asking her, but sometimes we want to know, ya know. [Frances laughs] I asked her, "How was the funeral? How was the wake?" She said, "It was all right! It was a cheap coffin." Oh, it was funny! So I told my kids, "You better buy me a special coffin so they won't see a cheap coffin." And I was telling my grandkids, "You don't go to see what the dead person looks like or what the coffin looks like, you go for the family. Pay your respects." Then Lorenzo said, "You never practice what you preach," teasing me.

I heard a joke the other day. This lady told her husband to go to the store, and she told him to get soap, a head of lettuce, milk, and Top Job. So the man was at the store, scratching his body all over, and the manager came up to him and said, "I'm sorry, you'll have to leave. We can't have that kind of behavior around here!" And the man said, "I'm just going over my list. Head of lettuce [Frances scratches her head], soap [scratching her armpits], milk [her breasts], and Top Job [her bottom]."

It is a lonely life when you lose your husband when you are young enough to be a wife. But when you get past that, it's fine, ya know. Like me, it doesn't bother me. I'm glad that I have a home, nobody tells me what to do, that I have all that, ya know. But again, sometimes I feel I can't pound a nail into the wall, and then I need a man. And if I ask somebody, I have to pay them!

When Jose died [Frances inhales deeply], I, we let our house on the reservation go. It was, it was just a house. It got worse, was almost falling down, and then I decided to fix it, so that's when I sent Lorenzo to be there, because he couldn't stay with us in town because he wasn't registered to live in my house. I sold tortillas because in the evenings I was, ya know, ironing—people used to bring their ironing. I worked all day and ironed at night, or I'd make tortillas and sell just to make [softly] extra money.

The years in between, they were years . . . and I understand now how I didn't fit in with the white people, but then I thought, well, that somehow I'll get used to it. So I did, I got so used to it. I like Tucson because I like people. I met people—it doesn't matter where, but I met people—on the streets, at a bus stop, anywhere. They were nice to me and I could talk to them. Just the other day I was thinking of a lady I met at a bus stop. She was telling me about how strange she felt when she first came to Tucson, and that now she was getting used to it. She said she was getting to be happy. And I was thinking that this is a big thing for us people. We can meet people and like them, and we can be happy. Or we can just stay away from them. Sometimes I feel that way, that I could just stay away from people and not be bothered with them. But then again, it makes it kind of hard, because I like people and I like to help people—what little I can offer, because I am not very good at a lot of things. So she was telling me that she met a lady who was crippled and her husband had cancer, so she'd buy groceries for them and help her clean him up. She said that made her happy. And I thought, how can it make her happy? How can it make her happy when there's two sick people there? It was strange to me, but after a while I thought about it, and finally I understood what she meant.

Those years in between I did domestic work. And I sold tortillas from home. And another thing I'd do is sew in the evenings, I would refashion the material to make clothes for the children. And then one day somebody told me from the school that my children are dressed the best. I can't believe it now, I can't do anything like that now.

There was a Mexican lady next door who took care of Linda then, the older kids were in school. We got the children's pension six months later, and my widow pension. Mildred took care of the children in the evening. Juanita was in college but then we ran out of money, so she had to go to school in Phoenix. She never did finish college. Mildred was the one that raised Linda. Christy, I raised her. Linda was her mother, too. Wherever Linda goes, Christy would go. Sundays we go to the movies, all of us. That's the only thing, because we didn't have a car, we sold the truck. My son was too young to drive and I wasn't a good driver.

After the kids were grown, I had those foster kids. That was the seventies. I got this girl that had trouble with her aunt's husband. At that time the foster child didn't get much. By the time you got the groceries and everything . . . She must have been about sixteen, I had her until she finished school, about two years. The other one came soon after. They have a little baby about two years old, but when I went to see the welfare, they said I couldn't take it because I was already sixty.

I worked for eighteen years. I stopped when I was sixty-two. I had three surgeries during that time, so I decided not to go back after that, because I had hernia. I did some demonstrations, but when I met you, I really started doing them. I used to baby-sit and do domestic work for Tom Bahti, and sometimes demonstrations. He would buy my baskets. So, after that I still work for him until I retired. What kept me going was church, and friends, and work. I went to Santa Cruz Church on Sixth Avenue, but I spent more time at St. Nicholas Indian Center, teaching the elderlies how to sew, make flowers, *cascarones*, and they would give me groceries for that.[1] So that helped. The kids were grown, and Mildred was married and Juanita was working, so it was easier. The kids would joke, saying that when you turn eighteen, you start getting poor. They stopped getting their pension when they turned eighteen.

It wasn't that hard, because, you see, I have friends. Like I told you once, you look at people and some are just people. One time I was getting off work and it was very hot, and there was man sitting there waiting for the bus. I was sitting on the bench in the shade because I knew that man, he was a drunk, too. So I went and I sat down. He shook hands and he said, "Well, Jose didn't mean to leave you, his time came. When our time comes, we can't say no, we can't stand back, we have to go. But he's happy wherever he is, he is looking down on you. He'll make it, he'll make it." I always remember that man, he's a drunk but he had good words. It really helps. From that day on, when I see a drunk, I say, well, maybe he's a drunk, but he may have more sense than any of us.

It was hard at nights . . . , but another thing, it was good for me, I was tired and I'd just go to sleep. Some people don't sleep. . . . And in the morning I'd get up and feed the kids, and burn the toast [Frances laughs]. I just go on and on and on. Just like a book. And one time, I told you about it, I was cooking and listening to the radio and the announcer said there were ten fatherless children. That really woke me up.

Frances's paternal grandparents, Jose (E-o'oho) and Salomina Francisco, outside their home at S-koksonagk.

Frances and her mother, Amelia, photographed at a
studio in Tucson in 1913.

Frances as a young child,
wearing someone else's shoes.
Photographed in Arizona about
1915.

Frances and her husband, Jose Manuel, in Tucson about 1948.

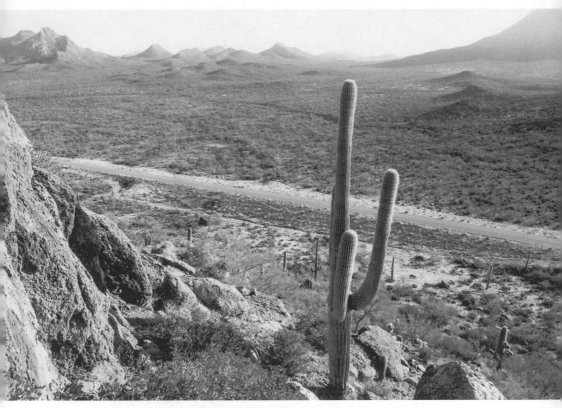

The desert around San Pedro.

Frances's "Indian kitchen" at San Pedro in 1980.

The church at San Pedro in the 1980s.

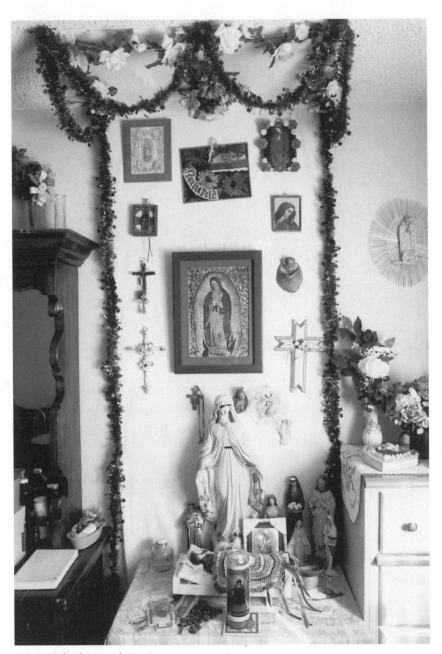

Frances's bedroom shrine in 1999.

Frances and her daughters Linda Sanchez (left) and Christy Manuel on
Thanksgiving Day, 1999.

Frances and her granddaughter Amelia Quiroga in 1999.

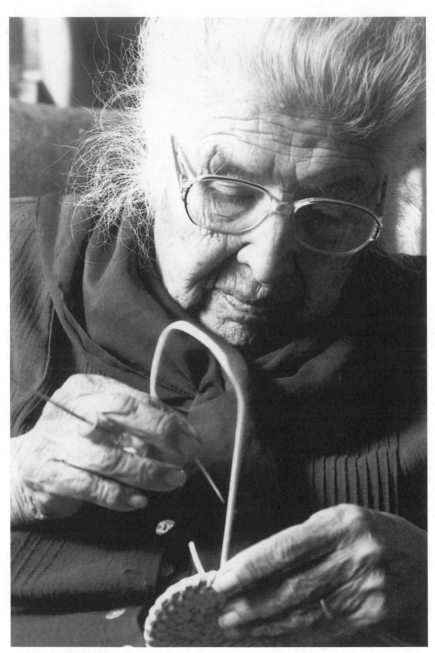

Frances making a basket at her home at San Pedro in 1999.

Part III ◇ Homecoming

San Pedro, 1981–Present

I believe a lot of things, and sometimes I don't want to believe a lot of things. What was it Amelia said? She was reading something in a book and told me, "Ya know, an elephant will go back to where they are from, like where they live, and if they are away from home and they're gonna die, they go back to that place and die." "That's what I am doing," I said. "I'm over here and maybe I'll die here." Her eyes got so big! (1987)

One evening Frances and I were sitting outside, talking about the night sounds.

"It was summer and we were sleeping outside, the four of us: Amelia and Denise [Frances's grandchildren, then small], and Lorenzo. You know, I'd sit inside and work on my basket, and they'll be out there supposedly sleeping, and one time I thought, 'I think I'll go out there for a while and come in.' And I went out there and the girls were there. I said, 'What are you doing?' 'We're counting the frogs [toads]! We counted seventy.'" Frances laughs.

"Oh, they must have counted the same frogs over and over again," I said, laughing.

"But they can't sleep late because the sun comes up early. I don't sleep all night, I'll sleep for a little while and then I'll come in. If I'm alone, I'll stay in-side. Before it gets dark, I'll close the shades and lock the door and I'll be here. Lorenzo used to go out and not come home until later. Two or three days, then he'll be back. That's the way it is in the desert, especially when you live way out in the middle of nowhere. You hear all kinds of noises," Frances said, yawning.

"It took me a while to decipher the sounds. Like the sounds of the horses banging against the water trough. And then there was the cat, it sounded like La Llorona," I said, not letting on that I had been scared.

"That must be Geronimo [the cat]," she said, knowing I was scared.

"Last night that dog was running so fast, it looked like a person flying. Graveyard [the dog] was really howling. And the horses were snorting!"

"Sometimes when the spirits are around, the horses make that sound. And when one of the dogs howl, they all howl," Frances said lightly, trying to scare me now.

"Then the coyotes start, and then the dogs and the horses. And I don't know what this big cow was doing in the desert here to the east. He was so loud! And then the dogs would start again."

"It must be a bull, then."

"Yeah, everything was echoing. And the birds, and Lorenzo's snoring."

"You were asleep but you weren't sleep. I feel tired after that kind of night," Frances said sympathetically.

"Yeah, I feel tired. Remember that night when Yellowstone was here, he was going back and forth, and the other horses were making loud noises, too?"

"Especially Chato, he makes that noise. Sometimes when the truck comes and takes the calves to the market, and the cows will cry! Sometimes it keeps me awake. They make noise, too."

"*And last night we heard the owls,*" I said softly.

"*We hadn't heard the owls for a long time, maybe a year. My heart slowly shivered,*" Frances said, remembering.

"*There was one far away. . . .*"

"*Seems like one of them was just flying back and forth. There were two of them. One of them had a big slow sound, and the other was real far. What are we supposed to talk about? Let's get it over with and then go to sleep,*" Frances said in her usual way.

7 ⟨·⟩ Getting Used To It

Dear Debbie,
I just came home from town. There is nothing to see
downtown, it's hot and dusty. It's little bit cooler round here,
nights are cool. I haven't done anything here. I've been living
here for seven months. I haven't really talked with anybody
round here. I work on my basket and take walks, watch TV,
eat, and sleep.
  And now I'm back to earth.
  I think I can start doing things. I went back to teaching and
I'm glad. 42 years is a long time. It was like starting a new life.
  (from an unfinished letter written between 1981 and 1985)

I applied for the house [with the tribe] and it took almost ten years before I
got it. So I had to swear that I would come back. I came back in 1981, when
I was sixty-eight. I had a big ceremony for my housewarming. It started
little and got bigger and bigger. I had saved a lot of money and sold some
cows. We had Yaqui Deer Dancers, Pascolas, and Matachinis. They danced
all night, until seven in the morning. The traditional [O'odham] dancers
only danced a short while—I have a picture of them. But somebody stole
my check, and whoever stole it took it [the photo]. Someone mailed it when
they found it, but some of them were missing.

I wanted it to be part religious, and part tradition, that's what I want. So
it happened, I got the Yaquis, and I got some singers and a dancer, and mu-
sician, and the Matachinis. And I killed a big cow, everything. I saved my
money and got everything, flowers, whatever. And I told my relatives, they
helped me. We had a shrine made up, so when the time came, the dancers
came to the house. They came first and the horses, four horses were there,
started at the church. The others came from the old house, went around,
and came here and went around, and came over there and went around,
and came back. You know my procession—the horses walked from there
to here and to the church. They say a lot of them didn't like it, why was the
horse in the procession? But that's the way I want it. There were about six

or eight hundred people who came for the ceremony — to eat and to dance. We had a dance and all that — chicken-scratch.

The next day the people came over and gave me some of these things, like that one over there with the little ducks — they were my housewarming presents. You can see these things hanging on the wall [pointing]. When we bless the house, we build the fire in the stove and we save that. I still got the ashes. Whatever we do, we save it. A medicine man blessed the house the night before. So it's a good foundation house.

I came back in '81 [Frances laughs]. I moved back home because I was retired, I was retired and I had to . . . well, I could have stayed in town. But my house was done, and I had to come home. Because if I didn't live there, it would be given away to someone else. So I had to come home. [Frances speaks softly and slowly.] And it took me two years to get used to it. When I came home, those people that I associated with were gone. These young people, you've seen them, they're there, but we don't see them. It was strange. It wasn't like this, we were more, more on the friendly road. But I'm bad at those things. I can't go visiting anybody. I don't really blame them, because there were so many things that they wanted to do. They wanted to get ahead, and I guess a lot of drinking, they got hangovers, and they don't want to be out. There's a reason why we're not together now. Maybe they have nothing against me, they just can't get along with me because I'm so different, and they're so different. I don't know how else to put it. I can't tell why, I just can't get used to it [her voice fading]. It wasn't lonely. It was something about the reservation. I like the reservation. I wasn't proud. It's just something about that, [softly] I couldn't get used to it.

I had a lot of things to do, and then still, that wasn't enough for me. It was so hard [Frances's voice fades out]. Somebody would come and say [in a high pitch], "Oh! You got such a pretty house," and "It's so pretty!" And I think, if I got a pretty house, then why am I so unhappy? Because every day I got up in the morning and it was the same thing. The same thing. And, um, in Tucson, you see different people, you want to go over here, you're gonna do this and do that, we're gonna make this and do it together, or, you know, things like that. You always have somebody you look up to, somebody you say to, "What are we gonna do? Are we gonna do this, or what shall we do? You know, all those things. But here, [in a high pitch] I was just here! I didn't go to town, except to buy groceries, for over a year.

I think I could have gotten cleared away, you know this, but I had no time for that like I do now. I didn't understand why I felt this way, but I just didn't have any real interest in anything. And later on, I asked myself, Why do I feel this way? It's not the people, it's me! I'm not interested in the people, I'm only interested in the people in town. Or only white people. And that's why I thought that it wasn't the people, it was me. And later on, I let go, I thought, if I'm going to live here, I'll live here. When I let go, I thought, well I am here, I might as well enjoy it. And then I started to enjoy everything — like which way the wind is blowing. I hear noise. My grandfather used to say when you are alone and hear noise, those are your friends. The things on the ground are the best — it's going to lead you somewhere. It's the things you see and hear on the ground — they are the ones that give you the courage and the strength to go on. I believe it now. I listen to those little noises, they are my friends. There is something crawling on the ground, it's going to lead me somewhere. I just accept the things and then I feel better about it. I was really longing for town. I was really, it wasn't the people! They say the people don't come to see me or anything. What would they see? What would I talk to them about?

I'm glad I got over it. I'd rather be here than anywhere else [Frances laughs]. The air — I love that most, the air . . . I don't care for cloudy days. I like rain, at a certain time, but not these cloudy days. It doesn't mean anything, it's just cloudy, that's all. But I'd rather have rain, and windy — I like wind. I like the cows and the horses. I don't care so much for the cows because I don't see them, but the horses, I do. Let's stop, I'm gonna work on my basket.

8 ◇ Lucious

Today is April 11,
1987,
the night is so still,
so quiet,
so comfortable, not a sound,
we can only hear our own
heartbeats.

We took a walk over by the church,
only the dogs were making noise
running around,
and we thank the Lord that we can still walk and that we can still see,
and when we get home, go to bed and relax,
and wait for the morning
while the night's rolling on.

I thought by now we'd be closer to the present. . . . We have . . . I thought of . . . We have a lot of things that will come. . . . Like first [slowly, sadly] I thought I was going to have my grandson, Lucious, for my own. He was a hard child to control, a difficult child. So I thought I would take him, [slowly and sadly] maybe somehow I could. . . . I thought this would come later, but I think we're ready for this. And I worked on a basket—a maze, and I sold it and I bought a horse. I paid for the horse, and I told Joe [another grandson], "This is yours, I got this one for you." That was fine. And the next thing, I made another maze and I sold it, and I got the cows [very sadly] for myself. The horses started developing right away, [softly] but the cows didn't. So when Lucious died, it broke my heart. Nothing meant anything to me.

I thought this would come later, but I think we're ready to talk about the wake. The reasons why it really broke my heart is because I didn't understand that he had problems. But then that didn't really get into my head, you know, I really didn't think it, it was that much [softly, inhaling] until after he died. That was, that's why I was so hurt.

[Inhaling deeply] He killed himself. [Inhaling] Hung himself. Yeah, it hurts. It still hurts to talk about it, but we have to talk about it. Well, they told me, the only way is to talk about it. My friends told me to go to counseling, but I didn't for four years. I made a big ceremonial for his fourth year [death] anniversary, it's just about ten years, March third. I just felt that way, like doing something for him, for his wandering soul to find rest. Because we did, for nine days we did the ceremony, but I wasn't there, I wasn't really there, I was too much in a sadness. And a year anniversary, a year, we did the same thing, but I was still . . . still, what would you say? Not clear on that. So four years I did it. When we were gonna plan this, this was gonna be a happy occasion, there wasn't gonna be any showing of sadness. So I told the man to do the rosary and the singing, and he told me to just buy white flowers so it'll be a new start. And, ahm, like the pure beginning, that's what I did. And we had the ceremony, the singing, and also the dancers and the clowning. I think everybody had a good time on the day of Lucious's fourth year anniversary. We had food, we had everything that we always do. Everything was blue like the sky, and the white flowers and the candles—only eight candles, because sometimes we put too many candles and one day somebody said that it was too hot, so we just had eight. And some saints and a cross—those saints that I have: Blessed Mother, Saint Francis, Josephine.

After the anniversary, it seems like the load of heaviness came off my shoulders, so I feel better now. And I think, he's . . . I hope that he's somewhere being happy now. That's how . . . how I feel now, I'm not sad. I just feel that he's somewhere happy and looking down on us, seeing that grandma's still around [Frances laughs]. That's the way I feel about it. So from then on, I do things, I work with my two hands, and I buy things—not for myself, but for the house or for the horses. Like when I go someplace, I buy something for the horses, for Lorenzo. Like I bought a halter, two halters in Ohio; in Oklahoma cowboy town I bought ropes and reins; and, ahm, wherever I go, I buy things for Lorenzo, for the horses.

9 ◇ The Owl Sickness

Frances's granddaughter Amelia Quiroga recorded this story
about the owl, one of Frances's stories from a long time ago.
Using Frances's words, she titled a term paper for a college class,
"My mind goes around and comes back to where I started."
Frances gave me the piece in 1997 to put in the book.

In my days I was told these things. It must be true. This story happened in Magdalena, Mexico. We used to have a wagon train that would go between our village and Magdalena. When the people arrived in Magdalena, the men would talk all night long while the women prayed. There were two young men who were scouts that led the wagon train. They would ride their horses and have an extra saddle horse along in case one of their other horses got hurt or tired. Once when they came to Magdalena, the two young men went to visit some people in a village close by where they were having a celebration. They left their horses with the wagon train. A few days later the wagon train left to continue the journey back to the villages in Arizona. The people from the wagon train left the horses behind for the young men, so they would have them when they returned. Unfortunately, the horses got away. The young men went to follow the wagon train in hopes of catching up to them. They went to the man that owned the camp and had been keeping the horses while the wagon train was there, and asked him how long it had been since the wagon train left. He told them that it hadn't been too long, about noon. One of the young men said, "I guess we have to follow them." And they started walking toward the wagon train. It got dark and they heard an owl making a high whistle sound up in the air. One of the young men was gifted and could see into the future, and he said, "Let's ask the owl where the wagon train is." The other man said, "A bird can't tell us anything!" Then the first young man whistled for the owl to come down. The owl flew down and landed on the ground in front of the young men. The first young man could see into the future and the other one could not. The first young man said, "I am going to talk to the owl. You must stand behind me and don't look anywhere. When I pull my arm back along my side, you can take a quick glimpse. Just look down. Don't look until I touch you." So he started talking to the owl and asked where the wagon train was camping for the night. He told the owl, "We don't have any tequila but I can offer a cigarette." The owl took the cigarette and started smoking fast. The owl told the young man the wagon train was not too far from there. The people were camping between two hills and they are around on the other side not far away. The second man that was standing behind the first could not see anything, but he could see the light of the cigarette. Then, the first young man who was talking to the owl pulled his arm back along his side to touch the young man behind. The young man who was standing behind looked over the first young man's shoulder to see the owl. Instead, he saw a man standing there wearing a beige shirt, and then he fainted. The first young man reached over to help pick up the second young man. He said, "What happened to you?" The second man knew what it meant, and that he hadn't just seen an owl.

One night Frances was sitting outside and called to me to come hear two owls—there was one big and one little one. "Within four days," Frances said intently, "if nothing happens, then we'll forget it. Someone may die, something good may happen, or something could be avoided." Luckily the owls went away that next day, leaving as suddenly as they had appeared. But the episode left us shook up, because it had reminded us of the owl sickness Frances had a few years before, when she almost died.[1]

I'll talk about the owl sickness, when I started bleeding. They have a rare kind of sickness, even the doctor got scared. Something to do with the kidney and a vessel that connects to the kidney.[2] He says I was very lucky. He says I could have bled to death. I really got scared, even the doctor got scared. And I heard this noise. . . .

It was in the evening, and I was over Alice's [Frances's neighbor] and we were sitting outside talking, and then we heard the owl. And Alice said, "Here comes the owl again," and I looked up there, he was coming. And here's the house, the other house. I was sitting and Alice was sitting. He comes like this and he was going to [speaking somberly, in a deep voice] sit on the wood facing that way, and then he just went. Then he came back and sat on that mesquite tree. And I said, "I better get home." It was getting dark. "I better get home," I said, because the owl might scratch my face, so then we stood up. She stood up and I stood up, and she said, "Here it comes again." Here it comes again, and it went like this, up and down in that big tree right there. So I started going and it felt like it was sitting just over there. I started going and it seems like I was going, but I wasn't moving forward. That's the first time I really noticed it. It was a big owl. About a foot, and big, yes. And pretty soon there were two of them, and Lorenzo hit one with his slingshot. I guess he never did come back . . . just the one. He'd be sitting on this post, sitting right there or sometimes on top of that [pointing to the post]. And, ah, so it came and I closed the door, closed the shades. And then one time we came late from town and it was sitting on top of the *ramada*. That was the first time I really noticed it. It didn't bother me, I just saw it sitting there. But it didn't bother me until that time it sat on the post. Once you see it, you think it's pretty, or it means something—a relative or a friend that's already gone.

But this one, it's too much, he just made me mad. It's just too much. Just before the dark, he'd come and sit there [her voice rising], you know. He'll move back and forth, sometimes to the church and to Alice's, just back and forth. I guess he stayed all night. When I was sitting outside, I knew he was around, but I didn't . . . Then pretty soon I heard something, you know, like hen or a bird on the ground, and it was sitting right there. Then I said [quickly], "I don't know, I can't understand, why are you doing this? If you meant to tell me something, why don't you just tell me I'm gonna die?" So Lorenzo started coming. I don't know. And pretty soon it was sitting way up there. [Frances's voice becomes deep and hoarse.] The owl really made me upset, and that's why I won't go out. He'd be sitting over there before the sun goes down. Ever after the medicine man came, he came for over a week. Then he stopped coming.

I had my worst sickness when I had the stroke, and I didn't know it. That's when I lost my [sight in one] eye. Usually when I get sick, I get kidney infection, bladder infection, headaches—little things, but this one was really bad. Oh, and one time [Frances laughs] I got sick when we went out, it was a really hot day. We were eating and eating and eating, that was in the morning, and in the afternoon I didn't feel good. I was sleeping outside and I couldn't sleep. I felt funny, I was cold and I was hot. So I came in and it was on a Wednesday, because Tuesday and Wednesday I didn't get up, it was in the afternoon I started shaking and shaking and shaking, just shaking, and they would put more blankets. That was the only thing that helped. Johnny and Jimmy [Frances's grandsons] even put a mattress on top of me—that mattress was heavy, so I could hold the shakes, ya know. So I started shaking and I told them to hold me down. And this went on— Wednesday, Thursday, Friday, Saturday—and Mildred [Frances's daughter] came that Saturday and just went to that house and went to the dance, didn't stop by here. I was really sick. And, ah, Sunday, Joe [one of Frances's grandsons] came in, and he said he was going to walk to the road and get somebody to take him to Three Points, and he was going to call somebody [softly, inhaling], they could come to see me. So I was holding onto that because I was really sick, because I hadn't eaten anything since I got sick. Then I found out later that day that he was passed out at the other house.

So the next day, that was Monday, I guess somebody went over there and told Lorissa [Frances's neighbor] I was sick. She came over and said to get ready, she was going to take me to the hospital. So I [slowly, softly] put my clothes on, and here Lorenzo and John [Frances's grandson] had gone to Three Points and called somebody, maybe Mildred or somebody, and told them I was sick. I was taken to the hospital, so Mildred started off to Sells. When I got to the door of the hospital [in Sells], I opened the door and I just dropped. So they came running with the wheelchair and all that, before they got me to bed. Oh, I was so tired, I wanted to go to bed but I had to go office to office and then Mildred came in. She said she was going to take me to town, so they gave me some papers and took me to [St. Mary's Hospital in] town. They put me to bed, and it was so cold. That was another real sickness I had. So they say, with all those sicknesses, that when it's time for me to go, I'll just go [Frances laughs], because I went through all these sicknesses. I said, "Oh boy, then I don't have to suffer!"

I had my kidney problem before that. This one started in October or November. It was two months before we ever got the medicine man. He came and he left, left while he was still coming. After a week it went away and I haven't seen anything. [In a lighter, softer tone] I guess he did something. We heard him talking to something. We went around the house with all these men—mostly men that were drunk. Went to all the houses. They had to go for the whole village to see if it was anything. They went to ask somebody if some dead person was . . . [trailing off] and I said, "Well why don't you ask Jose?" Anyway, the medicine man was talking—I wish you could hear sometimes when they talk to the spirits! You can't understand what they are saying [with slow and belabored speech]. That's what happened. He cleaned all the houses, the village, the church. *A'ada*, cleaning— it gets rid of the bad spirits, sickness. Everybody paid him, collected ten dollars from every family. So it went on and on. A lot of things that happens to people—[with difficulty] I don't believe it, I just forget it. I say they imagine things like that.

You have had a lot of hard times.

Oh, yeah, I had hard times. I had hard times but I don't really call that hard times. A lot of Indians have had hard times, especially with babies. They [inhaling the whole sentence] died from smallpox.[3] Also died from whooping cough. But what a lot of people might think is hard times that we had isn't hard times at all. Like when you carry water on your head in a bucket, put it in a tub for potty water and in another for drinking water. And sometimes you go and get water in the evening and put it in the tub and the next day you get more water. You wash diapers on the washboard, wash and wash and wash, and rinse, rinse, rinse, then hang them up. You know, when you just think about it, you have washing machine, you have a hose, and you just turn on the water. When you just think about it, it isn't real! But it is true because I used to do that!

I used to carry water on my head, I'm very strong on my head. When I came here, I'd go after wood with Lorenzo. He'd take the wheelbarrow and I'd tie me some wood and carry it on my head! I quit doing that when I got older. But I'm very strong on my head. One time Lorenzo was talking about how much I was carrying on my head. I told him, "I'm going to walk on the dike so people can see me!" Okay . . .

10 ◇ Lorenzo: Horses and Song

I said to Lorenzo, "It's Eastertime and the police are coloring
eggs. You can rob a bank and nobody would even know it!"
So he said, "I have to stay home and make sure nobody steals
my birds." I bet Lorenzo's asleep now and everybody's
stealing birds.

How would you describe Lorenzo?

Lorenzo is a cowboy, a real horseman. He always has his hat on—a straw
hat, and dark glasses. He doesn't say much, but then he'll surprise you with
something funny. But he could be mean, could really tell you off. I leave
him alone when he gets drunk. If he's mad, he'll just get up and go. He's
been like this all of his life, so I'd be a fool to try to make him mine. That's
why we didn't marry, this way we won't be hurting each other.

Lorenzo came in . . . I think it was 1958. He didn't have a job, so I sent him
over to the reservation to take care of things. That's when I decided to fix
my house [on the reservation], because it had gotten run-down after Jose
died. Joe was the one who said, "Why is he staying all the time?" "Because
he doesn't have a place to stay." "Well, can't he build a house?"

When he's drinking, all he'll talk about is horses. I'm always interested,
and he'll talk about the open range, a corral, a rope, or whatever will go
with the horses. If he has money, he'll just buy things for the horses. I feel
that the horses are just as important as people! When I was listening to the
TV the other day, it said in there that if anybody is so close to a dog, a person
should go see a psychiatrist. And I thought, I'd better go see a psychiatrist!

We were saying the other day, Lorenzo never really makes us laugh, but
he'll say something serious and it'll be funny, ya know—it sounds real
funny. One time I hid his bottle and he was looking for it, he was looking for
it, and he said, "Come on, show me my bottle, what did you do with it!?"
And, you know, in the old days a little kid would say, "*Nana* [I'm hurt], I
want my bottle!" He said, "I'm *nana*, I'm *nana*!" We laughed!

Lorenzo used to live with a lady by the name of Jenny. Once he had a horse and he named her Jenny, and he was telling me, "Jenny did this," and "Jenny did that." And I said, "Oh, that means you still think about Jenny, that's why you named your horse." I just said it! It was just there! Everyday talk. And one time we were here [Frances laughs], all my kids, all my kids — Mildred, Florence, Linda, and Christy, they were all here — here, you know — talking about something, and "Oh, your horse got out! What's her name, Jenny?" And he said, "Oh, Mom doesn't like it." And I remember I said that. All those girls laughed. "Mom's jealous!" That was funny. So the horse was never called Jenny after that. She works in the hospital, ya know.

One time it was a cold morning and he came in, he said, "I'm going to Three Points, I'm going with these people to Three Points." I said, "Why don't you build a fire before you go?" He said, "No, just lay here, I'll be right back! I'll light it for you when I come back." He came back in two days. I was getting after him, I was getting mad, and he said, "There was decay under you!" Just like Jimmy, he was supposed to come and he never came — I wanted him to fix the cooler. I said, "I wish I had a gun, I'd shoot you," and Jimmy said, "What for? What are you going shoot me for? Poor me!"

But if I ask him something in the morning, I don't know if he realizes how strong his words are. I wish he could hear himself sometimes, because he never says anything kind. Like he'll say, "Good morning," And then I'll ask him something, like "Does your hand hurt?" And he snapped, "Of course it hurts!" He used to get really upset about the horses.

One night Frances and Lorenzo were up late, trying to chase Yellowstone away, then up early, trying to corral him. By that time Lorenzo's old horse, Kiowa, was gone.

We heard these horses fighting, so we went over to see. Lorenzo said, "The horses are fighting." So he went out and chased them away. The next morning, in the morning, I was cooking breakfast and I saw the two horses out by the corral. I said, "Well, there's two horses now and they're fighting." So he went out, and chased one of them away. And the other one was going round the corral, and it would go around, and it would run the other way. It took a long time, and finally I couldn't stand it, so I went out to help him.

We finally got him into the corral. He was the neighbor's horse, they call him Yellowstone. We have an old horse named Chato, and they don't like each other, they always fight with each other. This time he wasn't there, he was out on the range, but we had a mare, I guess that's why he was around. He didn't want to go home, so later on, Lorenzo was so upset. So I asked him if he wanted to go to the neighbor and tell him to come get the horse, so he did, but he wasn't there. I guess the horse is still there. And I said, "Where's Kiowa, did he get out?" "You don't see him there!" So I knew he was upset [Frances laughs].

There is a good chance if it was tomorrow or the next day, but he's been gone for weeks. It's hard to catch because he knows where to hide. He's smart, he just roams in that open range. Lorenzo knows where he roams, but he can't ride a horse. He doesn't know it, but he can't ride a horse. The doctor said, "No more horse." We have to find some horses, because the other horses ran away, too.

I have feelings for the horses. To me, when I think back, I had nobody! These kids here, when they stay here, they get bored, because we're too old. I loved my grandmother, but I needed something else! There was nobody, so I turned to the horses. They didn't talk to me, but I felt close to them. We just had two that I really cared for then, a girl and a male horse. And I think horses understand. They really do. We spend money. We buy hay and buy hay, we just keep Chato here because we want to see him. He's out on the range, he's gone out on the range, I know that he likes to run around. We'll have to get somebody to find him and bring him back. We just let him go so he could have some running around. He's been corralled for years, for years, three years, always there. And now he's running around on the open range! Retirement! [Frances laughs.] Somebody said they saw him and he was skinny. Maybe he was skinny because he's been running around. Before, when we let him go, he'd go for a while and then come back, but this time he didn't come back. I felt sorry for myself because I always like to see him in the morning. I'd look out in the morning, I'd look out and he'd be right there, looking up with a diamond on his forehead—all his sons and his children have diamonds on their heads. I used to look out there and Chato would be standing there with a diamond on his head. And when he left, it was sad.

Monalisa was born May 1, '87, he's the joy of our lives. Like a human being born, although he's got four legs! [Frances laughs.] We love him, and we love him, and we're gonna try to keep him till he gets bigger, then he can run around with his mother. So we'll see how we'll do about our horses. Caballero is here, maybe Joe will come and train him, if he's really coming.

A lot of people think horses are devils. When I had my housewarming, I had four horses in the procession and people wondered why I had the horses, because it was devil against God, ya know. Why is it that St. George has a horse, and St. Ramon the *caballero*? And St. George was a doctor. I don't think horses are devils.[1] We ourselves are devils. [There is a long pause.]

Did I ever tell you about the little boy? There was this man, he was a bad man, he was doing a lot of things like I don't know what they call it, but in Indian we call ha'icu ha-da:s, ha'icu ha-da:s, it's like if I say I'm gonna do this, and the San Pedro people will be in a lot of trouble, the animals will be hungry, we won't have a lot of rain. That's what they call ha'icu ha-da:s. And another thing, *hiwhai* it means witchcraft. That's what they think he's doing. It went on and on — I get mixed up right there. They said there were three people together doing this. Three medicine men working together. And, ah, well, they killed the three men, and anyway, left two little boys and their mother. A little while after that, the mother died, so there were just two little boys left. They used to go around, the oldest one carrying the youngest one on his back. They go around and they go to people's houses and beg for food. And I guess at that time they don't have the religious belief in forgiveness. They threw things at them, sometimes they threw food at them. It was hot and sometimes they wouldn't get anything for days. So one time they were around and they got tired and they laid down in a wash where there's a lot of soft sand. They were crying because they were hungry and they went to sleep. And pretty soon this youngest one woke up and saw a man standing with a shiny face, it was so shiny. And he couldn't see because it was so shiny. And finally he got both of his eyes and he could see, and it was a man with a bow and arrow.

So he told him to get up and to put the arrow on his brother four times, one in front on the shoulder and the other in back on the thighs. And he didn't want to do it, he didn't want to do it. And he kept telling him. And finally he did it, and he turned around, there was this beautiful horse. Really beautiful. And the man told him, get on and ride that horse. And the people

were nice to him, and tried to buy the horse. And they asked where was
his brother. He was riding his brother. That's why they say the horse is our
brother.

If someone is doing real good, we're jealous! I always feel like that. Like
it's in another story. Mary was a good girl. But this snake comes and, ya
know, does something and she has a baby, but it didn't say anything about
the devil. Aren't we all a little bad? Who is better than another one?

Some Papagos think it's a demon. I don't know whether it's true, or if
they just made it up. I never did think that the horses are devils. The horses
are human beings—part of us like anything else, that's the way I feel, because I like horses. So the other day I was dreaming I had this beautiful
horse we used to have long time ago, and it died long time ago, we called
him Tony. And I said, "Look at Tony, look at Tony! He's come back, I wonder where he's gone?" In the back of my mind I knew he was dead. After a
while I turned around and there was this man standing there. He said, "We
are trying to get some water, but there's no water at the well." I said, "The
water is shut off there, why don't you go to the big well, you'll get some
water over there!" He was a horse but he was man. I didn't think anything,
I never did get scared or anything by it. I was telling Chato, "You are bad
bad bad," even now he understands when I talk to him.

A long time ago we had special songs for the roundup, like this one:

He wesi yosi name ñ-ṣa:yakime
he wesi yosi name ñ-ṣa:yakime
siwone tonolime
kume si-ya ñ-ab ʻo we mawa-ke si wañi wu:puḍa
ṣopol ʻi-ñi-wuliṣepa
[Who can put the halter on me
Who can put the halter on me
The halter glows in the dark
Can you put your hands on me and tie me
Above my head you tie the knot
Shorter you tie me]

You know, Lorenzo is a song-dreamer. He dreams songs. Lorenzo sings
about everything, especially when he's drinking. He even has a song about

when his wife divorced him. My grandmother used to *sing*! I'm forgetting those songs now. I wanted to be a singer, but my voice sounds like a train coming [Frances laughs heartily]. Lorenzo sings a lot. When he gets drunk he'll *sing*!

My grandfather, my half brother's grandfather, he was a song-dreamer, too. He was singing this about when he goes to war: This is not a legend, this is real, this is on this Earth. When they are ready to go to war, they run and they fast. There has to be a leader, two of them, so when they are ready to go, they sing all night. They say they walked by night, in the morning they hide out. So he tells in his song, starting at night, and it tells where they are going to be at dawn. I loved that song, it was a beautiful song, I remember that:

> *Kuc gam hu hi-meda-ha*
> *kuc gam hu hi-meda-ha*
> *si'al ke:kam ñeina ka hi:meda-ha*
> *ku:c 'al ñ-i:-muidañe wa pi 'ape tahamka-ha*
> *ku:c 'am 'o s-kaidam 'o himeda*
> [Over there walking
> Over there walking
> Rising early in the morning and walking
> It makes my heart feel sad
> Walking loudly]

This is a legend, a little one. Before that, when they were getting ready, they would be making sure—I told you about that black thing that has so many legs, he couldn't make enough shoes because he's got so many legs. So he couldn't go to war. They said he's been making the shoes but not even half of them were done, so he couldn't go to war. Is the tape on? So the song goes, it's about Rattle Mountain:

> *Ṣawiku:ḍe nonowha:ŋ*
> *ṣawiku:ḍe nonowha:ŋ*
> *wa:ṣ 'an ñumal 'i-wawañhi:me*
> *ku:ñ 'am wui cem cukaŋ*
> *-hida*

cewhai nonowha:ŋ
ku:ñ 'am wui cem sisiañ-hida-ha
tuanam nonwhaj wui taṣai cem ceṣajida
[Rattle Shape Mountain
Rattle Shape Mountain
way over there it lays low
there the night will fall
long mountain
toward it the dawn will come
at Acorn Mountain the sun will rise]

It's so interesting, so sad, too. I suppose when I go to war, I might think, ugh, they might kill me, so I'd turn around and go back. I put up a dance for the dance group [the Desert Indian Dancers] about that, but I don't think they'll be using that now.

Ṣawiku:ḍe nonowha:ŋ
ṣawiku:ḍe nonowha:ŋ
wa:ṣ 'an ñumal 'i-wawañhi:me
ku:ñ 'am wui cem cukaŋ
-hida
cewayoyakame nonowha:ŋ
ku:ñ 'am wui cem sisiañ-hida-ha
tuanam nonwhaj wui taṣai cem ceṣajida
[Rattle Shape Mountain
Rattle Shape Mountain
way over there it lays low
there the night will fall
long mountain
toward it the dawn will come
at Acorn Mountain the sun will rise]

I can imagine the way they are walking at night. I wonder if they think about snakes. When you go to war, I guess you don't think about it. [Frances hums the tune.]

"You always used to sing," I say.

We always used to sing.[2] I never just sit down and sing like I am now. I'll be doing something, working and singing, riding and singing, going in the wagon and singing.

I asked Frances if she was going to teach her grandchildren the songs.

If they ask me, I'll tell them. I was taught never to volunteer anything unless they ask me. That's what I was taught, especially the legends. That's why I said that nobody ever asked what was it like. I'm not saying that . . . maybe they don't have time, or maybe they just don't care. I don't know which, I don't know. And sometimes a person will ask me at the wrong time, like my niece was asking me to tell her something about the rattle, and I told her it's not clear. If I was gonna think about it, I'd think about it, and tell them really the way it is, not just get here and there. . . .

Frances taped this alone during the time I was living in Madison:

[Tired, sadly] Today is Sunday afternoon, May 5, 1985. Donna and Skip [Deborah's friends] just came and brought your bed to me. I will just tell you about Lorenzo. It was Saturday morning, he got up at nine o clock, he came and told me he was gonna round up the horse, but he wanted somebody to round up side by side. So he left and he found somebody to round up. He came back and wanted some water. The horse won't stand still, so I got him some water. He even asked me what time it was and I told him. It was eleven o'clock, so that was the last time I saw him that Saturday.

So the next day was Sunday. We had a meeting, and at the meeting at about twelve o'clock I asked Cisco and Junior if they had seen him. He might be somewhere drinking and the horse would be tied up somewhere. . . . They said they haven't seen him anyplace, or the horse. At about one o'clock I told them, "Maybe you can try to track him down, him and the horse, maybe . . . I'm kind of worried because the horse is not steady yet." So they went out. At about nine o'clock they came back and told me that they found the horse, that it was dragging a rope. So I knew that he was thrown off somewhere. I asked them, "What shall we do? Shall I call the police?" They said it'd be better to call the police.

So they went to Three Points and called the police and came back and told me [Frances inhales, slowly] to wait for some policeman to come. So I waited, and about four-thirty a policeman came and asked me all kinds of questions, asked me about the range. I told him, "Look, I don't have any ideas because I don't go around." And I told him there was water holes all around, I don't know which direction. By just that time a man came over from the other ranch and told me that the horse came over to the ranch. They were trying to get him but he runs away, so I told him the man could tell them better than I could. So he told them where the water holes were. So the police said, "You go and I'll follow you and look around there, see if I can find him or find out something about him," he said. So they left and I waited and waited, and about eight o'clock he came back. He told me he went all over where his car could go but no, no luck. He said he didn't see him, but he said he was still gonna go back to that ranch and follow that road that goes to the highway, maybe he might be walking. And just then they came in again and they said they got the horse and got the saddle, brought the saddle. That started worrying me this time. Of course I was worried, but this was worse. But then I never did really think that the people would care. Two ladies came and sat with me. Of course, Alice was here all the time, and another lady, and they left and another man came over . . . they sat.

At about eleven o'clock I told them, "You better go to sleep because the police said that in the morning they'll call—I guess there's a group called the Searchers and I guess they were gonna call from town. And also tell the other ranchers to come so they'll have a wide search. So I told them, "You better go home and go to sleep. Remember they said they were gonna come early, so we have to get up early." So they went and I tried to sleep. I thought [very slowly] the morning would never come, and then I looked at the clock, it was the same time I had looked before. My clock hand wasn't moving, so I got so mad I threw my clock away . . . and then I waited, I waited, and I waited until finally the morning came. I waited after I got up and waited outside, and soon Alice came over and we sat there. The men had already saddled their horses when a truck came with all the horses. I didn't realize that Cisco had come and Ramon went out, too [cowboys, Frances's neighbors]. They said they were gonna go out and they were gonna start and how wide they were gonna spread. So they went out. About five miles from here, where the new well is, I guess the pickup slowed down and this man was sitting in the back. Somebody said, "Stop, stop! I think I heard somebody yelling." It was just a little mesquite tree that he was under. He crawled over there and he laid flat on his back from eleven-thirty until seven o'clock Monday morning. It was hot during the day and at night it was real cold. I guess the vultures would come and circle around, thinking he was dead.

But he came back. He had been lying in the desert for three days. He broke his rib, crawled under a mesquite tree. The vultures came, but somehow he survived. He dislocated his shoulder and broke some ribs. The hired cowboy, Antone Rios, found him. I have a poem my grandson Sonny wrote about his accident. It's somewhere . . . [Frances shuffles through a drawer in the living room]. Here it is:

You never know what the day will bring,
The sun goes up and the sun goes down.

"I'll be back," was what he said,
Got on his horse and away he went.

The sun traveled a good part of the day,
when the horse threw its rider, to the ground he lay.

Broken ribs and dislocated shoulder,
Flat on his back and the day grew older.

For three days and two nights,
His only protection a tree that he used to block the desert sun,
And the animals who came to see.

The buzzards flew over and knew he wasn't done,
Coyotes came but wouldn't have none.

There must be a saint for cowboys in distress,
for a cry was heard and this he blessed.

Fellow villager had found the hurt cowboy and the rescue would
    soon follow,
Now he rests in good hands.

And ride and sing tomorrow,
You never know what the day will bring.

And the sun comes up and the sun goes down,
He said, "That's why I sing."
    Sonny Antone
    April 14, 1992

*Lorenzo died seven years later, on February 28, 1992. He was approximately
seventy-eight years old.*

He had a lot of things, emphysema, cirrhosis, and other complications. We
had the wake and the funeral [slowly] in the evening, it lasted all night. I arranged for the horses and the dancers, Desert Indian Dancers, to take him
from the house to the church, and to the grave. They call him [the horse]
Chato, that's his son Tony running around. He was running yesterday. He
looks pretty good. But Jimmy said I should shoe him because he just cut
his nails, now he's running around.

   Chato was tied up all night. I felt sorry for him because he had to stay all
night with all that commotion. The priest came for funeral service. . . . And
they eat and they go. It was a long night. We stayed up all night. [There is
a short silence.] I miss him. When I come home, I miss him.

*Some of our best times have been singing. We used to sit outside at night,
and the two of them would sing! Lorenzo played the gourd rattle with grace
and strength, a powerful combination. Lorenzo had a really deep voice, while
Frances's is high-pitched. It was a harmonic effect I could listen to for hours. But
after a few songs, Frances would yawn and say, "Time for bed!" They used to
tuck me in, slamming the stuck door of my camper. "Don't be scared!" Lorenzo
would say.*

   *Once, at Frances's bidding, Lorenzo took me on a roundup with several other
men of the village. I didn't ride well, but it didn't seem to matter to my horse,
Night Mary, a seasoned workhorse. Weaving in and out of river washes and
ravines, she'd chase the calves back to the herd, a herd of seventy-odd cows
running through the river washes back to the corral. At lunchtime we sat under*

an old mesquite tree, eating beans out of a can, just like the movies. We were gone all day, returning hot and dusty as the sun was setting, triumphant as we herded over a hundred cows into the village corral. Frances was waiting with fresh chile and tortillas. It was like a dream that Frances wanted me to know, something she had always wanted to do herself. After that, Lorenzo would smile at me knowingly. "You're a cowgirl. Remember when you rode in the roundup?" Frances's family is so attached to the horses they corralled that it can be said that one of the ways they reckon times past is according to which horse was around:"Oh, yeah, that's when Kiowa was around." Some of the horses have been named after people, like Jenny and Antonio (Frances's grandfather).

While one would be hard-pressed to get them to talk about it, Frances and Lorenzo have worked hard to sustain and revive some of the old traditions. For example, they started a dance group, for Lorenzo's songs. In the sixties it was called Scratching and Skipping. "Something like that," Frances says. Frances bought the cotton and old sheets, and Lorenzo made the birds with the hangers. And Frances put Lorenzo's songs to dance. Originally there were twelve people in the group, including Frances's grandchildren, John and Lucious, and Frances's nieces. Later the Desert Dancers got started, and Florence and Danny Lopez, Frances's daughter and son-in-law, took over. Frances taught the children how to dance. The group has performed in Phoenix, Santa Fe, Florence, Sells, Ajo, Coronado, Fort Huachuca, Green Valley, Tucson malls, festivals, rodeos, Flagstaff, and all over the reservation (see "Awards and Recognition").

11 ◇ Making Baskets

> I said that my grandmother taught me to make baskets
> .
> Well, I did make baskets and,
> later on,
> I found myself liking making baskets
> and to me
> basket weaving is relaxing.
> And
> I don't know how to put it but it's THERE
> [Softly] you're all together when you are making baskets
>   there are no other things
> like if you're cooking you are thinking about something else,
> or if you are washing or walking you're thinking about something.
> But basket weaving is the only thing that you are all there
> .
> And sometimes I think about it
> and in my imagination
> it SHINES
>   from above
> and it tells how to go about it
>   how to do
>   what color to use
> .
> And it seems to work that way
>   it seems that I don't make mistakes
> like when you sew you put the sleeve on the wrong side.
> But as long as you are all there, there's no mistakes.
>   (1987)

My recent life is the same, I get up in the morning and do the cooking. If I'm lazy, I don't do anything, I just do things that have to be done. And, um, if I really feel like working on baskets, I'll just soak the yucca and wait. Sometimes I don't get to it until afternoon. And some days I work and some days I play. But I'm not the kind of person who goes to somebody's house to sit and talk. That's the way I am from way back.

I'm not the very best basket weaver, there are others who make prettier baskets. Sometimes I wonder how they feel. Are they doing it for money, or do they feel the same way I feel when I make baskets? Especially when, like, if you say, "Make me a basket and be finished at a certain time." I can't do it, because my hands and my mind don't move that fast. So I really don't care for orders, but I do take them. It takes me a long time to complete a basket because my hands and my mind don't move that fast. You have to learn a lot of patience with basket weaving. If you try to hurry, you make a lot of mistakes. That slows you down because you have to go back and correct your mistakes. If you just relax and take your time. . . . It may not be the way you want it to, but if you work on it, it will come to you. But if you try to jump ahead of yourself, you cannot do it. That's life!

Recently I went to the doctor because I am losing my sight. I lost the sight of one eye, so I'm using just one. I went to the doctor and he said my eyes are not better, no worse. I asked him why my eye hurts when I sew, and why it doesn't when I make baskets. The doctor laughed, and he said, "That's because you know so much in your mind that you don't really see, you just go on making it." I wanted to test myself, so I made really tiny baskets to see how I do. It seems to me that it's just the same as when I was using both eyes. That's what gives me courage, because when I first found out about my eyes, they gave me five years, then three, and now I only have two years before I go completely blind. But I'm hoping that it will be a mistake, that I won't go blind in two years.

I started your basket, Debbie. I started with that, and I wanted to make it real round. That's why I left it until I really got a hold of it, so that it'll be round. Because if you're not careful, it's gonna be crooked.

One afternoon Frances was sitting in her living room with a string of bear grass between her teeth, making a beautiful, finely woven basket with the "man in the maze" design. She looked at me hard, like she was getting ready to tell me something important. I had learned to listen carefully to her words, for when she talks about something, there's often a hidden message. For Frances, basket weaving is a metaphor for life.

Maybe it's not the right word. Like, right now, I could sit down and make baskets. Somehow, I want to make a basket. Maybe I'll do something else—

it's just like going back. Like, I'll just go with them to Sells for a ride, or I've got some ironing to do. [Frances speaks firmly.] We'll tell stories when it's there, not when you try to make it happen. Like you feel like baking a cake and it comes out real good. But if you say, make me a cake, no. Like you get up in the morning and you are ahead of yourself. Like you say you're gonna feed your family, and I'm gonna do this, I'm gonna do that, gonna do that—it won't work that way! But if you just get up and feel good and [slowly, firmly] don't load yourself—that's what I do, I don't put a big load on me, because if I can't complete what I planned, I don't feel good about it. I learned a long time ago that this is better—that's the way I am! And I am a lot happier now. When I was younger, I planned things and it would never work out, and I'd get upset. Like this morning, I got up and I said, "Well, I'm gonna hang the washing, or I'm gonna wash my hair, I'm gonna either make a basket or iron." Well, I didn't make myself sit down and make a basket, or sit down and iron. I'm gonna make a choice, or just go to Sells with you for a ride!

When I did domestic work, I worked by the hour, so I had to budget my time, do this for a certain time, and do that and do that. In the evening you are so tired because your motor runs so fast. And, sometimes, the time goes so fast and you're so slow—that upsets me. And, another thing, I'm happy about it. Some people will say, "I hope this happens," you know. I'm hoping something, but I don't hope for a certain thing because when I'm hoping for something and it doesn't happen, I'm disappointed. So I'm just hoping for something—I don't know what I'm hoping for but I'm hoping for something. Like when I pray and God doesn't give me what I pray for but he gives me something else.

So when I pray in the evening, I just pray for the family, the people that need help, the people that are alone, the people that are hungry, the people that don't have any homes. So it's just like you get the stuff off your shoulders, and you're lighter and you go to sleep. [Frances chuckles.] That's the way I feel and imagine things.

There's one bad thing about me. Like if I go out there and sit out there under the *ramada*, pretty soon I think, "Why am I sitting there? I should be doing this." That's one thing I can't get rid of, it's just there! Like if I just go out and sit and relax—that's why sometimes I get so tired, I don't give myself time to relax—I'm thinking about something that has to be done.

And another thing, like if you're thinking about something that happened fifty years ago, and you're thinking about it. You can't mix those things with the present.

I was thinking the other day about how much I like Tucson. I still like Tucson, because of my friends. Anytime anything was wrong with me, they were right there, they asked me if I needed anything. I still have a lot of friends and I still come back to Tucson. Right now I have those basket weavers, they are learning to make baskets. Most of them are my friends. I go out to a lot of demonstrations and I meet people, they are my friends, too. And the people that I have worked for are my friends, too!

My best friend was Norma Musser. She was in the service, they call them WACs. She's also a widow. She's my friend because she is like me, she's kind of loud. And, ah, she jokes and she likes the same things I like, so I call her my friend. Another lady is Sharon. She's in Los Angeles now, but she writes. I have a new friend, her name is Thelma. She became my friend just lately, but you could tell that she is your best friend. She doesn't do like, ah, I don't call that best friend when they go out of their way to do things. She doesn't do that, but she is my friend. And Peggy, and Mary Ann — she's managing the Tuesday afternoon class. And an elder lady, Celeste Burrell, she's my friend. And the rest are my friends, too.

Friendship is very hard — it's not easy to make friends. I have known this ever since I was a young girl. Maybe it's because I don't know how to make friends. I have to study a person a long time before I call them my friend. In our ways of telling things, like, they say you can't call someone your best friend. You may think you have a best friend. To use the white man's words, your best friend will stab you in the back. My grandmother once said to me that it's very tricky to make friends. She said sometimes you have a friend, a real good friend, but it's not your friend — she just wants your husband, and someday you'll find out it's your husband's friend. And another thing, if you have a child, somebody would want to hold him, want to carry it — that's no good either. For the longest time I wondered, what does she mean by that? Then I heard that I had a friend, a cousin, this young girl always goes over there and picks up the baby and takes him home, for years, until she found out she was pregnant. All this time she was playing around with the husband. This lady told me herself, "My best friend went to bed with my husband." She came home and saw it. That's when I understood what my grandmother was saying. She said you cannot call someone your best friend, you can call friends. And a friend is someone you can go along with and you help each other, and you can disagree and agree, that's the only friend that you will have. When it's over, it's still your friend. It's not your friend when you argue like . . . Emma and I used to argue and get mad at each other, and really tell each other off, but we're still friends now. If you have a friend, you call just friends, not just one. That way you won't worry about it.

So if I like somebody, I don't really show it, because it wears off and it's just too much. And like, they say, "Oh, I like you," and it wears off, it doesn't mean anything. So if I like somebody, in my heart I like them, but I don't go saying all that. Oh, I follow them around. Like I said, the Indians don't believe in kisses. But when we go to the village and somebody's nice to me, I hang onto her until she gets tired of me.

I was just talking to the kids about my tools. One of my tools is Maria and the other one's Missy. And old Charlie, and Nancy, and, um, Herman. You know, Herman gives me a lot of trouble. When I left Idlewild [California] and I was coming home, I left him under the bed, and I got him and put him in my purse, and couldn't go through the gate because I had a knife in my purse. And last year when I went, I lost Herman in the shop. When I was packing, I told Lucinda [a friend] that I lost my hammer. I think we left Herman over there. So she got to the phone and called, "Herman's missing," and everybody's running around looking for Herman. There was a man, a crippled man. He was with me the last time we left because we were sitting talking about . . . what do you call that? Ceramics. We were watching them bake them. So I thought, we'll ask James Campbell. So he was the last person that was there. So here, everybody was running around and so James Campbell had the hammer, and he was standing there holding it in his hand and everybody's running around. He heard somebody say that Herman's missing, and he said, "Oh, I have Herman." So they called me back and said

Herman's been found. [Frances laughs.] They seem to be really interested in Herman, where is Herman? He gives me a lot of trouble, so I leave him home now.

I think when you talk about baskets, what is there to talk about it? You tie a knot and you go around and around, whatever's in your mind, you're just thinking about it when you are doing it. It's not like when it's broken and you fix it, when you do different things in the basket, it's not there. It goes round and round, the design is in your head — what color you're gonna put in, how much bear grass you're gonna put in, if you feel you need some more, it's just that. Unless I give my whole head to the tape, it'll be a lot. Because it's in my head, not on the outside, it comes when you are working on the basket. But the outside is something you hear, something you listen to, somebody's talking about.

[Frances leans forward.] I don't know if I told you about this thing, how I feel about baskets. I heard from this lady, she's the leader of this arts organization. They had a meeting. I didn't hear it from the horse's mouth, I heard it from this lady, and she told me. She said they talked about it, and one thing she wanted me to know is that they said this man is traveling all over the reservation to Hopi country and all over, and he sees their work. Everywhere he goes, he finds the work is not the same as it was years ago. And they said they are not really proud of their work, they are in a hurry to get it done. To me, I feel that . . . I think I told you about the speaker in Idlewild. That got me thinking about the work we do, whatever talent we have, we are supposed to really take care of it and do it right, what is given to us. And everything else is not working the way it's supposed to and everything is not the same. What I think about the basket is that nowadays, young ladies, even older ladies — I'm talking about us. When they see pretty things or pretty house or pretty furniture in there, they feel like making baskets to get some money to buy these things. So they are not really careful, they just hurry to get the things that they want. That's why the baskets aren't the same as they were before. Because at that time, there was nothing. Ladies took their time, do their work, what was given to them. They work with their eyes, their hands, their mind, their thoughts. They work hard, their body warms and the sweat — that's the real thing. Nowadays we hurry. Like me, I'm hurrying to save some money to buy a sandwich. So this is what I want to say.

If you go and ask somebody, like suppose someone says, "Well, I'll talk about baskets," she'll put something just to make it interesting. I don't want that, I want the real one. That's the way I feel about it. So when I go to demonstration, I just talk about what comes to my mind. At demonstrations sometimes I don't feel like talking, but I feel I have to talk. Sometimes they ask dumb questions, like "Do you buy this? Do you color this?" It's not really dumb questions, because they don't really know. And they ask something way far from the basket weaving, like "Have you ever ridden in an airplane?" and that kind of thing. One little girl asked me, "Are you married?" [Frances laughs.] Some little boy asked me, "Where do you buy your clothes?" I said, "Well, I make my clothes. I can't buy anything big enough for me!" Sometimes the teachers ask dumb questions, too.

At Idlewild, I like to visit the people that I meet there, the other Indian women. We tell jokes and all that. But there's not too many things to talk about baskets. And another thing I'll say—I'm not criticizing, but my students may not understand that some of us may not be meant to do something. Like maybe James might want to ride in the rodeo, but if it's not in him, he can't make it. Or if somebody wants to make a basket, if it's not in her. . . . She'll try, which I really respect, people who try but can't make it. And some—like I have new student, she made a beautiful basket the first day, and I was surprised. I guess people just have to have the ability to work with their hands, she was one of those. Another lady's been with me since Fort Lowell, and night classes, she's very good and very neat. And another lady is one of those kind who is very good in a lot of things, but she's been working on a basket for six months; she's trying, and she's put a turtle, but it looks like a lizard. And I have to learn how to answer them, I can't just say, "Oh, it's good." That's not in me. But I say it when I really feel it. I watch everyone, and how they are working. And if I see one, I feel any minute they are going to ask me a question. Because I've already seen their work. It's very hard, but I have to tell the truth.

These basket weaving ladies, they are my friends. They are my students, but they are also my friends. Some of them have been with me for fifteen years, remember? We laugh! I don't usually say much, because they keep talking and talking. . . . All those ladies talk a lot. Our night classes, sometimes I don't even get home until ten-thirty. The security guard [at the Tucson House] thinks, "Where's the old lady been all this time?"

Frances recalls that her fingers bled as she learned the ancient art of O'odham basket weaving from her grandmother at S-koksonagk. But with much practice, the craft became an integral part of Frances's way of being in the world. Frances has demonstrated and taught classes and workshops at schools, recreation centers, and arts and cultural organizations all over the United States, including Idlewild, California; Dayton, Ohio; New York City; and throughout Arizona; and has won many awards for her baskets.

Part IV ◇ God and I'itoi

Speeches from the Heart

Thinking of a white person—
[Quickly] Well, that's the way I feel sometimes
gets mixed up with an Indian
.
But then
why am I trying to change?
I finally get down to think,
Why am I trying not to believe what my people believed?
I'm an Indian!
   (1982)

Much of Frances's sense of who she is lies in the teachings of her grandparents: their speeches, songs, stories, and legends. "Get up and run," they admonished, "you may meet something that will give you power—a bird, a mountain lion, or a coyote." This respect for living things lies at the core of Frances's beliefs.

For Frances the "old ways" also include Santo himdag, *the way of the saints. Like many of her people, Frances is a devout practitioner of a Southwestern version of Sonoran or folk Catholicism, with its saints and sacred images, Mexican-style churches, Spanish hymns, feast days, and, following her grandparents, a strong personal religion.[1] Frances's life story invokes sacred shrines and pilgrimage sites from both the O'odham and the Catholic traditions— places, rituals, and sacred events which have deeply influenced her way of being in the world. These include the town of Magdalena in Sonora (a former O'odham village where there is an annual curing festival in honor of St. Francis), the Tohono O'odham Children's Shrine at Santa Rosa (where two children were sacrificed to save the world), and the ancient O'odham Wi:gita and wine ceremonies. O'odham Catholicism encompasses the teachings introduced by Spanish Franciscan and Jesuit missionaries as they were interpreted by Frances's ancestors over a hundred years ago. Frances's grandmother, Salomina, was a devout Catholic. Today it is not uncommon for a medicine man to recommend a church service as a cure for illness, and both traditions are called upon to bring rain and to achieve success, healing, and well-being.*

Frances was born of the border and its unique history, for the Tohono O'odham share a sixty-four-mile border with Mexico, and a common history with much of northern Sonora.[2] The border is a place of confluence and contrast: over several hundred years, Frances's people have incorporated rites, practices, and beliefs of Spanish conquistadors and priests, northern Mexican ranching and cowboy cultures, along with diverse influences from Tucson, a multiethnic urban center where Frances lived and worked alongside U.S. Mexicans, blacks, Chinese, Yaqui Indians, and Milga:n.[3]

Chapters 12 (a speech) and 15 (about medicine men) were directed by Frances, whereas chapters 13 and 14 were directed by question-answer sessions. This format worked best for Frances, for among her people religion is practiced with humility and is rarely talked about openly. "People will not believe you, anyway," Frances says, only half-joking. We taped these chapters toward the end of our work together in 1987. We offer them to illuminate Frances's personal religion and some of the teachings that have been important to her.

12 ◇ Christianity

One time I was listening to two little kids arguing if St. Francis
was a god, or if there was a God up in Heaven. Before I knew
it, they started to throw rocks at each other, and I said, "Does
anybody come over and teach you about God? I'm not the one
to teach you." (1982)

*The tape recording which follows is of the speech entitled "Papago Encultura-
tion into Christianity," organized by the priesthood of San Xavier for their annual conference on religious education. The event was held at the Tucson Convention Center in 1982, and the audience, Frances said, included lay O'odham
as well as the priests. Frances's speech was transcribed in its totality from the
original recording.*

I was asked to speak here, I don't know why. They know very well that I
don't know a lot of English, I know very little. If I say something that I don't
mean, bear with me, because somebody might get mad if I say something I
don't mean. I guess I'll have to talk about the roots of the past. The roots of
the past was, for me, by my grandparents. These were the two people I grew
up with. We lived out in the middle of nowhere, with desert surrounding
us; there were no other kids around. What I learned, I listened and remembered—we had no choice. Nowadays, you talk to the younger generation
and by tomorrow what you said will be forgotten. What I'm going to say is
about these ways.

A few years ago a missionary came to my home in San Pedro. He was
talking to a friend of mine, and asked him if he knew of a prayer, one of
our prayers. I don't know if the man just didn't want to tell them, but we
do have prayers, our own prayers. We have as many prayers as the Catholic
religion has. We pray to the sun; we pray to the Great Spirit, the Maker; we
pray to the Earth. In all those things that we do, there are prayers. Of course,
we don't call it prayers, we call it something else. We even have prayers for
the hungry, but right now nobody knows that prayer. When the old people
die, a lot of things will be forgotten, and I am sad for that. But I guess it's

all right because a lot of them don't think it's important. It is important to me because we had no choice, we had to remember what we were told by the old people. We didn't have a choice, no matter how much we hated to listen to them preach, we had to listen to the stories. We had to have the preaching, and then the stories. Or we had to listen to a legend, and then to be preached afterward. There's a lot of things you hear, it's supposed to mean something.

I remember that we didn't know anything, my people didn't know about the Catholic religion until later on. My grandfather said that the Catholic religion was about this high [Frances gestures about three feet high] but we got it right in the middle. But he also said that we cannot go back [to the old ways] because it isn't meant for us. We never forget. My people learn about Jesus and the Church; they are true Catholics and respect the Church. My people believe God and the Church in their own way. Our old people are old-fashioned. Like me, I'm old-fashioned. I believe in the way I learned in the very beginning. When things started changing, I think that my old people got sort of confused. Because they learned the way they were taught and believed it was the true God, it was the true religion. Everything in it was truth. And when things start changing a lot, the old people got confused, because they wondered which is the truth, which is really the truth? And they have to look for the truth again. Maybe then they will truly understand. Maybe they'll change again, who knows?

We believe that when the Spanish came, my people learned prayers from the Spanish. They prayed in Mexican. But after I went to school — I went to school when I was twelve years old, I went to first grade when I was twelve years old. I was taught catechism. I learned to pray and thought that was great because I understood what I was saying, like "I believe in God, our Father who art in heaven. Hail Mary full of grace." I knew what I was saying. But what are they saying in Spanish? That was a problem for my people. How many of us understand what we are saying in prayer? How many of us understand? So I think that it is good that they want to teach the Indian prayer now. But I think it's too bad I can't learn, I can't even say it, I don't even remember. . . .

I was asked to say a prayer for graduation, for about seven hundred people, and I wanted to say it in Indian. There's a man who writes Bible in Indian, so I went to this man, and he gave me a tape. Every time I cook, I turn it right on. I learned it! So when I got up in front of all those people, I forgot about it, I went blank. I had to use my own words! But I guess I did it fine. So that's the way it is. I cannot learn, so I have to talk coming from myself, from my own thinking. That's the only way I can talk to people, talk to an audience.

When I was a little girl, I never did know Christmas, so we used to go to a place called Ko:m Wawhai — that's where I was born; we used to go there and spend a few months. I guess it was Christmastime one year and they were going to have a dinner and ceremony. I went to where they take the offering to say the rosary prayer and I saw this bowl with candy in it, and my grandmother said if I stay up until three o'clock, I can have some. Imagine how sleepy I was, but I stayed up for those oranges and candy. It was the first Christmas that I remember. The next day they gave me an old belt as a Christmas present. It was an old belt, but I enjoyed it because I never had a Christmas present. That was great, that was something that I remember now. Seems like it happened last year, but it was years and years ago, in 1913 or somewhere along there. So it's a long, long time. I'm glad I remember. You remember something that happened sixty years ago, and then you don't even remember where you put your purse, or what you went after in your room. But I remember my grandfather would say something, and I remember just as clear as it happened right now. But I don't know why I forget where I put my purse. I don't feel bad to be old because I think it's a lot of fun to be old. You do funny things and you laugh about it.

To go back to religion. I met a lady, she was an old lady. As I said, my people believed in God and they believed in their own ways. So I met this lady, she had a lot of dogs — so many dogs that she didn't know what to do with them. She said, "Oh, I have so many dogs, they are so much trouble. I am praying to St. Martin to help me find homes for them." At the time I thought it was kind of silly to pray for that. So a month later I saw her again and I asked her, "What did you do with your dogs?" And she said, "Oh, they all have homes now." And, um, well, I'm not going to think it's silly. I have to get a candle and light it to St. Martin. What I mean is that they believed in that in their own ways.

Another time a lady had a colt. The colt was so sick I thought it was going to die. I told the lady, and she said, "I know it. But I'm praying so hard that the horse will live." So a couple of months later I met her and I said, "What happened to the horse?" "Oh, it lived, it's still around," she said. So that's what I mean, we do silly things, but maybe God doesn't think it's silly because he answers. He made the horse well. We can pray, and of course God can do anything, and that's the way the Indians believe.

When I was growing up, my grandmother used to tell me about this religious church and about God and people, and there was always a saying that someday there will be many roads to follow. Someday there will be many branches to climb. Of course, at the time, I didn't know what it means, but it's today that things change. The service has changed, the people have changed, everything's changed. I would like my son-in-law, Danny Lopez, to read something I wrote many years ago when I started seeing how things have changed in our church:

> I like the little Catholic church that stands upon an Indian reservation in the quiet country where the friendly Papago Indians meet. It may not have a gilded dome or spires standing tall or any wonderful designs to the doors or walls. It may not boast of windows stained with scenes of holy art, but it always extends to all a welcome from the heart. I like the little church because it struggles every day to keep on going. And to serve the gentle souls that pray. And most of all it has such sweet and peaceful air, which we cannot help but feel that God is really there. (1962)

That's what I wrote. There was this lady who was in Sells, that like now you read the *Papago Runner*; well, I thought I'd write something. Well, I wrote about my daughter getting married to Danny Lopez. So it sounded real good, so I added something else, and that sounded good, too. So I said, "Why not write something about our beliefs, our church, our village?" So I sent it to the lady and she said she cannot print it because it was too religious. I didn't understand, so I thought, "Oh well." What I wrote about was the way the people feel at the time. They say that when you walk into church, you feel that God is there. I believed, I am not a very good church person but I go to church whenever I can, but I am, um, I am great in talking to God every day, maybe every hour. Like if I go to sleep without saying my prayers and I wake up at about two in the morning, I say, "Oh, I forgot to say my prayers," and I get up and pray. Or if there are a lot of people, I get excited and I forget to say my meal prayer, I'll remember when I'm washing dishes, and I start praying. I learned to pray in 1927 when I was going to catechism, that's how I pray. I cannot say "Holy Spirit" because something might happen to me, I say "Holy Ghost." I cannot change, that's the way I believe. When the temptation gets too great, I start to say, "In the name of the Father, Son, and Holy Ghost," because if I say "Holy Spirit," I might still tell a lie. I think many of us are still holding on to what we learned from the beginning. Of course, there is no wrong in the way the new generation thinks. There's no wrong in that, I'm just trying to understand. If you stand on your head in church, I'll try to understand that, too. So I'm trying. But I guess a lot of my people are old-fashioned. They want to stick with what they learned from the time they started learning about Catholic religion. It's very strong because my people are very great and true believers.

When I was a little girl, we hardly ever ate meat. We never had meat except maybe once a month when maybe my grandfather would kill a rabbit or a deer. And my grandfather says on Fridays we shouldn't eat meat. So I asked my grandmother, "Why shouldn't we eat meat on Fridays?" "Because your tongue's gonna get long," she said. So I believed that if I eat meat on Fridays, my tongue's gonna get long—it's already long! And, um, she used to say, "If you sit home, God doesn't want you to talk about people. If you don't have anything nice to say about your relatives or about people, just don't talk about them." And I asked her why, and she said my tongue was going to get long. That was the teachings of people. They teach you in a way that you get it through your head and you remember it. And when I grew up, I thought, "What's the use of talking about someone when they don't hear you? I'll go to them and say it." That's the way I was taught. I think my grandparents were great and wise people. I'm not saying they did nothing wrong, because there's wrong somewhere, but they taught me right. Maybe that's why I am very happy, because I do what I was told.

A lot of things, they fall into a pattern, that's what they told me. And I didn't believe it at the time—"That's not going to happen, that's not true." And one day, I told her that we were going to steal some watermelon. I didn't think it was stealing because I told my grandmother. She was half-asleep and I guess she didn't know what I said. I said, "Grandmother, we are going to steal some watermelon." She said okay. So I went to a watermelon patch with some kids, some kids went way into the middle of the patch but went back because the owners were coming. I was the one who started it, so I was crying and my grandmother asked, "What's the matter?"

I said the man spanked me. She said, "Why?" And I told her, "I was stealing watermelons." She said, "That's what a thief gets!" That's the way, if we do something wrong we have a correction right there. They don't do it the way we do with our kids, where they do something wrong at school and then maybe a day or two later we are spanking them. They don't know why! I think that's the way, that's the way my grandmother taught me. Sometimes I wish that I had closed my ears, but now I am glad that she raised me this way.

We had a cross like a crucifix, a picture of St. Francis Assisi, and a picture of Blessed Mother. These are the only saints I knew about when I was a little girl. Then later I learned about the Sacred Heart—that's another one. But I don't feel I have to pray in church to pray, I pray anytime I feel like it. Like my grandmother, she prays, I wish I had learned the prayer about the night. When we sleep on the earth floor each night, she'd start praying, "The darkness is rolling . . ." on and on. I have a daughter, Danny's wife, who says I have to teach her first before I can teach somebody else. So . . .

When I was about twenty years old, my grandfather said that fifty years from now it will be just like a leg, or a wheel that will roll and everybody will jump and grab it, and try to be something that they're not. It will hit hard and the people will be confused. The world will be full of hate. The world will be dirty, there will be no shame. The people will forget, the children will forget their language. Sometimes I wonder, how does he knew things in the future? This is today, the children are not talking Indian. So that's what they mean, we'll try to grab that, we'll try to be something we're not, white people. Like we are now, we dress like white people, we talk English. I talk a broken English, but I talk English. That's what he means to be something you aren't. I know I will never be Milga:n. I will always be a dark brown Indian, no matter how much I try. I try to do what the Milga:n does, try to do that, but I will never be anything else but Indian. I am very proud of being a Papago, and I know where I came from and I know who I am. That's what I want my children to know, to know who they are and where they came from.

To go back to my grandfather, how did he know things were going to happen? He never did go anyplace, he was always there, always home. He never did talk to a white man because we lived in the middle of nowhere and no white man came around. But he knew. And another thing, he knew about the clouds. He used to say the clouds are white from the south and from the north are bluish white. When I went to Cincinnati a few years ago, I walked around because the plane wasn't there. And I looked, it was raining then and the sun started coming out, and I see this bluish beautiful clouds. And when we were flying over the White Mountains there were pure white clouds. I get goose pimples when I start to think about how my grandfather might have known that. The old people knew these things. I told you that my grandfather said that things would change, that there would be many roads to travel and branches to climb. How does he know? I wish I had something like that. The other day I was watching TV and I stood up and looked out my window and there were people just sitting around. I wished I could be that Incredible Hulk and get the people and tie them up and then leave. All of the sudden I felt that way. Then I thought, "I just want to be myself. I don't want to be a medicine woman, who cares! I'm me!" That's what I told myself, I am happy with being me. I am happy with what I believe. I don't think I am doing anything wrong if I forget my prayers sometimes. Is that wrong? If I talk Indian, I talk all day without stopping, but I was taught by the Catholic Sisters that God talks to us once a week. But my grandparents said different, I'll stick with that.

One time I was listening to two little kids arguing if St. Francis was a god, or if there was a God up in Heaven. Before I knew it, they started to throw rocks at each other, and I said, "Does anybody come over and teach you about God? I'm not the one to teach you."

When I was a little girl, I caught whooping cough and almost died, that's what they say, anyway. I probably just went to sleep or something. They took me to Magdalena in Mexico to ask St. Francis to make me live, to grow up and be a simple person. I am a simple person. And they prayed to the Blessed Mother that if I get well, I will always have long hair, so I have long hair now. That's the way that I believe. If my grandparents did something for me, I respect it. If they baptize me Catholic, I'm going to be buried a Catholic.

One time I asked one of the Sisters, "Do all the saints always want a dance?" Like we say, we are going to have a dance for saint so-and-so. She said no. I'm glad, because I have a lot of saints, and if I have to put up dancing, I'll be dancing all the year. My poor saints are just there, I light candles for them, I pray to them, but they have never had a dance. They are probably bored to death.

We are trying to go back. If we go back, what's covered up in layers and layers underneath, would any of the younger generation care to believe that? If I could, I'd go back to sixty years ago when my people were strong Catholics. When Father Ventura [Bonaventura] used to come around with horse and buggy, everybody would kneel down, like a foreign custom, like he was a king. That's how much respect we had for the priest and the Church. I'd like to go back to that, my people were really strong believers. I like that. I'm talked out.

13 ◇ The Church at San Pedro

Deborah: The hymns were all in Spanish, right?
Frances: We didn't have any hymns in Indian, only Spanish.
Deborah: Do you remember them?
Frances: I remember, but I'm not going to sing it!

In San Pedro the yearly round of church activities is encompassed within the seasons and rhythms of the Catholic liturgical calendar, and births and death anniversaries of loved ones. The church is the center of these activities. The Jesuits began to baptize the Tohono O'odham in the 1600s, but there was no church in the region until the 1880s, following O'odham involvement with the Franciscans. By 1920 most villages had a one-room adobe church with a large plaza, where people practiced their own version of the area's Sonoran Catholicism.[1] On this Palm Sunday we could hear the hymns, in Spanish, from across the plaza. I asked Frances to talk about the old church services at San Pedro, and turned the tape recorder on.

They had different services long, long time ago, but not anymore. It's kind of hard to describe it. . . . Well, I remember when they . . . I thought this was beautiful when they used to celebrate Holy Cross. They used to make little steps, and in the evening when they go in procession to the cross, it's got steps, they'll have the procession go over there and put the cross there. Usually the man and the woman will carry the cross there. That was a long time ago, they don't do it anymore. They would carry the cross and the arch and all the saints, the candles, and things like that would go, and the musicians and the singers, and when they get back to church, they'd go sing and the person ahead of the procession will go and there's a prayer and a song, and they'll slowly bring the cross on the first step. Then they'll move back and the others will bring the cross down the steps, and start singing and then go down to the ground. And the men will be standing on each side and they'll cross their hands, like this [crossing her arms across her chest]. That was interesting to me. And after that they'll pass out [in a high voice] little tiny biscuits. And after that the dance will start, the eating will start.

And in the morning, the one, the very first one will be way in the back, and the second one will be the leader next year. Like a step, and that's the end. There are five of them, Jose and I did it — his father was in it, so we got to do it.

And on Easter, on Holy Thursday, they'll have a procession — that's when they'll burn everything, like the palm that's got old, they'll burn it. Like if there are old saints, or whatever belongs to it, they'll burn that. On Friday they cover all the saints with black, and Saturday they throw flowers . . . like the Yaquis do.[2] And on the second day of November, All Souls' Day, we decorate the graves, light the candles, and in the evening put the food. Two years ago we put the food right here [at the house], and with the tarp around it because there's no room. One time I was sleeping and I heard something and looked up and there was the dog standing on the table, eating the bread! [Frances laughs.] So last year we put that chicken wire all around it, and that was fine. We light candles at the house for the family — my-father-in-law, my mother-in-law, my stepmother, all those that I think they come [Frances laughs].

Jose is here. My grandmother would do this, she would decorate the grave, clean out the graves and decorate. And she'll cook and she'll put it out, like if somebody's gonna come and eat, put it out — watermelon, and chile, green beans, roasted corn, and coffee. [The phone rings.]

Okay, anyway, they put out the candles and they prayed and about midnight they say they went back to the graves. And that's the way I grew up, and when my grandmother died, I did those things. So I do the things that they did, and it just went on, because I just grew up with that. And sometimes I wonder, why? Why are we doing this? When my husband was alive, I said, "I wonder if they really come and eat what we leave them." And my husband said, "Well, don't stop doing it, so when I die, be sure you cook me chile with string beans. If you don't cook it, I might really get hungry, and really die." So I said, "I wonder if they really do eat," and he said, "When I die, I'll write you a letter about it." He must have lost my address, because I haven't got a letter yet.

They used paper flowers and candles. And now it's too much. The last time I saw an All Souls' Day where they put out clothes. It was too much, too out of place. Maybe I'm the only one who feels this way, I never did tell anybody how I felt. This one lady told me that she thinks that my kids used to ask why they didn't eat or drink this, so I was telling one lady, and she said, "They don't really eat, they just come and smell the food." Another lady said she saw them come and bless the food.

We didn't have church on Sundays, but we had St. Peter, All Souls' Day, Holy Cross, Christmas, and Easter. Later on, people bought statues of St. Francis. Alice's grandparents were in charge of the church, then Alice and her son.

Frances looked at me for direction, so I asked her if she remembered when the church was built.

I guess I was too small, it was already there when I came. My grandmother always helped, but my grandfather was never interested in the church. They were remodeling. And they used to carry the dirt, women carried the dirt in baskets on their heads, bringing it over and walking back and forth, and the men carried the water in barrels. We don't see those wooden barrels anymore. They used to carry water in them, and bring it to the church. They mixed it with the dirt and used their hands to put it on the church. I remember, I used to go over there and they would chase me out of the way, [in a high voice] "Get out of here, you are in the way!" I'll be out, and then I'll go back again, you know how kids are.

That was about 1917. I was about five then. My grandmother would cook. She was a good cook, so she'd make something special to eat. [In a high pitch] And I don't know why they'd eat in church! They used to put *main*, they call it *main*, mats, they made it out of desert spoon leaves. And they'd bring their food. That's what I liked about it, to eat.

Later on, it was remodeled again. I was told that when they first built the church, this lady—a medicine woman—blessed the church. They say she baptized the church. She was a powerful woman. When she prayed, she met God, and talked to God. [Frances laughs real loud, and Lorenzo joins her.] He doesn't believe it! Remember her, Lorenzo? Tonol Wo:po'im.

Lorenzo said, "Oh yeah, I remember. She's pretty old!"

She'll say, "Well, this saint wants a fiesta." People would get ready and do that. We used to get a lot of names from it. One time she took a little statue out, it was from her heart, they say. People used to call San Pedro "Sa:nto-

Wiwpul" [a play on the village's Indian name, Wiwpul]. Sa:nto E-wiho means "throw out a saint," because it came out of her heart. She probably put it in her mouth and threw it out. Or they called it A'atapuḍ Momotk, "the one that shakes." She's the one who blessed the church. And then later on, she told them the saint wanted a fiesta, and she went out and then was dancing with this statue—I didn't see it but I just heard about it. They used to call the saint Sa:nto Niño. [Both Frances and Lorenzo were laughing real hard.] It was a big story.

Laughing, I told Frances that I thought it was an interesting story.

I guess it was, but to me it was an embarrassing story [still laughing]. To me, it just doesn't seem possible. [There is silence for a few minutes.] And then, later on, I think two Fathers blessed it. I think I had two kids then. There was a Father Regis, used to come to my house. We would feed him, you know. And one time he said, "Why don't we remodel the church, it needs it." So we talked about it, and we talked about it. And then finally we had a meeting. That was after . . . , years before they split up. The church split up because a lot of people didn't believe that lady [the medicine woman]. There was a house where they kept their saints. They used to have dances over there, too. So this was after. So we had a meeting, and of course, nobody said anything. And then after the meeting I heard that I shouldn't be the one trying to do something different for this church, because they built it themselves, and I just came here [after marriage]. That was the end of that thing. Then I moved to Tucson, and some other Father came and told the other lady who was just married here, too, so they got started. The Father from San Xavier Mission helped. We pitched in. We used to have a club, the St. Nicholas Center in Tucson, and so we put up money for that, too. Later on, after it was finished, Bishop Green blessed it. He was from town; he came and blessed it.

They just come when it's special, holidays and things. And then about some years ago. . . . It's not too long ago that they built the church you see now. So they built this one—we call them coyote workers. They're from here, they built that. It came from tribe, the money came from the tribe.

Having seen Frances spend a lot of time in the church, I asked her to talk about why the church is important to her.

Well . . . it's important to me because it's a church, that's all. Sometimes I go in there and rest, rest and think—important things. I respect the Church, I respect people that do things for the Church. If I can help, I will. And, like if I say, there's certain things I'd rather have in my home, like Santa Guadalupe, I'd rather do it in my home. I give a dinner, a procession, and pray. So that's the only thing I do. And I don't ask people to put something in. Like feast days, we donate twenty dollars from every family. At Christmastime I do it myself, too. But if they have something, I have to donate, too.

I think . . . It's just me, I don't think anybody else. Like if you go to church; you go to church, because it's Sunday, you go to church. Too many people, too many things going on, so you listen, and sometimes you get a lot of what the preacher says, and sometimes you don't. Sometimes it's just talk. And it's not the same as when you go into church alone, and you pray and you pray, with all your heart. But church—"Oh, that one's got a pretty dress"; I think if you really want to worship, you should go alone. One time somebody was saying, "Well, how come you're not married?" And I said, "I don't meet someone to marry." And they said, "Why don't you meet someone in church?" What do I do, go and look around? There's no good-looking men! That's me, I don't think anybody else feels that way.

I do respect the priest, I really do. I think what we are doing now, we're trying to make a little money on the side to help the priest. You see, the priest pays his gas to come over here, and there are maybe about eight people in the church, what we put in the basket, that's his money for that. Sometimes somebody will put twenty cents, or a dime, or a dollar. That's nothing! If somebody's sick or if somebody dies, we call him to come, and he comes for mass and again for the funeral, four times! Coming and going, and coming and going. We are selling *cascarones*, wreaths, and flowers. We've been selling right along! We made thirty-three dollars, and then we spent it and now we're making some more. A lady came and wanted eighteen wreaths, for May third. We all buy some, and the Sisters buy some, and people in the village buy some.

"I'll buy one," I said, picking up a red and yellow cascarone.

Oh, it's a dollar. To me they are pretty. Okay, that's about all for the church. Unless you have questions.

14 ◇ My Saints

I believe in St. Francis
I believe in Blessed Mother . . .
I have Blessed Mother
with hands like this holding EVERYTHING.
I believed in Santa Lucia that has four eyes

.
Oh, I believe a lot of things,
a lot of saints

.
Saints . . .
Like . . .
I started my shrine at my home
at my old home

.
That was years ago.
I used to DREAM about
the saint
    Blessed Mother
that sometimes I'd be walking
and then I'll see this SAINT,
Blessed Mother
[slowly] standing against the rocks
and all between the rocks

.
Do you ever go to that shrine at my house?
It looks like her.
    (1981)

I believe every saint—I just believe in God, that's all. Like if some other
preacher would come to the door, I'd say, "Well, I'm a Catholic and I believe
in God, too, so it's all right. If you're working for God, I believe it. Thank
you very much." I don't get mad at them like some others, you know. I'm
a Catholic and I'll never change. My parents baptized me as Catholic and
I'll stay Catholic until the end. [Frances speaks firmly.] And I don't want to
know more about it. Like they say if you join these other things, you will
know more about God. I think I know about God in me. Knowing all those
things, I don't think it'll help unless I want to become a Sister [laughing].

But I hear things, you know. And, what else? Because my grandfather says we'll never know from the very beginning, because we weren't Catholics until later, when the Spanish came. That's all, that's good enough for us. Every night, every day, I pray. At night I do a little prayer. It'll be just whatever I feel like saying, that's all. Like if I feel I should do this for the church, I just go ahead and do it, I don't want to be asked.

In my bedroom I have Blessed Mother. Those hands like this [Frances folds her hands]—they are holding everything. It's the story of it holding people, protecting people. To me, it means she's holding everything, everything, and it's gonna stay that way. The shrine at the old house is also Blessed Mother. When that lady gave it to me, she was coming with a blanket wrapped around it just like a little baby [Frances laughs]—it was so cute. She gave it to me, so I respect her, you know, to go out and buy a saint for my housewarming. St. Francis Assisi is my favorite, too, I don't know why![1] [In a high pitch]. It's just something that, when you see something and you just like it, I liked the saint. It's also because when I almost died from whooping cough, my grandmother promised that she was gonna take me to Magdalena to ask St. Francis to let me live, and when I grow up I was gonna be a simple person. I wish she hadn't said that! [Frances chuckles.] She also prayed to Blessed Mother. That was when I had whooping cough; it almost killed me, too. So she prayed and prayed to Blessed Mother, and promised that I was gonna have [Frances inhales] long hair. I must have done something wrong, that's why my hair's coming off in the middle.

My hair started coming out a long time ago, before my husband died. We went to a place, to a funeral, and the lady that died had her hair done, and one of her sisters asked if I had an extra hairpin. So I just took one of my hairpins and gave it to her to use it on her hair, a big bone hairpin. So my *sweat* and my *odor* is buried, that's what the medicine man said, that's why my hair came off. They couldn't do anything about it unless we take out the dead person [Frances inhales]. Yeah, they tell me that the dye does that, but it was like that before I dyed my hair. Then Juanita gave me a little hair to put on, but it feels funny, so I don't use it.

I didn't know anything about the Yaquis until I moved to Tucson—we go to the Easter ceremonies. But then, one time, Christy's hair was bald on top, about this big [gesturing a few inches]. We would take her to the doctor, to the nurse, to all, and then one day Lorenzo told me, "Well, why don't you take 'em to the Yaquis?" So I took her, they told me to come, that the Chapayekas,[2] they will do some healings for her, so I did. I took her, I took her over there and [inhaling deeply] they did all those [rituals], and a month later, the hair just came out, like you throw a whip on the ground, so black. So I got interested in them. So every time I do something on my own, I always get the Yaquis there, too.

Having often wondered, I asked Frances why she rolls her hair up in little balls and saves it.

My grandmother says that if it comes off, you should bring it, so I bring home my hair. The bad people could use it, or if I die, I have to look for my hair and bring it home. That's what my grandmother dreamed about my mother, that she cut her hair. She doesn't have the hair that comes off. My grandmother went and threw it off. And one time she dreamed that there was hair *all* over, and there was a man picking it up, and my grandmother told him she was dumb to throw hair like this. So this is my job, every morning, to roll the hair up in little balls and save it. "If you weren't so dumb, I wouldn't have this dirty job," so she told me not to leave my hair anywhere. So I always bring it home.

Then I asked Frances to talk a little bit about the old religion.

Well, I just believe the things that I was told. Like, ah, I believe that whatever is on this Earth, is what is said in the beginning, like especially cactus, you're not supposed to start the cactus plant, my grandfather used to say, it grows on its own. Little things that are running on the ground, you should let them live. You know I believe that, and I believe [firmly] that there's something besides God, not God.

They say it's confusing, they say the Maker. Like I'itoi, it's God, and it's confusing. Like if you talk about God and pretty soon you switch to I'itoi, you confuse them right there. So it's just better to believe that there is something besides God, it's above, whatever it is. I'itoi is part of God. Jesus and the Holy Spirit are part of God. And like the sun, you look at the sun and say, Dear God, it gives us light. At night, you see that night's rolling in, you believe that there's darkness. I don't know how to explain it. Do you want to ask me some questions?

"Maybe you could talk about Coyote, about animal spirits," I said.

I always believed in Coyote, he's clumsy but he's always a powerful one.[3] Spirits can be animal, coyote or owl, anything. That's what I believe. I think I have a guardian angel. Like a *ju:kĭ maḍ* [a little red bug], "rain child," a human angel. I know I have one. And I also believe, too, in a prayer when you say Holy Ghost, now they say Holy Spirit, the white dove, like when you pray for people, my son, my daughter and grandchildren way back in Ohio, I believe the dove carries the prayer to them. There are certain things that sacrifice their lives for us, like deer and rabbit, things we eat. Like the Yaquis, they respect the deer because it's sacrificed. That's what we do with a cow, we pray that you sacrifice your life for us, and give the reason.

"And you pray for rain," I added.

Everybody prays for rain [Frances laughs]. I pray to the only one God. They have different things, like a frog, the little red bug they call *ju:kĭ maḍ*, the long black thing with legs, the woodpecker, that's their job for the rain. There's a lot of things like that in the old ways. Like we were taught to pray, not just [in] church. We were told that it comes to your heart. Like when you are walking in the desert, you pray—it's not just church. It could be anywhere, because your heart will tell you where. One time Lorenzo was walking in the desert from the highway, trying to make a shortcut in the desert. It was hot, and he was sweating and he thought his heart would go because there was no breeze. "Maker, give me a little breeze," he said. And in maybe two seconds a slow breeze started coming. So that's when I thought it's true what they told.

I asked Frances to talk about the ceremonies her grandparents performed at the house, but found that she didn't want to talk about it.

Like if it's a hot day, my grandfather would put a feather out. Or my grand-mother would put the saints out, it's for rain. I can't speak for other people, what they believe, I don't know! I can't because I don't know! People don't talk about it. I don't think about it! I believe, I believe, that's it! I don't think about it, I don't talk about it. I feel it's better that way . . . because none of the people now want to hear about it, like the legends. . . .

So I asked her if she wanted to talk about how she got the shrine for Blessed Mother, on the hill by her old house.

I wanted to have it built. It took eight years. One time I was talking to a Mexican guy, he was a drunk, and he was a pusher, too. And I was talking to him about it, and he said, "I'll do it for you!" I thought he was smoking and he was drinking, that he just said it, so. . . . One day he came over to the house, to my house in town, he said they were ready to make that one, and I said, "Well, I don't have the money to buy the stuff, you know, the cement, and whatever." You see, he was working for some kind of construction, he had a lot of white cement, and I had wanted it to be built with the rocks. So when they came, they got started, and they said they didn't want me to go over there until it was finished! So it went another eight months, and, ah, one day he came and said it was finished. Because they'd go over there and just get together and drink, they'd go over there and other people in San Pedro would come and help. It was about two years ago that my house was finished. I got the saint for my homewarming. We had a big, big ceremonial, and we had that [saint] in front of the church. And the wind was blowing, and there were some ladies supposed to be taking care of her, and they let it go, so it fell down and broke right in half. The ceremony wasn't gonna stop, it was going to go on, and it did! And I put it back together. Now it's covered with lace, it's been there years and years. One day Mildred went over there and glued it together. That how it started.

A cow bellowed from the corral, breaking our silence,. "And you go to Magdalena every year," I added.

My grandmother used to go to St. Francis [Magdalena] every other year, but she didn't do like they do now. They rode the train and they went by wagon. They left the wagons at Nogales and then rode the train from there. That's how I remember. But I also remember that sometimes we would go from there on *that* side, and then go to Magdalena and camp out, ya know. I remember that later on, we'd go to Nogales and then go on the train and camp out. They'll be a lot of people camping. What I like is to see the fire. There will be fire going that looks pretty — that's all I can say that interested me then. We go every year.

Well, this is not a legend. I read this somewhere a long, long time ago, that St. Francis was born in Italy, and he has this church. And pretty soon the people went ahead and modernized the church, and St. Francis, a simple man just like me, he didn't want to live in that modern house. I know how St. Francis feels, and about his simpleness. So he said he was gonna leave and travel a long way. He says, "The birds are my friends and the wilderness is my hope." I think that's a very beautiful thing, so I like St. Francis, he's a simple man. I ask for things and I don't know if he's gonna give it to me, or give it to me in another way. Whatever I ask for, he gives me something else, that's how I feel. I never feel that St. Francis doesn't answer my prayers, but it's that way.

15 ◇ Modern Medicine People

I wish I could believe everything,
but I cannot

I don't know what's in me,
but I cannot.
Maybe I'm wrong.
I cannot make myself believe in
everything

I believe in medicine men

I strongly say that,
I believe in medicine men.
And I believe what we're told
on this Earth

I believe the darkness, I believe the light,
I believe the wind, how it works, how it . . .
like they say, the wind has little roads,
big wind or little wind,
storms.
And I believe that

I believe the clouds,
stars,
    moon,
or what I hear

It's just like putting a puzzle and it falls into a pattern.
I believe that in my mind.
    [1985]

Sometimes Frances talks deeply about conflicts she feels between what she was taught and how she experiences the world, for example, how she feels about some of the "the modern medicine people." She explains how medicine people obtain their powers from animals and other powerful objects or beings. If they are offended and their rights transgressed, the same animals and other power-

ful beings and objects that bring gifts can cause illness; the medicine man is called in to diagnose the illness. Following the diagnosis, a singer will sing to the animal for the cure. But some of the new medicine people are different; their powers, initiations, and techniques are not the same as they were when Frances was growing up.

Frances makes the point that the powers of the medicine man are similar to the powers available to all of us. She tells the story of how a little boy was able to take care of his mother by gaining power from the desert animals. Once again we hear the teaching received from her grandparents: to pay close attention to all living things, even "the little things that are crawling on the ground," for they might give us a gift of insight or power.

A young man was married to an older lady, and they would hunt together. They had a little boy. The man died, he was killed by his older brother. [Frances speaks slowly, with feeling.] The wife was so sad, and, as you said, when you're really sorry, you have grief. And I guess that's why she got so mean.

The uncle would be coming home with whatever he kills, deer or whatever, and the little boy would walk by him and say, "Uncle, uncle," because they were hungry. So one day he came home with another deer and he took the inside out and took some kind of meat that's supposed to be very good, and put it on his belt. The little boy went to meet him, and he was walking by him, and just then the meat fell off his belt. The boy got it and took it home to his mother, and said, "Roast this. Cook it for me over the open fire. My uncle gave this to me." But his mother knew that he'd never give them anything.

The old man came over and asked about it, and his mother said, "I don't know anything about it." He said, "I know the boy got it because he was the only one with me. I know he got the meat." So they gave the meat back. So they decided to leave, to go away from that uncle and live somewhere else [speaking slowly], to do the best they can to get along. He was just a little boy then. They went that night, and it was windy, so they couldn't see their tracks because the wind was blowing so hard. And it went on and on. When they came to a mountain, they decided to make their home. The only thing they could find was what they collected in the desert. And that's the way they lived.

One day the mother of that little boy went to look for something else to eat and found a whole ear of corn. I guess the birds got it from the fields and left it there. So she took it home, and when the season came around, she planted it and they got corn from it, and they ate. They got some more ears, and planted more and more. The little boy had gotten older. He must have been about eight years old. He went to his mother one day and said, "Why don't you make me a bow and arrow? I saw something peeping out of a pile of wood, I want to kill that. Maybe we can eat it." So she said, "You can't kill a pack rat. It's got a hole in the ground and when it sees you, it'll run in and run in. Older people kill them, because they know how to do it." He was too little. But he kept on asking, and he made a bow and arrow. So he went, and he brought back the rat. He said, "I killed this." He just opened it up and took the insides out.

The next day, the boy said, "Why don't you make me another arrow? There's something out there with a cotton tail and I want to kill it." So he went there and came back with a cottontail rabbit. He took the insides out and put it away.

The next day he went out, came back, and said, "There's something there that's got long hair with pink ears, make me another arrow." And she said, "No, you can't do that. It's a rabbit and it runs fast, jumps fast. The older people know how to do it, how to get close to it and shoot it, but you can't, you're just a little boy." And so it went on and on. He went there and got the rabbit. He brought it home and said, "Here, I got this one. You said it was wild and runs fast and jumps fast, but here it is." So she wrapped it up and put it away, took the insides out.

The next day, the same thing happened. The boy went out and then came back and said, "There's something there in back of the mountain. It's like those jumping cactus when its dry, there's something out there with the dry jumping cactus on it's head." It was horns. And the mother said, "That's what they call *huak* [deer]. He'll feel you when you come. It's also fast. It'll jump and run and you'll never catch it." So he went on and on and on, and finally made another arrow. He came back and he was going, he was really going. I don't know what they call it, but it's like when a cat is stalking something, we call it *wi'ahi*. And finally somebody whistled and looked back — it was a lion. And the mountain lion said, "Let me kill it for you." And he told him not to tell his mother he killed it. So he put blood on his arrow and went back to his mother. He said, "Look, I killed this big deer." He never told her that the lion killed it. That's the way it was told.

[Frances speaks firmly.] When a boy is growing up, he should get up and run, do whatever young boys do. Maybe something will see you and like you and give you something. We both live here—we're both women, and Jimmy's here [Frances's grandson]. Fifty years ago or seventy years ago, even if Jimmy was a little boy, if you got your period, we couldn't let you come in, because on account of Jimmy. You could stay out someplace and we could take food to you or water to you. That's to keep him pure. Anything that's got power will like you and give you something—that's what happened to this little boy who met the lion. So anyway, he came home and he cooked the things and they ate them. He cried and she cried as everything came back to them, how hard they had it, how mean the uncle was, and how much sadness there was when her husband was killed. Everything came back.

That's what he was singing. And another thing I didn't tell you. From the beginning, they didn't have anything [Frances inhales deeply], so there's something that's along the road, when it rains, when it's summer rain, the grass is tall like this [gesturing]. They made it into a rope and that's what holds the bow. That's supposed to be from the beginning.

From then on, he killed, because he was far away from the village. And another hunter came to this place and said that a deer was dead somewhere. This man went to see it, to see why the deer was dead. He found the arrow still sticking there and took it out. He saw that it was a different point, a rock point that he knew nobody uses it in that village. He went to a meeting in the village and told them he found this arrow in a deer, and asked if anybody knew where the arrow came from.

There was this old man. That's why there's the old saying, "The world won't be going around if [speaking slowly] there's no old ones, no young ones. There was no old ones, no middle-aged, no young ones, and no children. The world won't go around." That means like if I didn't know something, I'd go to an older person to ask her. That's what it means.

So there was this old man. He said, "Well, I guess you didn't find out who this arrow belonged to, [Frances's voices gets louder] but my guess is—do you remember when a child was mistreated? Maybe that's him! He grew up somewhere and that's his arrow." So here was this old man, this mean old man, the boy's uncle. He said, "Well, why don't you give it to me and I'll take it? Give me that arrow and I'll go to see my nephew and have some meat." So he gave him the arrow.

The uncle went looking for them and when he found them, [slowly, softly] they saw him coming, so they weren't going to face him. The old man was trying to say, "Here's your arrow," but they wouldn't talk to him. He got the message and left the arrow and went home. And that's the end, there's no more after that. It's like when we call *da:m ce:* [to get even], and now there is no more, ya know, no more bitterness.

The boy knew that the uncle has a cane that's got roots. It's just a stick with a point on it, old people always have it in their house. Like I have a saint. They worship it; anyway, it's got roots. That one's got *roots*.

The boy got some sticks and made a design they call *giñskud* [an O'odham stick game, a form of gambling], I have them somewhere, those sticks that you play games with. The game is like this. You say, "I saw some bird's eggs." But I know it's not time for the bird to lay eggs. Then you say, "Well, I'm going to go get it, and I'll win." And he broke his nail, and I said, "I didn't know the moon was there," and he said, "It's not time for a new moon." Then you hold that broken nail, and you say, "Look, look at my hand, then you'll see the moon." So then you win. You lost two, then you say, "Put that stick away. It looks like it's looking at me." Then you say, "No, can't do it, it's got *roots*." And here, that gopher had already bit off the roots of that stick. "Well, I'll move it," and he got it for him, so he got a round stick he had and he sang this song:

Hemu dai susuliga
Hemu dai susuliga
Hodai dapinime culi t-abai susuliga
[There I throw the sticks
There I throw the sticks
On the smooth rock I throw the sticks]

And he hit it far. It went as far as the air and came back, and he hit the ground and made that noise, and the man fell backward, and he went so fast, he got the sticks and he said, "'A:nai ñai -suliŋe-ga 'a:nai ñai-suliŋe-ga [There I throw the sticks]," and he hit it again. It went farther up and hit the ground so hard it threw him back a second time, and he jumped up and got the stick. He had a hard time getting it, and he said, "*'A:nai ñai -ṣuliŋe-ga 'a:nai ñai-ṣuliŋe-ga* [There I throw the sticks]." And the boy hit the sticks again. And they went farther up and hit the ground, and threw him up a third time.

He almost jumped up and got the sticks. He almost didn't get up. And he hit them and they went farther up and the uncle fell on the ground. They call *sic sic*, you know it makes that noise, so the uncle fell down and he never got up. So the boy got even and he went home. The boy was coming home and his mother saw him, and he was dancing with that stick. Because there was no bitterness.

My grandfather told me this story. I didn't use to like his stories because he was always preaching, like "Get up and run," and he would say that things are flying above, or things are running on the ground, things would see us, and see how pure we are, they might give us power. Whatever power they have, like a medicine man, or a singer, or whatever. Like becoming a medicine man would come from a buzzard or a coyote. One time somebody told me about this man who wanted to be a medicine man. An older man told him, "It's not easy to be a medicine man. You have to go through a lot. You have to suffer a lot before you can become a [Frances inhales deeply] medicine man." Well, anyway, the man still goes after the older man. And finally, he said, "Okay. We're going to go to a big mountain." And they went there and he said, "You stand here. And we'll go over to that cave." And on the way he went to that cave and got a stick. The old man was standing beside him and said, "You watch for whatever comes out. It's gonna come out and come in between us. If he wants you to be a medicine man, he'll go around and around and around. You will feel like it's gonna squeeze you to death, and you'll have to take it."

[Speaking softly] So, he stood there, and pretty soon, a snake came out from the cave, about this big [Frances gestures five or six feet high] with eyes huge like this [Frances gestures to show large eyes]. He came out and he came closer and closer. So the man ran away. He didn't want to be a medicine man. [Softly] I guess that's what they do.

Even a rock, even a rock will be powerful. There's a story about that. I wish I could remember it. That's why I say nowadays that there's no *really* medicine man, because they didn't get the power that way. Maybe they got it from drinking too much and they have those DTs, and they think that's what it is to be a medicine man. Oh, they are medicine men, but not as powerful as before.

So I didn't want to hear stories from my grandfather because I didn't want to be preached [Frances laughs].

Like I was telling this lady, this man came over, I was just sitting. He said, "I want you to tell me something, tell something about this purification dance," ya know. And, ah, so I told him, "Well, purification means when your first period comes, your body changes, it changes, and you change into a smell like fishy smell. So they have this dance and they go back and forth and the sweat goes out and they breathe out. And in the end, they are pure!" That's why the lady has to have the period and go out and leave for four days, then wash herself, wash everything, then leave everything before she goes back. That's to keep the man pure. But now if there is no pure, there is no pure men now. Because they get their period and they eat, they drink right there. That's the reason why. Like if the little boy's growing up, he's supposed to be pure, so the powerful things in this world will meet him and give him power. There will be a gift from them. Anything. Now there is no pure. That's why there are no good medicine men. Before, they were good, and they were good hunters. Because my grandfather told me that when he would go hunting, if he came home with a deer, ya know, comes home with a deer, and she had her period, she won't eat the meat. And I said, "Why is that? What does that got to do with it?" And he said that the next time, if he goes out hunting, well, whatever he's hunting will smell it from miles and miles away.

Whatever my grandmother told me as a child, I believe that and sometimes I think, "Well, I don't know, seems like it's—I wonder if it's true." But then I still go back to believing it because . . . it's just being an Indian, I guess.

I want to tell now of my own experience. Jose was alive then, my cousin. He's still living. They had a little daughter, she was so sick, so she went to the medicine man in Si:l Naggia. There was three medicine men there so they went to one. This one told them that there was no hope for her, so they came over and told us. She's my niece and my godchild, too, so I said, "Well, we'll follow you and be with you," ya know, if it happens, so we went to San Xavier. It was close. We went over there and we stayed that night. The next night was . . . no, we stayed just one day and that night was New Year's Eve. The other medicine man, he's still alive, he's real old, he's still alive now. And I don't think we should give his name. I guess he was at the dance and then the grandfather of that little girl went to, went over there and got him. It was after midnight, the new year already came. And he'd blow, and he did whatever the medicine man does. And he said, 'cause we were all there, he said, "There's nothing wrong with her body, it's just fine, it's her head. Ya know, there's a soft spot on the top." I guess everybody has it, it just hardens up when we grow. The whole thing fell, and it's just sitting on her throat. That's why she can't swallow, and, ahm, so just find somebody that knows how to pick it up.

Okay, well, I guess they took him back to the dance or whatever. But I guess they left for Si:l Naggia, the one, the grandfather and grandmother, because just before the sun was up, they came and brought a lady—a lady. And she went in and saw her, she came back, she got a pan of cold water; it was January and everything was cold. She got a pan of cold water and she was putting it on her head. I don't know whether she wanted to get cool or something, she put her finger in her mouth. Ya know, sometimes you could hear the bone sets, that's what it sounded like. She threw up a whole lot of blood, and she said, "This is what I like, it's gonna work." And, ah, so she said, "Well, our forehead is like this [Frances places her fingers on her forehead] and this all came out, so it's just sitting there. So when I lift it up, these things go back in [gesturing with her thumb and pinky]. And it should be all right." I don't know what happened. Because we were sitting up nights and we were sleeping, and she was all right! I think she ate something, when we got up in the afternoon she was eating beans and crackers, and now she's about this big [gestures about five feet wide]. That woman at the powwow, she was eating when we were standing there, that's the one.

I asked Frances to explain what happens in the ceremony.

Blow like the cigarette, just blow and feel it. And I always imagine things like, if you are a medicine man, when you look at something, light shines.

And you see it and you know. I think that's what it's like. [Rapidly] I'm not a medicine woman, so I wouldn't know, but that's the way I imagine. Light shines, they say his eyes, because he's kind of blind, like me right now. So he must have some power. He was kind of blind, but he saw it. That's what I believe, because when he's really a down-to-earth medicine man . . . , like, um, something happened.

One time when I was young, somebody had an argument with my uncle. My uncle died long time ago. He said, "Well, if you're a medicine man, why don't you put a curse on 'em, and I'll ask you to take it out, and if you don't take it out I'm gonna kill you!" They weren't really . . . , they were arguing, ya know, and I thought, could he be a medicine man? I used to think, how could he be a medicine man? That was when he was young, ya know, I didn't believe he was a medicine man until the time when we took Lorenzo and he was so sick. And he said something to do, what did he say? I forgot. Not too long ago, he said something about the eagle, the hawk, we should get some singers for the healing we call *wuso*. So we never did. It was the pills [that cured it]. He said he dreamed that somebody cursed him. He said, no, it wasn't like that. The hawk caused it. We have a lot of things that cause us sickness, just being Indian. We have owls, snake, snake coils, horny toad, hawk, and, ahm, those woodpeckers, and, ahm, a lot of things! It's our sickness. Now the doctors believe that when you're sick, they give medicine and medicine and medicine, and pretty soon the medicine doesn't work. The doctor will say, "Maybe if you want, go to the medicine man," just to cure his conscience, that's all. But we didn't get that. He was saying the other day we didn't get the singers because we never have time for him to do it. I said we'll have time after that Pioneer Days.

What else should I tell about the medicine men? I think I said in the other tape about how they become medicine men, but well, when a child's born, they say when a child's born, a mother takes care of it. It goes to sleep and has the warmth of their body, and it's warm and takes care of it. Like a baby should be when he grows up, and the house is pure. Like the women get sick and goes to the hut. And there's nothing in here, ya know. Well, when they get, I don't know how old they have to be. The father gets him up and tells him to run. Then they'll run. Maybe the powerful birds, whatever, will meet you and give you his power. That's how they got to be medicine men. But if you get the power from something, you have to go through a lot before you become a medicine man. You could be hurt, you could be, ya know, a lot of hard times, like sick, or blood. Then they become medicine men.

The person gets to be a medicine man whenever it is given to them, sometimes when they are just little boys. This little boy in the legend — [quickly] we shouldn't talk about it, snakes are out.[1] The boy said when he was trying to kill the deer when he was a little boy, and the lion was in back of him and killed the deer and gave him his power, that's what they do. You can become a powerful hunter or you can get *whatever*, not just the medicine man.

And, um, there's a lot of things that it's hard to say. Like I told you, Debbie, already that I cannot believe everything in this Earth. [Slowly, with conviction] I cannot. I tried, but I cannot. What I believe is the voices of my grandparents. It seems that they were old, and they came a long way on this Earth. They've seen a lot, they feel a lot, and they go through a lot. And their voices, it sounds like the things are real. And after I hear a lot of things, the same things that my grandparents told me, but I don't have the feelings of the sounds that I hear from my grandparents. Like, a lot of time, I believe in medicine men, and I believe in other things. Like the old ways, I believe that. But, ah, maybe about twenty or thirty years ago things really changed. I don't know how long ago it started, but it changed so fast, I think it was too fast for my mind. I cannot make myself believe, I tried. Like I hear things that happened on this Earth. Just a lot of things I can't begin to explain or tell in every detail what happens. But in my mind I hear it. That's why I cannot believe the modern things now. I hear a lot of science fiction. Of course, in science fiction, it tells that a person can write and act on it, and in their imagination it is true. In our ways they don't tell anything about it.

There was a nightmare far away toward Nevada. I heard from a medicine woman that she could hear the girl by doing the distant feeling. Nobody can even imagine how many times I tried to believe that. It's just like you're testing yourself, and then every time I test myself, it comes out different. And then you go back to the same thing, you backtrack yourself to the same thing — it wasn't like that in the very beginning. Like if I say, "I'm gonna grab that bird out there with my power." I can say that, but I cannot do that. Because I don't have any power. It's a made-up thing, I'm sorry to say it. But the old saying, if you believe it, it's true. I don't know. I wish I could believe everything, but I cannot. I don't know what's in me, but I cannot. Maybe I'm wrong. I cannot make myself believe in *everything*. I believe in medicine men. I strongly say that, I believe in medicine men. And I believe what we're told on this Earth. I believe because I was told a long time ago. I believe because it happens right in front of my eyes! And I believe those things. A lot of things I believe because I've seen it happen. But I cannot believe the modern medicine people [slowly] that can do something. Maybe they can . . . but . . . I cannot believe that.

I knew a medicine man, he's gone already. And he said he was gonna make this woman a medicine woman. He was drunk, they were both drunk. They were going to inject a cigarette rolling paper into her wrist. When he was blowing it and sucking it, you could hear the paper going into his mouth. So we said, "You didn't put it in there, you put it in your mouth!" He denied it, so finally we wrestled with him and he opened his mouth, it was on the roof of his mouth. That's the way I imagine things, I guess. I question.

My son in-law said, when he said that this man's time is coming, a lot of things is foretold. Like the coyote stands close to the house, or the owls sit on the roof all night long, the star boy fell—all those things. And a lot of things they say, you go to the east, and there's prickly pear and all that. That's what they say. To me it could be just a tale.

I question everything. I'm Indian and I'm always going to be Indian. It's there—no matter what you think or believe, it's just there! It's just being an Indian, I guess. Okay, that's all.

Oh, and another thing. Debbie, this is what I'm talking about that they call it "Hohokam." I guess there were people living a long time ago, living there. That's where they're going to dig up, clear up for farming. So they found some bones, so that's when it started. The medicine man is telling us what to do, telling us how to bury them. The runners are going to *run*, the singers are going to *sing*, the dancers are going to *dance*, and whatever our tradition is going to happen right there. I guess I'll have to go along with them!

And another thing. I'd like to ask somebody, "What is Hohokam?" In all those legends I never heard of Hohokam. I heard of something called Wu:ṣkam. Wu:ṣkam. They are the people that were living and were moved into the water. My mother-in-law used to say that they didn't walk, they were running all the time. [Frances yawns.] I don't really know about Hohokam. To me it means "gone." Like if my vase is gone, "*Huhugam!*"

I mentioned that some archaeologists are digging Hohokam ruins.[2]

They are digging all those bones, and having ceremonies. They had one last Friday at the mission. I was talking to Louise, and I said, "Why can't you just bury them instead of doing all these things?" There was a hill where my mother was buried. The ladies went there and got pieces of broken pottery and they were saying there was a village there, and I said, "Maybe." I'd like to find out. One of my students' husbands told me he found some bones over there, and I said, "That was my grandfather's bones!" And he said, "Was your grandfather two thousand years old?" [Frances laughs a good, hearty laugh.]

Part V ◇ Reflections

Things That Connect

We're not supposed to tell this kind of stories in the summer,
it isn't good for us.
Snakes are out!
So I'm just telling
the little stories,
this is not the real one.
The real one is the same,
but it's longer than this one.
Snakes could bite for telling stories in summer
.

If snakes hear us,
they'll come over and bite us
or bother us,
so that's why we don't tell the stories
[softly] in the summer
.

But a lot of things . . .
The power is *down*,
it's not as strong as when we were doing . . .
Their power is not as strong
.

When we did things the way we were supposed to, it was
powerful.
But now it's weakened.
I hope it doesn't happen in the summer,
  that the snakes doesn't hear me,
I hope they're deaf now because they're old.
  (1990)

We've heard Frances talk about "little stories." "This is not a legend, just a little story," she'd say, embedding a story "from the Beginning" in her everyday talk. Like everything that is sacred, O'odham legends have their own time and place, their sacred texts and contexts. In the past legends were told over many nights, and only in the winter months when the snakes weren't out. The O'odham believe that snakes are the guardians of secrets, of secrets from the time of the Beginning.[1]

One day in early April 1987, we were eating lunch and Frances began speaking in a somber tone. I quickly switched the tape recorder on as she nodded and began:

Long ago they would set us down and tell us the stories, the stories and all the things that are connected to them, the *Ho'oki a:gida*. And now they are all gone. I don't want the [full-length] legends in the book. They tell them over and over in different ways, and it changes—it's changing and it's going to change more in a modern way. I don't want that, because it's been told, it's been in books. Every one of us has different stories or different language, and it comes out differently. Like the Children's Shrine. It's not as strong as it was before, because it's gotten too modern.[2] If I had my way, I think we should keep it the way it was, when they discovered how to take care of it. It was very beautiful before, because there were just about four rocks, one for every direction. It didn't have those dolls there. It looks like a shrine where somebody's buried. It's changed too fast. It's good they put toys there— they were children. But all these years, whoever took care of them, they just had the four rocks. And every four years they put new sticks there, but the rocks stayed there.

That's the way I think about all those things that have been told. The legends have been told a simple way, then pretty soon somebody else tells and adds a little more to make the story more interesting, and more and more. That's why it's not real anymore, it's not what we were told when we were kids, it's been changed so much and so fast, it doesn't have the feeling that it had—it's faded. It's too modern, the words are just put in.

Maybe a long time from now, maybe fifty years from now, things will be changed in a different way. But this is a good time to tell about how I feel about the new generation. Of course I can't do anything about it. But maybe someday somebody will read it and maybe get something out of it.

I think it is going to be better when the person tells the things that happen, remembers what happened in their life. I'm sure everybody has these
stories. I think that's what should be told! Legends have already been told!
It's already been spoiled. When my grandfather told stories, in some places
it tells embarrassing things, but we shouldn't laugh. Today people laugh.
My grandfather would get really mad at us if we laughed, call us "silly girls,"
so we don't laugh, we're not supposed to laugh.

I had made up my mind years ago I was never going to tell stories again.
Then pretty soon I thought to myself, maybe I should, because things will be
forgotten. I'm already forgetting things, and it's bad, because I am making
myself forget things. Reaching back now, it's not there. I understand now
that that's the way things are going, they are buried and they are not there —
no matter how hard you dig. It died a long time ago. Even before people
who knew more than me died, it died. It's just like if I had planted something, and it's going good, and pretty soon somebody comes and snips off
a little flower, snips off a little flower, like that. The beauty of that plant is
gone. Like that, the beauty of the stories are gone. The only things that will
survive are the things that are written in the books. But these legends will
be a fake. That's the way it is!

*Legends were supposed to be told in a certain way: in formulaic, powerful
words, spoken with care over many sittings. For Frances, these words and their
contexts disappeared a long time ago. So Frances tells the "little stories," like
tales told to children who are too young to sit through the longer ones. Frances
believes that the power of the desert serpents has decreased, because we are no
longer doing things the way we're supposed to; this throws the world out of balance. So after a while Frances decided to tell the shorter stories, thinking that
maybe the snakes are not as powerful as they were when she was growing up.*

16 ◇ I'm Not Sewing, Just Telling Stories

This is the story about the lady—I
Told you a little about it.
I'm not sewing,
I'm supposed to but I'm not.
I'm just telling STORIES.
One time—
Once upon a time
there was a lady . . .
(1981)

One time, once upon a time there was a lady. She was beautiful. Nothing was good enough for her, no man was good enough for her. So one day, the Maker made a man and gave him all the power . . . and what shall I say? He made him a wooden ball, like this kickball, in Indian they call it ṣoṇgiwul. The Maker made the ball while he was sitting right between Kitt Peak and Sandy Mountain. There's a lot of rocks, he was sitting in an opening between them. The man was racing with this kickball, kicked the ball and it went right next to the mat that the girl was making. So she grabbed the ball and put the ball right under her skirt. He came and said to her, "Where's my ball?" She said, "I don't know, I don't see any ball around here. I'm working on my mat and don't see any ball." He said, "You got it! I kicked it right over here and you got it." She said, "Oh, no, I didn't get it. I didn't see it!" The man thought, "Well, I'll just go home." He turned around and started going, and she said, "Come get your ball, here's your ball." She tried to reach under herself and looked under her skirt, but she couldn't find it. He was standing there watching her, and knew right away what had happened.

Nine months later a baby was born with long, long fingernails, and everybody was afraid of her nails. When she got bigger, she would fight with the kids. Each time a child would cry, her mother would spank her. At first she didn't mind, but then finally the mother spanked her so hard she suffered, and she left home. She went way over to what's now called Posa Verde [Many Dogs], which at the time was called Cedagĭ Wawhai, Green Well. She made her home there, living there and hunting for whatever she wanted to eat. And then pretty soon she started on people. First she started on kids. Every time a baby would be crying, she would be right there, saying, "What did you do to my grandchild?" She'd scratch the child, open her stomach and her intestines would be put around the house. This went on and on. People were trying to figure out how they were going to get rid of her, how they were going to get her out. But they could not find a way.

Finally an old man said, "Well, why don't you go to the person who did it, because he's the one who started this." So he went and found that man, and he said he'd come in four days. But in four days nobody came. So they went to him again, and he said, "I'll be there in four days." The people waited and they waited, but nobody came. Again he said, "I'll be there in four days." It just went on and on. And finally one old man said, "I don't think he meant four days, I think he meant four years!" So all that time the witch was eating up the people, and finally the man came and told them what to do.

They gathered up the wood, and did all the things the old man told them to do. They went to her home and invited her to come and enjoy herself with them — they said there's going to be a big dance. So she jumped and ran around and got her skirt and was tying it, dressing up while she was dancing around. She sounded good when she danced because she had hoofs and bells around her ankles. So she went like this to the dance with this man. And they danced and danced, and every time they gave her a piece of bread, she would sit down. They put some tobacco in the pipe and were passing it around, and told people not to inhale. All this was going on while the other people were getting the wood and rocks to make a door, and then another door, and then a gate all around the place.

Finally, she went to sleep so the man they call I'itoi [Big Brother] carried her on his shoulder toward his cave at Baboquivari. And she woke up. So the people danced again and again until she went back to sleep. The man carried her again, she almost woke up, so they started dancing again, and she went back to sleep. So they went in the cave and put her way in the back of the cave. They put the wood and then the door and the wood and then the door, like that until they were out of the cave, and they started burning it. When the fire started, she was jumping up, shouting, "Why are you doing this to me? I was having a good time with you!" This is what she was yelling. And so she died.

I guess at that time when something happened like this, they do something for revenge, so they ate her. And there was an old lady, an old lady. Usually in our ways if somebody butchers a cow, an old lady will come and sit, and usually they give her some and then she'll go home. So this old lady came and sat and sat, and nobody gave her any meat. After they ate, the people went their separate ways. So the old lady crawled over to the rocks and found a few drops of blood. She got them and rolled them up into little balls and went home. She put them in a little hole and told her grandsons to go over there in four mornings and see what happens.

So after four mornings they went over there, and there were eggs in the place where she put the blood. They went home and told their grandmother, who said, "This is why I put them there. In four mornings you go over there and see what happened." So after four mornings they went over there and there were little birds, like little pieces of cotton. "Oh, yeah, that's what I wanted them to be," she said. "In four mornings you go over there and see." So after four mornings they went over there, and came back and said, "Those are the prettiest birds I ever saw." "That's what I want them to be," she said, "so after four mornings you go over there and bring them home." So after four mornings he went over there and brought them home. That's what people call peacocks, 'ado, they have pretty feathers. That's the blood of a witch.[1]

"The story of Ho'ok," Frances said, "shows that we can take care of our children just so far, but we can't keep their hearts, especially now. The father is too strict, controlling and mean," she explained; this is why the daughter is violated, and turns out the way she does. The ironwood story, below, also opens with a girl who is too proud and is violated, in this case bearing twins. She repeats the message: extreme pride will reap nothing but trouble. "A person can be proud inside, but not outside," Frances is fond of saying.

I'd say my life is interesting, but that's coming from me. I don't know if anyone else will think it's interesting. It sort of makes me scared [to record all of this]. Sometimes I think, maybe I'm crazy! Like I look out the window and I think, "Oh, that poor tree. I wonder what it's thinking, or that poor bird, it's hungry, I wonder if it needs some water." Or "The poor cactus, I wonder if it's cold." All those things—I don't know. . . . Or if something is running, a little thing running, I think maybe it's meant to be here, so I just let it go, unless it's something I know to be dangerous. The other day I was out there trying to clean some bear grass, so pretty soon this big bird started to eat the meat. There was some meat hanging there, so I thought, "Look at the greedy birds eating the meat!" It was Mildred's meat and I thought, "Oh, it's such a little bird, maybe it won't eat the whole thing." [Frances laughs.] So I never told anyone. She finally got them off the line. So those are the things, so let's change into a story.

Okay, we'll talk about the ironwood. Well, there was a girl, a really beautiful girl. She was kind of like me when I went to town and I learned a lot and I earned my own money. I knew how to dress up and I feel—maybe that's the way she feels—nothing was too good for her; she was too good. That's all she thinks of, and nobody, like boys, was good enough for her. So that's what my grandmother used to say [firmly]: "You can be proud. [Softly] You can be proud, but not outside. You can be really proud inside, but you have to be proud [slowly] from the bottom up, not just halfway." And she said that, "Some proud girls are not proud underneath." You know what that means. Well, that's what this girl was. At that time I didn't understand, but after I was forty years old, I did. Well, this girl was like that.

One day she was resting, ya know, stretched out on that *main*, what they call *main*. It's a mat they use for the bed, like that rug right there [indicating with her eyes], they sleep on it. Pretty soon a great big cloud formed up, and a drop of rain fell. She got bigger and bigger, and nine months came. Twins were born. Twins were born. As they grew up, they asked, "Who's our father?" And it went on and on, and finally, she told them, "The Cloud is your father." So years went on and they wanted to see their father.

Well, this is not the long story. There is a loong looong story about it, and there's a short story. There's a little short story, and that's what I'm telling.

And, finally, the twins said, "Well, we're going to see back east." "It'll take you a long time to get there, but if you really want to go, you can," their mother said. So they set the date and they went on their journey. They went on and on and on, and, finally, they got to this round house, and there was the Wind. The form that comes first, and then the rain, they called it *jegos*, because it came first and then the rain, because the Cloud was blind.

First they went to the Wind—he was older. They were brothers, Wind and Cloud were brothers. They went in to see the Wind, and they said, "My uncle." The Wind said, "If you are my nephews, why don't you blow the air, and then I'll know it's you." So they stormed for a little. Then they went to their father, and said, "My father." And he said, "If you are my sons, you roar—you know, make noise when it rains. And so they did. So they lived with him there for a while, and he told them, "Why don't you go back to your mother—your mother needs you more than we do." So he got them ready for their journey. It was rainy season, and he said, "Well, if you are going, if you get into the storm, don't run, just walk. If you get the rain and lightning, don't get under a mesquite tree, get under an ironwood tree." It's got something to do with electricity. The ironwood is hard and strong.

They went, and finally, the storm came. They were walking, and the rain and lightning came. They couldn't stand the rain and the lightning, so they went under a mesquite tree. The lightning struck them both and scattered their flesh all over. And that big mountain over there—S-cuk Du'ag, there's a lot of *'a'ud*, century plants,[2] and that is edible, too. You know you cut them and bury them. Those little boys turned into that so the people can eat it and use it for food. There's a lot of them on that mountain over there.

So that's how Cloud killed his sons. So ironwood has something to do with the electricity. So this is something you could tell Jimmy [Frances's grandson] about the ironwood.

There's another story about the ironwood. When we had the flood, there was this boy, a young man. He started coming from back east. Whenever there's a young girl, the boy started coming and he sleeps there in the morning. They know how he was, but wouldn't say the name—it's like a dragon in the Bible. But it's a young man, I guess it changes shapes. Here, it eats the young girls. In another story it's a saint. You see that saint right there [St. George]? That was a snake that comes and does the same thing as this young man.

And there was a powerful man they call Siwañ. He had a pretty daughter and he knew the boy was coming. So he went out and got the *hanam*,[3] its almost like the jumping cactus, and he put it between his daughter's legs. So he said to the girl, "When he comes home, he'll go to bed, and do what he wants to do. When the boy does that, he'll feel those stickers and he'll let go. You turn around and you do this to him with that ironwood." So the girl did that to the boy.

So the man developed a baby. In the morning he took the baby, and here people already knew, ya know? So when he went to where the people were, they said, "Well, where's the baby? We want to see the new baby." Here he left him somewhere [softly] and went over there without it.

So he went back to get the baby, and the baby was crying. The semen was his tears, the baby's tears. And in the morning the baby was born from a man. That's the end of the world. And that's where it comes from—from that girl. Because her father told her what to do—it tells in the story. Why do we think it's dirty? Why do we think it's so wrong? Who are we? Always dirty, always talked about, made fun of. But in legends it's not. She did a smart thing, but a wrong thing came out of it. That's why the tears came, because a baby was born to a man. I can't end the world, but these people are powerful.

That's what the story says. You see, this didn't just start yesterday or today. It's in the world since the very beginning! I think it's very important, but I don't know how many people feel this way. People think they are nothing, they are dirty. To me, if I was making the rules, I would make the rules so that people would try to accept them the way they are, instead of putting them down. Because they are here! We can't do anything about it! We can't get rid of them. We could go out and kill them all, but I don't think that's the way. They still belong to God! They are God's children.

And now the new things came out, well, it's new to me and I still don't know what it really is all about. I still don't know about AIDS, because I didn't hear about it until just lately. And if it comes from them . . . , that's what they said. Some others say it comes from something else. We can't do anything about it. There are a lot of things that are just as bad. We don't really say anything about that. But if you just sit and think about it, or look around for it, we'll find that there are other things just as bad. That's just the way I think, but I don't know.

This is the story of a friend of mine that was, how shall I put it? Came into the world as an illegitimate child. We should call it illegitimate mother! This child was born to a young girl maybe fifteen or sixteen, and the father of the child was her uncle. So she stayed with him until she went home and got the baby. And the father didn't like it—he didn't like the baby for not having a father, or because it was his own brother's child. So when she came home with the baby—because she delivered the baby in a little house. . . . Anyway, she came home to the house after six days and he told his wife to get rid of the child.

I guess the wife didn't have the nerve to destroy the baby. She [the daughter] came home with the baby and he got a big stick and hit her in the back and she fell. There was a lady nearby who took the baby and ran. I guess the man thought he killed her, but he didn't. So the ladies got together and picked up the mother, and walked her around and walked her around, telling them to go someplace far away, because he might kill the baby and kill her. There's a place called Si:l Naggia, Saddle Hang. And she moved over there. She walked from Anaka to Si:l Naggia with the baby. She started after dark and walked all night, maybe part of the day. And [the child] lived there with these people. Pretty soon this man found out where they were living and he'd come and bring groceries and material for their clothes, and finally built them a little house, so she lived there raising her little boy. Three years later—the baby was three years old, she got sick and died. So these people got the boy and raised him as their son. He grew up to be a handsome man, and he knows a lot of things—from the dogs to horses, cows, horses, and everything. He is a singer.

The reason I am telling this story is because there is a legend, it's almost the same thing. These two girls were growing up, the father was thinking he would raise them and marry them off. Pretty soon these two men—they are twins—used to come. They were handsome men, but they were really those . . . what do you call them, that lives under the ground? They were gophers, they were really gophers. So the two girls come to see them, both these twins.

The two girls, both of them got pregnant. The mother didn't know and she found out too late. Anyway, the father was going to let them keep the babies, I guess he was thinking of some reason of his own why he wanted to keep the babies, but anyway, the babies were born and they were both boys. Somehow the two twins found out about them. A few months after they were born, the old man went to see the babies. I guess the old man was always watching, he wanted to keep those babies for his own reasons— he was going to kill those two men, the fathers. Finally one night they [the twins] came over to see the girls and the babies, and the father was ready for them—he killed the twins, the fathers of the babies. As he killed them, he also pounded them with bones and everything and put it in a storeaway jar. Once in a while he picked just like, what would I say, something like you keep pounded meat in a jar, that's what he keeps them in and he eats them.

Finally the two boys began to grow up. They asked their mothers, "Who is our father?" And the mothers wouldn't tell them. And the next time they asked, "Who is our father?" Again she wouldn't tell them. And the next time they asked, "Who is our father?" And the fourth time, she told them.

One day they were eating what we call *poṣol* (meat stew). The old man was eating their father's meat and they wanted some, but he wouldn't give them any. Anyway, they stole some and tasted it. Tasted like meat, like ground meat or something. And they asked their mother, "What is grandfather eating with the *poṣol*?" So it went on and finally they asked again, so she told them that their fathers live way out where the sun comes up. They wanted to go see and they said, "No you can't go, it's too far," making all kinds of excuses not to go. But they wanted to go, so finally they told them that their fathers were gone, their fathers were dead. But they wanted to go and find out how they died.

Finally, they went all the way back east, and when they got there, there was a lizard lying there in an old broken-down house. They were asking themselves, "Where could my father be?" And the lizard says, "Did you know the old man killed them?" And so I guess right away they believed that. The lizard told them that. So they turned back, and tried to imagine their father, trying to make up in their imagination their father, but they couldn't. And a voice said, "If there's any bones left in us, we could build up from there." But there are no bones, they are all smashed up. So they never could imagine their fathers' forms. So they went home and asked their mother about what they found out. She told them, finally, that it was true, and the two of them killed their grandfather.

Once again Frances's message is that parents should not be covetous or controlling with their children. If they are, they will cause problems for them, and,

in the end, the living things of the Earth (here, the lizard) will put things back into balance.

I thought of something and now I can't remember. What was it? Oh, well, I'm not gonna worry about it. I'm not gonna worry my little head [laughing]. This is about a children's shrine, about the children who were sacrificed when we were going to have a flood. The water was coming out and was going to wash all the people, and the world. The water was coming and each time somebody would tell a medicine man, and they would go and study about how the water was coming up, and then go back and tell the people we were going to have a flood. So then another medicine man would be taken there, and every medicine man that went — eight medicine men went, and, ahm, every one of them said the same thing, we were going to have a flood. So an old man asked, "What are we going to do about it? How can we stop it? There's a lot of people, young people, some children just now born. They should have a chance to see the world, enjoy the world, to see what the world is all about!" So, another old man said, "Well, I guess we have to make a sacrifice ['*iagc*, "to offer"]." So they chose about eight men to go and they gave them a stick, to go to the families that have pretty daughters under twelve years of age. And some had to go to the people who have boys the same age. When they find them, they put a flower on them, marking those who were chosen to be sacrificed.

So that went on for days, all the while, the water was getting higher and higher. They came to a lady who had a pretty daughter, and she saw them coming. There was the squash had grown just about high enough to hide a person, so she rushed to hide her daughter under the leaves of the squash. Another lady hid her son in a rolled-up sleeping mat. And they went on, the men couldn't find him, so they went on. And finally they got two girls and two boys, and took them over to the place where they would be sacrificed, and they were all dressed up. The girls wore all pink and yellow and the boys were painted half black and half yellow. They were all so pretty! They threw them in the hole where the water was coming out. So there the water stopped and the people went on living. But these people, these women, the lady ran over to see her boy, to get her boy out. When she did, the mat was rolled up, only all she could see was the foam that comes when the water runs, when we can see where the water has been. She saw a lot of foam, and the boy wasn't there. And at the squash garden the woman lifted up the leaves of the squash and the girl wasn't there. She saw the same thing, the foam, so she knew the water had swept her away. Eight days after that, the woman was still going back to that spot. She goes back, back, she goes back, until finally one morning there was a blossom, a real pretty, fresh blossom. This is the design that you've seen in baskets. It's a long story. A real story is real long. This is a little story, what they tell us when we are really little and they don't want to go into these long stories, this is what they tell us. About the squash blossoms, you've seen them. That's how it becomes squash blossoms in the baskets.[4]

Later on, I asked Frances about the story, and she said that the flood came because people were not doing what they were supposed to do. "Like now, that's why things is going so bad, all the sickness now, all the crazy things [going on at the reservation]," she said.

"How could they sacrifice children to save the world?" I asked. "Because love for the children is stronger than love for thousands of people," Frances answered softly.

17 ◇ Murder My Dreams . . .

Frances: I've got dreams, but I don't have any power.
Deborah: It's secret power.
Frances: If it is, it's sure not coming out!
   (1987)

One day Frances sat down at the table, looked at me, and laughed. "I think if I could sit down and tell you everything that happens to me, you would have a long, long story." "Tell me just one thing," I said. "It's kind of silly, ya know, I think I believe it, though. Well, I don't want to tell it, I might just tell the WHOLE THING! Then I'll murder my dreams" [laughing].

Well, what I saw, when I first used to cry at night. This is the only thing, then don't ask me again, okay? I used to cry at nights and see all these things, and one night, I thought, "Well, I've lived on this Earth, I used to feel that if I can't see anything, I might as well be dead." I hate to hear that, but that's what I thought. I didn't tell anybody. I might as well be dead, ya know. And pretty soon I see these flowers, purple flowers, like the flowers on my saints—purple. I see these flowers, and I was looking at them, and I never thought about it. My eyes was looking and pretty soon it opened, it opened, a little bud, and it started opening. I was watching it open and pretty soon [slowly]—a real beautiful flower. Nothing. It was nothing sad. That's what. The next day I didn't feel sad. I just thought, "Well, if I'm gonna be blind, I'm gonna be blind! There's nothing sad about that!" The flower didn't tell me not to worry, the flower didn't tell me "You can see," or "you're gonna be blind." Nothing. Just that [Frances gestures with her hands, like a flower opening].

I knew it was from God. [Frances speaks louder, with feeling.] But to me, I believe in what happens, it comes from God through something else. I believe that. If I'm lost, pretty soon my dog will come around and lead me home. That was sent from God. Like the old joke, the old joke says this man was drowning and the Coast Guard was trying to help him. A man in a canoe was trying to help him, and the man said, "No, no, God will help me." Then the Coast Guard came and he said, "No, no, God will help me." And pretty soon the helicopter tried and said, "Hold onto me," and he said, "No, no," and pretty soon he drowned. He went to God and he said, "What do you mean? How come you didn't help me? You said you'd help me anytime I needed help. How come you didn't help?" And God said, "What do you expect? I sent three things to help you." [Frances laughs.] But this one's been way before I ever knew about this joke.

Things I believe really happens, I don't imagine it, it really happens. Like things in this world, like when you dream about people getting together in your dream, people that you don't even see anymore, people that you remember from a long time ago. If you see women with black clothes and black shawls covering their faces, that means death.[1] And at the time I didn't believe it, but it happens. Just the other day. . . . I knew a man. A long, long time ago I was a young girl, not really young but I was younger then, and there was this man who came over to my cousin's place. I saw him with his wife, years later his wife died, and I've never seen that man. Since then, maybe three weeks ago, I dreamed about these people. I don't know what they were doing, but I dreamed my father was there and the man was there. So just last Thursday I found out that the man died. So I don't know why, I wish I could see him again, I wish I could. I think he's about the last oldest man at Ko:m Wawhai, now gone. So last night I went to the wake and I saw him, and so I remember that way I saw him in my dream. So that's what I believe — it's true, ya know. I used to dream about dead people that's been gone a long, long time, I dream about. The next day I won't feel good. [Thoughtfully] I don't know if it's really this thing, I just didn't feel good.

And if you see green flies at your door anywhere, it also means death. Well, anyway, I'm superstitious, not like walking under the ladder or seeing a black cat, that's not our ways. But if you see green flies, that also means death. A long, long time ago when I used to dream about meat, sometimes I find a lot of meat on my table and the blood would be running down. So one time I told a Mexican lady and she said that's not good, that it means that one of your family will have an accident and then die, he'll be dead. And I thought, "Oh, that's not true." And I kept dreaming about it, dreaming about it. And finally my husband died, he was instantly killed. And from then on, I believe it. I'm superstitious about a lot of things.

I asked an old man one time why it is that old people know so many things that's gonna happen. He said, "Because that's the way it is! When you lay down, you will be meeting inside your head, just like when you go to a meeting and you learn about things. Heartbeats, too, you learn when you listen to your heart." That's what he said! And I thought, "How strange!" [Frances laughs.] He was a good speaker. He's been gone three years. Venito Garcia.

Our people, most of our people, especially old people, are gifted. And they know what's going to happen, or they know what happened in faraway places. Like this man was in town, and then he went back late at night. He was driving so fast that he turned over his car and killed himself. And this man way, way on the other side of Santa Rosa dreamed about this man, that this man was singing. He was just telling how he feels and how the people feels. So the song goes. . . .

[*in a high-pitched voice*]

Wa-wai-wa cu:cim nonowaŋ ṣoṣona
mui wapainomĭ wa si s-kaidame kukunu kia memelhime-he
ṣoig 'al ñ-i:bhai taka hekĭ hu pi 'al 'e-mamacime
ṣoig 'al ñ-a:nuhu muipa ñ-e:lino wa pi ñ-mamacime ka ñ-i:muina
    ñañe ñ-i:toime
[At base of Many Rocks Standing Mountain
Much metal loudly wrecked, you came here
My poor heart already feels that I am dead
Poor me, I am much unconscious, my spirit is gone]

This is what the man dreamed about this man that already killed himself, and then a few days later he heard that he was gone. This is the way the Indians do. I guess they have a little bit, a little bit of a gifted thing. Because one time — it was in June, I went to work, I used to work for Mr. and Mrs. Bahti, and they live out by Smuggler's Inn. So I usually got off on Speedway and walked south of Speedway to get to their house. So one morning I was walking, I used to go to work early because they go to open the store by nine, so I was supposed to get there by eight. So I got off the bus and I was going, the pavement road, I was following the pavement road and then

I saw this squirrel was run over or hit by a car and was right there and the blood was coming out of his mouth. And I thought, "Well, I'll push it over on the side so the cars won't run over it," so I did. It was in June . . . , July August September October. So in October my cousin shot himself, he was going hunting and climbed up Baboquivari Mountain, and, ah, dropped the gun and it shot off right on his thigh, and he bled to death. I didn't know, we heard it later on, and then we went to his funeral and everything. A few weeks later I dreamed about him. He was coming toward me and he was saying, "It really happened so fast. I just didn't know what hit me. It was just a little quail that got me and carried me over to the east," he said. The song goes . . .

> 'Al wa si kokomagĭ 'al kakaicu ko ñ-wañmehime
> sialig ko namekime ñ-i:muitake wa to beicukime
> [In the morning you meet me to lead me, my spirit you take away
> Little dark quail you lead me on]

This is what he said, why it happened in June, why it took so long before it happened. But it was the same squirrel that I pushed over on the side.

And another man, Lorenzo, you know him. Like I told you, my sister died from drinking too much. So he didn't know that my sister was dead. But he was asleep at somebody's house by the window, and he thought he woke up and he heard this lady singing right by the window, and this is how the song goes:

> Cu:ka ṣon-na ñeñei-wene-ta mana ñ-i:muita siwoname tonolhime
> ṣoiga 'ala ñ-i:bhei taka he:ku pi 'al 'e-mamacime
> do:k 'al wiñu hiosin kumuita ka-g 'e:na ñamui melopime-he
> ṣoine 'ala ñ-i:muipa siwonamo tonolhime hime
> [The songs of Tucson make my heart shine brightly
> My poor heart feels that it is already dead
> It is the flowery vapor of alcohol that I run to
> My poor heart it brightly shines]

This other man, a young man, was, ah, hunting on horseback and there's a mountain called Owls Nest, and he's around there, and he finally must have stepped on a rattlesnake. So the rattlesnake bit him on the leg. He thought, "I better go home before my leg gets swollen and stiff." So he went home, and he got home and that night he died. This man was dreaming about him. The man who died was that one that was singing, the man was listening to what he was singing. In our ways we believe that when we die, we backtrack to the places we've been, we have to go through that before we can leave, really go off to the other world. That's what we believe. So this is the song about the man who was telling that he was following his steps — that he was following where he had been, and the song goes like

> Cu:kuñe ko:oṣe nonowha gam hunikoiwa ke:hekaime
> cu:kuñe ko:oṣe nonowha gam hunikoiwa ke:hekaime
> kuñi s-hega wepeco m-al hime kam ho ñeida
> 'ine hasi cuhuge gamo yoina gamo cuhukugime
> he:kĭ hu da himikuñe kune kamo koinetamo ceñitohime
> [Owl Nest Mountain to the west it stands
> Owl Nest Mountain to the west it stands
> Below that mountain I walk to and see
> What is it that around the mountain it grows dark
> It is my former place that I think of]

When I slept outside, I could hear Frances breathing in her room. I often wondered what she was dreaming. She often tells me about her dreams in the morning, and we talk about what they might mean. Like Lorenzo, Frances gets premonitions. Sometimes her dreams contain a message for someone else, like the time Frances dreamed my father came to look for me. She didn't know yet that he had just died.

One morning I asked, "How do you know if the dream is a prophecy or not?" Frances said simply:

When you are asleep, I'itoi or whoever took a hair and tied it. You sleep and you sleep into this. You dream about something . . . it's like water, you put a dime in the water and it's light, it's not thick, and then you go to the second knot, that's when you dream about all these things. Real, real, like the green things, or you are running, or you feel good. This is good. And the third knot, that's when you have the nightmares, and the fourth, you're dead. Lorenzo's dreams were second knot.

18 ◇ A Lot of Things
We Don't Know About

A lot of things we don't know about
.

A lot of things don't work the way it's
SUPPOSED to work
because we don't KNOW about it,
we're not accustomed
to these things.
  (1981)

There are a lot of things we Indians don't know about. We were just desert people, we didn't know anything about money. We worked together, built houses together, planted together, talked together. If there was a problem, we'd sit down and talk about it and straighten the problems out. When the Spaniards came and taught us about the days of the month and the days of the week, and the dollar sign—time, that's when everything changed. If we needed help, somebody would come and help, we didn't think anything of it. Now we learn the dollar sign, we—that's what we expect, we expect to be paid, how much time I work, how much money. That's when they really changed. Everything else changed, the relationship and the acting. Everybody is so fast to get there or make money or . . . [her tone is slumbering, sad] or get ahead. That's all they think of, is getting ahead. That changed, and, uh, sometimes we plan things, too, and when the plans don't work, we feel bad, we get mad. We do something, and pretty soon it gets bigger and bigger, and that's why a lot of things are, ah, I mean a lot of people are sick, a lot of people go crazy—well, not crazy but nervous. Because of that.

When the day came that the land planning was paid the Papagos [in the 1950s], when the day came, a lot of people thought they knew about money, but they didn't. Because we didn't, we didn't have any money. We didn't know anything about it. So they kinda went crazy over the money [coughing]. When I was growing up, there were men, they can go out and work and support their family, and ya know, my grandfather, he plants summer and winter—that's what we eat—and he hunts—that's our meat. Then, well, it went on and on and on until—I don't remember what year. It was an open range, too. They didn't have any fences, ya know, you can go anyplace and you can do what you want anyplace just as long as it's on the reservation. The superintendent came and that changed a little bit. And later came the district, and changed more. That's why we have district S-cuk Du'ag—San Pedro, Ban Da:k, Ko:m Wawhai, Si:l Naggia, Kwin's Well. There are other districts, eleven districts in the reservation, in S-cuk Du'ag, seven villages. In a village we tell them what we want and how to go about it. Mildred [Frances's daughter] is the representative from our village. So that changed a lot. When Johnson became president, that's when the Indians started getting social security, and then later, welfare. And later came disabled and old age pension. The people really changed. They don't have to go out and work and support the family. They depend on that, they depend on the monthly check. They say we are just like a bird with an open mouth, waiting for the government to put, ya know, and that's when they started—like now, the people drink. They have more drinking. It also becomes more alcohol, all these things change.

We had a lady, I've known her since she was a baby. I've known her from the day that she was born, and when her mother died, when she was very young, the grandmother took care of her and at that time the grandparents had a lot of money. And so the girl can get anything she wants without even asking for it, and it went on. And, finally, the grandfather died, and then years—but not very long, maybe two or three years later, the grandmother died. She was left with an uncle and his wife. [There is a long, thoughtful pause.] I don't even remember when she started drinking. And she drinks a lot, and finally she met up with this fellow, he was young, too. And then they start living together. And somehow this man gets killed, run over, and she was alone. And she would go with whoever felt like going with her, and, ahm, and then she met up with this fellow, I guess, and then she started living with him. And they were really living like a husband and wife for a long time. Oh, yeah, they drank together, they drink together, but I feel that it was better that they are together, even though they drink. [Frances speaks sadly, slowly.] And then he died, too, last year. It was the same thing, and then she was alone again. The aunts and the uncle, aunts from both sides, were alive, living in that place, and she stayed for about a week. Then she went to town and never came back! And she'd roam around there! [Frances speaks very softly.] Finally she got sick, and went to the hospital on Friday morning, St. Mary's. And they found that she was very sick so they had to put her in intensive care. That morning she died.

It is just very sad because none of . . . , I mean most of our people are dying like this. And I should think they'd learn, the people would learn from this, ya know. But I guess it's very hard. I'm not saying that if I was drinking, that I'd do differently, I suppose I'd do the same thing! But I should think that by now my people should learn how dangerous it is to drink, especially the cheap wine, the cheap kind of liquor that they drink. And I think it's very sad when a person dies like this. That's the way I think. But I'm not saying it's easy to just quit drinking—I don't think so. The way I hear things is that drinking is a sickness. Maybe it is! You see, we didn't know very much about drinking in the past, I don't know who introduced it! Well! It's not that my people didn't drink! They drank once in a while when they go to Mexico and buy the tequila, but they don't just drink it right there, they keep it for a certain occasion. And another time they drink is in the wine ceremony in the first part of September. That's about the only time they would get drunk! But not all the time like now! They're drunk every day!

I was invited to an alcoholic meeting, ya know they have meetings, and they asked me to say something. I didn't know what to say! You see, I don't drink and I don't really know what the drinking is all about, but I figured because *my* husband drank, but my husband didn't die from cirrhosis of the liver, he died [softly] in an accident. These people, they drink so much, and um, they don't know when to stop, they just drink and drink and drink until they get so passed out and they don't know, don't know what they are doing. We don't know how to . . . We try, everybody else has tried—church tried, a lot of other organizations tried, but they still go ahead! I know a man who went to the Baptist church. Ya know what happened? He didn't drink for six months, and now [softly] he's drinking again. And another man didn't drink for twenty years, and something happened, he started drinking every day again. And, ahm, so it's very sad that my people are like that, but there isn't anything I can do about it.

A lot of things we don't know about. A lot of things don't work the way it's supposed to work because we don't know about it, we're not accustomed to these things. And the only thing that I can think of is we're trying to do what the white people does. But we'll never make it because we're not accustomed to it. We're not—it's not in us, just like alcohol, we'll never be able to make it because it's not in us. Another thing, we don't know anything about money. Because we don't know how to spend it, we don't know how to save it. I remember some Indians started to run a grocery store and never made it. And some people tried gas stations, they never made it because they don't know! Some people started a restaurant, they never made it. So I don't support—maybe, maybe in 1990 maybe some young person will be able to do it because they'll have more schooling and more education. But us, let's hope. That's my way of thinking.

Now, this Hopi man spoke at a meeting, he spoke about the reservation. When he was ten years old, he could run in an open range for miles and miles, then later on, they sent him to school and it seems like he was just in a closed-in fence or house, and a person right there says, "Stand up, sit down, go that way, go this way, go to bed, get up." It's like that. And it ruined his thinking. He doesn't think anymore like an Indian. And he gave up and he thought, "Well, if I can't have what I had before, I might as well not think." Because thinking of a white person gets mixed up with an Indian. Well, that's the way I feel sometimes. And then later on, right now I think I'll just go along, that's what I say. When they build houses, you think that's your house. But the insurance is right there. Or say, if you can sell the house, but you can't sell the land. How are we going to sell the house if we can't sell the land? How are you going to sell the house? There's a question.[1] And there's lots of questions. Colorado River is supposed to come to the reservation; it was going to be used on the reservation but now I don't think we can get it because it's too far.[2]

And, ah, there's this old saying that the Colorado River is there for a reason. So many things, I don't know which one is . . . What reason? Sometimes the Colorado River will be just muddy and sometimes it'll be just clear. And that's also for a reason. It never said anything in our legends that someday we're going to get the water for planting, or like irrigation water. It never said anything. But now we're going—a lot of people are going against it. I'm against it. They'll get it, but they won't have it for long, it's going to dry up.

Saturday we are going to have another meeting, what they call district meeting. I feel kind of nervous about it because every time we have a meeting, sometimes they get into an argument and they say things that they shouldn't. And by just listening to what they say, you always think, "They shouldn't be talking like this, at each other's throats. This is supposed to be for our own good!" For our people, they are our representatives, our chairmen, our officers. They are supposed to get the people together, to work together. And you know that's impossible, because we let that go [slowly] a loong looong time ago. We don't work together, we never agree on something. Somebody says that one thing and the other says the opposite.

These are some of the things that come up at meetings. Last Saturday we had a meeting and a man came over from Phoenix, an attorney. Some people bought land near the reservation border and they want to pave Coleman Road. Some of the men asked them, "Why?" They said that this should be avoided. But nobody did anything about it. And, um, one man said that there was a cow shot. He got there just a few minutes before it happened. I asked him if it happened right there, then why didn't he call the police? So the police can do their job. And another one said that they put a calf, an eight-months' calf, in the truck. Why can't they call the police? Why do they let the people get away with it? They are lost. We are lost on the reservation. There are police, there are lawyers, there are judges. The people are there, and the police are there. There are two hundred policemen that are supposed to take care of the reservation.

So I think that's why, I think we get discouraged because we don't understand. We don't know! Like one time we had some land somewhere on the other side of town and we were trying to get it back. There is the old saying that when the white people first came, they asked the Indians if they could live here, if they could live here for a while. Because they think that the Indians are so nice, they are so kind, and they do things with a smile. I think they do things with a smile because they don't understand—that's the way my people are. First time they smile, they laugh. They thought the white people were smart, so they laughed. Then they started living here and building things, they made a lot of things knowing that we cannot pay them, we cannot chase them out. We don't have the money to pay what they ask for what they build.

I think a lot of things we do about our land is because we don't understand. I remember one time there were two men arguing about land, some Indian land, saying, "This is my dirt, this is your dirt." They start the way we do it, we don't understand. And another thing, how are we going to sell the house if we can't sell the land?

When the white man came, we didn't have a lot of things they have, like all these different kinds of disease. We didn't know about it and so we didn't get sick. We didn't know anything about cancer, diabetes, TB, leukemia, all these things we know now that exist. Sometimes I wonder if it's because we know about these sicknesses that we are sick.

When we go to the medicine man and they try to cure the sickness, sometimes the medicine man will look over us and say, "Well, you have to go to the doctor, this is white man's sickness. If it's our sickness, I could cure it, but this belongs to the white man." So we go to the doctor and they look us over and say, "You are just too fat," or "You are just too old," or "Next time you come back, we'll have to test your blood, we'll have to X-ray you." All these things we have to go through at the doctor's. And sometimes we don't even find out what's wrong with us! Maybe the doctors know, but they don't want to tell us. Maybe we are dying. They ought to tell us, but they don't, because they are afraid we'll die of fear. So all of these things now exist. It seems to me that we are sick all of the time! Thinking of a white person gets mixed up with being Indian.

When I was growing up, I never really saw sick people, I never saw sickness going around. Only maybe once or twice a year whooping cough, measles, or chicken pox would come around. There would also be pinkeye, we had a season for that, and the little kids would get it. We lived in an open place and got a lot of fresh air, and we cooked over the open fire. We used the pottery to drink from — everybody drank from it — or we would be traveling and we'd drink from the water hole. Nowadays the little babies' water has to be boiled. We had little babies, but the water didn't have to be boiled! And nowadays people say, "Don't take your child over there, so-and-so has chicken pox." That's when they really get it bad. At that time, when I was growing up, there was nothing. We didn't have anything like that. So — the things are changing right before my eyes.

I'm going to say something not exactly what we planned. Now I'll say the world is going too fast, it's changing too much, and some parts is good and some parts isn't. I am saying this because I am old-fashioned and I'm saying this because I am an Indian. And an Indian is old-fashioned, that makes me more of an Indian than anything else.

One time I said to my grandson, he was a teenager, I said, "You should have this, you should do this," and he said, "Oh, that's old-fashioned!" "What's the new fashion?" I told him. He didn't say anything, he didn't expect me to be mad about that. And I told him, "The new fashion is to get drunk, to make a fool of yourself, and the next thing is you smoke, and the next thing you steal. Is that new fashion? I'll tell you the new fashion is no good." I was so mad at him! And from then on, he never said anything. He just listens, whether he likes it or not.

19 ◇ I'm Not Really So Good!

I don't want anybody to say about THAT

I'm just a person,
Just a person

I'm not that special,
I don't feel special.
I just feel
it's ME!
I'm ME!
Nobody else.
   (1987)

But I'm not all that good. If somebody reads this, they'll think, "Well, she's so good," but I'm *not*. I have done things that I'm not proud of, but we're not going to talk about it until way at the end, after they say, "She's so good." Then they'll read this and say, "Oh! This is no good!" [Frances laughs.] Really it's not *so* bad; most women go through that. I'm not a bad person, I'm just saying that I'm not all good. I have faults, too! So we'll talk about it.

"Like the one about the policeman?" I asked.

Oh yeah! [Frances laughs.] I went to jail just because I was fighting with a policeman—broke his nose. [Laughing] That's what the judge said, I broke his nose! I don't know whether I believe him or not. The judge, he said I broke his nose. "And why did you do that?" I said it was because I thought he was taking my husband. One person was hitting him with a stick, and the other was dragging him. It made me mad, I told him to stand him up and lead him.
   Then he asked me if it was my husband, and I said, "No, it was my cousin." "Where was your husband?" "Oh, he was somewhere." "Was he drinking?" I said, yes, because I couldn't say no. He was drinking. And then he asked me again if he was drinking, and that made me mad! And I said, "Doesn't everybody drink?" "Where does he get his liquor?" he said. At that time

they couldn't get it, they had to get it from the bootlegger. "Where does he get his liquor?" "Where Sam Manuel gets his, I guess that's where he gets it." It made me mad.

That's his son. . . . There was this man. He was gonna sell some calves to bail himself out, and he said, "You know how the cow feels when you sell the calf, you know how the cow feels?" So, me, with my big mouth, because I was already mad, I said, [in a high, loud voice] "How did these cows get into this?" So he pounds, to be quiet. I was so mad. I just looked at him. I wish I could grab him and break his nose again. [We laugh!]

And another thing. When I was working, after I lost my husband, and I was working, they were having a big day in Si:l Naggia and I wanted to go. So I knew people who live right there, so I thought I'd ask them to take me. At that time the lady brought her father—he was an old man. So I quit working and I got ready and we went. Somehow we were late getting in, and the man was drunk and was singing, we were sitting in the back of the truck. And I was singing with him, you know, just singing. And when we got to the place, his wife got mad because I was singing with him. And it went on. *Boy!* That lady didn't like me. And I feel bad about it because she didn't like me. Her daughter lives there, so she had to be there when things go on, like a fiesta. So I was there helping, I was there and she thought I was something, like a *fire* going.

So we sat down to eat, and she sat down right there and I sat down right here. So I said, "Pass the salt," and she slammed it down. Something clicked in my head, and I thought, "This is it. I'm gonna do something. It may be the wrong thing to do, but I'm gonna do something." Wherever she was, I was right there with her—we were working side by side. She didn't talk for two days, she didn't talk for two days. She was cleaning chile, I was right there. That's what I want. And then the third day she got sick and I was right there. I didn't do anything wrong! That was nothing, I was just singing with him. And I thought, "Now this is wrong," and I thought, "Even if I'm desperate I won't take a chance on an old man!" He was an old man! That was a good lesson for me. I was ready to face anything.

I think I already told you that after Jose died, I was gonna marry somebody. He wanted to move in, and I said I'm too old-fashioned, so I said we'll have to wait until the kids get a little bigger, because Christy and Linda were too young to understand. He used to come and visit me, but then one time he didn't come for two weeks, and I heard he was married to somebody else. My pride got hurt. I didn't care, but my pride got hurt that he couldn't wait. He was a younger man and I don't think he really wanted to marry me, he just wanted a meal ticket, that's all. And sex. I said I'm too old-fashioned. I was gonna marry him, though, we did plan to get married in March. Before that, he married [Frances inhales deeply] someone else. And for a little while they separated, then he was living with somebody else and pretty soon they separated, and he was living with somebody else. She died. And then one time we were sleeping, this lady was living with Lorenzo—she was living with him, too. So one day we were at a dance, and we were sitting there and Lorenzo was standing in back of me, and she was dancing. As soon as she saw Lorenzo standing there—boy! She called me all kinds of names! I was so embarrassed at what she called me, and finally, [laughing] I just went and got her on the hip and then I hit her, and she got loose and went around so I followed her, and I got her. I was really thinking I was gonna beat her hard, and I knocked two of her teeth out. Linda came running. "Don't you call my mother like that!" She started hitting her and the police got her, and so I told him it's not her fault, it's me, I did it. Well, finally, they let her go and they said the best thing was to take her home. [Laughing] So we had to go to court! After court the judge said, "Well, I'm not going to fine you anything. I'm just gonna say that I suppose I'd do that if my mother was being called dirty things!" Oh! You never heard a lady being so dirty! And in front of Lorenzo!

That man from Ban Da:k, they lived together and then she died. Then one day he killed himself, and I thought, I'm so glad it's not *meant* for me to marry him. I don't think I could ever live like this lady, how they drink together and do things together.

When Lorenzo used to drink, he used to get mad. He used to say, "The people are scared of you." I said, "I'm sure glad they're scared of me." That's the way I am, outspoken.

20 ◇ Two Hands: Making It Lighter

I have TWO HANDS.
I can still do things for myself
.
One day
I won't have them
.
That's when my children comes in
.
I'm not asking anything from you girls
but someday I'll say you do this for ME
you do this for me
.
when the day comes I will . . .
I hope the day will never come
.
I have nothing but my two hands
.
All these things
like the ANIMALS we have,
they come from my two hands
.
The only thing,
I have two hands
.
and I buy the horse
I buy the COW
.
Amelia's got cows because of that two hands.
   (1987)

Debbie, it's now Thursday afternoon, May third, and I'm talking about my horses. My late husband had horses, and when he died, we sold all his horses. [Sadly, slowly] We didn't have any horses. When I was supposed to move back to the reservation, I thought, "What can I do, there'll be no home because there will be no horses!" So I decided to buy a horse. So I made a basket of a man in a maze, and I talked to my cousin, he was willing to sell me a MARE, so I bought the mare, I bought it. She was good enough to stay around here, she didn't try to go back to Santa Rosa. From then on, the first colt was a mare, too, Morning Star, because she was born when the morning star was just up. So I gave it to my grandson. The second one, my other grandson; the third one, my other grandson; and, uh, the fourth one — they all had their horses. "So this is mine," I thought, the horses that came later were mine. How I felt about these horses was because that's what I grew up with. I talk to them, but they don't talk back to me, but that is fine. I feel that if there is no horse, there is no home.

Well, later on, I decided, "Why do I have horses? I don't have any cow! What will the horse be good for, just looks? Just roaming around?" And so I decided to buy a calf, a heifer. And I worked — here goes my work again, and I made another maze. And another one. So I sold the two baskets and I got the money and I bought a heifer. Lorenzo had a horse, a mare, the little horse came, and he gave it to Christy, so Christy had a horse. And later on, when the roundup came, somehow the little horse got hurt. She wasn't walking right and Lorenzo sold it. He came back and asked me, "Should we give the money to Christy or should we just buy another horse?" So I said, "Well let's just buy her a calf, even if it's just a little calf, but she'll grow up." So we did. We put the money — I put a little money in it, too, so we bought another calf from another man. So that's how it started. Amelia's going ahead of me, which I am kind of jealous. She's got . . . That's the way things go. And I can proudly say that this is mine. There was no rich uncle, there was nobody who helped me buy my animals. So right now they are running around on the open range, and there's two horses in the corral all the time. Then they get bored, so we turn them loose and put some more in. So that's the way . . . They've been eating out my home, but it won't be a home if I didn't have horses around. And so, that's the way I'm living here. Somebody may think I'm crazy just having horses for looks. Some are tamed, and when people come around, they ride horses, which is very good because they need the exercise.

The hard things just go with something good. That's why I accepted, a long time ago, that I want my family to be just so and so and so, and I'll be happy. What little time I have, I want that, and I'll be happy. But no. You'll never, you can't have that. There's always something to fight about. That'll give me a bad feeling, always. And, ahm, I used to think, I used to feel that, I wish that . . . , I wish this one would . . . , Florence would stop by, I wish this one would stop by, and sometimes I hear Florence is over at Sells, Florence is over at Big Fields, and I used to think, "Why? Can't she swing around and come see me?" And I think, "Well, I can't say 'Come see me,' what would I say? I have to wait until they feel like coming and not ask them to."[1]

Sometimes I feel that nobody cares, and I'm not doing anything any good for my children, so they don't care, ya know. And then pretty soon I think, "Well, I've heard *that* before." The birds get big and fly away. They're gone, and have their own families. I was telling you, I'm sure they care! They care! But they don't have time, or they are young and they don't have the feeling that you have when you get older. So I feel that way. Things that happen to me hurt me, and then I think about it and think about it, sometimes I push it away and stop thinking about it. And I never once thought—like Emma says they don't love me, after you raise your kids, they don't love you. I'm sure they do! That's what make things easier. But I said once, to my ladies one time, "Next time, next time I'm gonna come back to life, I'm gonna have children and let them marry orphans, not marry those with families. So I can have them to myself."

I have eleven grandchildren and four great-grandchildren, and there's two on the way. I'm loaded with all kinds of grandchildren, that's what I told you. It is important to me that maybe someday my great-grandchildren will know what kind of a grandmother they have. How poor the grandmother was raised. Ya know, I'm kind of proud of that, ya know, being poor, being the way I was. I'm proud of it! I don't know why! [Laughing] Somebody else would be ashamed of it. Sometimes my dress would be torn, so it'll tear again, it'll just get smaller and smaller. Okay, let's stop here.

Some days ago I was looking for something in my box where I keep my old recipes. Not that I cook with recipes, but I have a lot of them. And I found something that I want you to hear. I think it's very good. I had a friend a long, long time ago, it's just one of those things that this nurse, she was a war nurse and she was an old nurse, and she liked me. We talked together, she told me things and I told her things. Well she told me this, and I told her to write it for me, and so she did. And it's—I think it's very good, I'm gonna read it to you:

Even though I clutch my blanket when the alarm rings off each morning, thank you, Lord, that I can hear—there are many that are deaf. Even though I keep my eyes tightly closed against the morning light as long as possible, thank you, Lord, that I can see—there are many that are blind. I had a bad morning, the toast burned, the socks were lost, there was too much noise and too much running, but I thank the Lord that I have family, there are many who are lonely. I come to breakfast and see what little food there is on the table, but then I thank the Lord because there are many who are hungry.

I don't know why she liked me, she was a nurse at the sanatorium where I had TB. I'd go to her office and I'd sit there, she's the one who told me a lot of things. A lot of things that I remember, and, and she gave me a little card, that's where it says that. It is so beautiful. So real, and so *true*. She'd read me things. She'd read it just like you're reading a poem, you know.

Yesterday my heart was so heavy, and I know why. But, then . . . This is a special prayer that I always say whenever things upset me. It always comes to me whether I'm sitting or walking or laying down. Whatever I'm doing, it comes to me like, ah:

> Lord
> Above,
> you look down on us,
> on me,
> and give me strength
>   give me courage
>   give me understanding,
> that I'll understand my people.

[Frances speaks slowly, with feeling.] I'll accept what they give me even though sometimes it hurts. My heart was heavy because I have a good friend and one of my loved ones said something that really upset me, and I hope that God looks down on us and eases the things that hurts, eases the things that's heavy—that's all I ask for my friend. I've been going through this ever since I was sixteen years old and I wanted to be a [church] singer, but one look at me and I wasn't the right person. So that's when I really remember my prayer. This is what I'm saying because someday somebody will be on the same road. But if it comes out, he'll read about me and he will understand that there are people who go through also, there are people that are facing the same problem, there are people that feel the same kind of heaviness. So, that's what we ask the good Lord to give us, strength to go on, to face up to what's pointing at us, to face people that are maybe not against us, but something that's in life that happens to everyone. Like you get up in the morning and you are ahead of yourself. Like you say you're gonna feed your family and I'm gonna do this, I'm gonna do that, gonna do that. It won't work that way. If you just get up and feel good, and [slowly, firmly] do what you can do—don't load yourself! That's what I do. I don't put a big load on me, because if I can't complete what I planned, I don't feel good about it. I'm hoping for something, but I don't hope for a certain thing. Because when I'm hoping for something and it doesn't happen, I'm disappointed. So I'm just hoping for something, I don't know what I'm hoping, but I'm hoping for something. Like when I pray to God, God didn't give me what I pray for but he gave me something else. Like in the evening you don't pray for a certain thing, you just pray for the family, that people that needs help, the people that are alone, the people that are hungry, the people that don't have any homes. So it's just like you get the stuff off your shoulders and you're lighter, and you go to sleep. [Frances chuckles.] That's the way I feel and imagine things.

We forget and we make mistakes, but that's life! When I first learned this . . . it's really hard. Like me, I'm here. What I do is what I like to do, and if I don't feel like doing this, I don't do it. And I don't go places and say, "I did this, I did that, this person says this, this person says that." I don't like to make up stories. What makes me feel that being the kind of person, I think that's why life is not hard for me. I can go back and talk about how many disappointments, how many letdowns, how many falls. But I'm not thinking that's hard life, I don't regret. I think I live my life the way it was given to me. I never say life isn't worth it. It's a big, wide world, and nobody can do anything about it. So I might as well accept it. When I was younger, I used to plan, but it doesn't work that way, I'd get disappointed. Now I just feel that if it happens, it happens. Like I was telling you, if those men come and build my corral, it will be. But I'm not thinking, "It's gonna happen, it's gonna happen." I'll be disappointed, but I'm not gonna die. What is there to change? Life is life! No matter what kind of life! Either way you take it, whether you . . .

"want to cry about it or laugh about it," I added.

Yeah. I used to never cry, but one time I said [laughing], "I think the only time I ever cry is when somebody dies!" And somebody said, "No, you're not! You'll be sometimes smiling when a dead person's there!" I don't remember that! But one time I was coming home from work and somebody was teasing me about something and I went around and I was smiling, and I said, "So-and-so died." And the kids looked at me and said, "Then why are you still smiling?" Here I was smiling at that person and . . . That's the way my life is. It's no more than . . . Well, what can you gain about crying? You can't change if you try to be serious. My grandmother says you can be proud inside and not outside. I think that's what I am. Okay, that's all.

Is the tape on? I was about sixty or seventy and my eyes were bad, and I had gone to the doctor, the government doctor, back and forth for about a year, until they told me that in two more years I was going to be blind. I came home and I cried, I thought, "What can I do? What can I do? What is there for me when I can't *see*?" And it went on and on. One day I thought, "I've been in this world for seventy years, I've seen a lot [slowly] and things aren't going to be any better and they aren't going to be any worse, even if I don't see." So I accepted it, and I started practicing being blind. I put a towel or a diaper around my face and I walked around. First I stood at the end of the room and looked at things, studied the things. I looked at my dishes and my pots and pans, and then go outside and see, and then I started tying my eyes and walked around. Sometimes I'd trip on something, forget it's there. Every time I was alone I did that. And it seems like when I started feeling sorry for myself, it went away. I guess I was thinking, "Well if I'm gonna be blind, I'm gonna be blind!" I just went on for months, I think.

One day I went to California to demonstrate baskets, even though I couldn't see. I don't know, the doctor told me I can see better when I'm making baskets because I know so much of it. So I went to California and

I taught them, and then my boss took me to see two doctors. They talked about it, they said, "You may not see good, but in another ten years you won't be blind." So my hopes were higher than ever. It turns out I had glaucoma.

So I'm very grateful that I'm seeing better now. I can't see very good without my glasses. But I guess that's the way you have to do! You accept, and that's easier.

[Frances laughs a hearty laugh.] I hope it changes, because every time I think about the newspaper, the movies, the trees, I want to see the bright light when I'm dying. [Laughing] So a lot of things have changed in seven years.

You try not to think of the worst, but it's there, it comes. Like I was telling how I had the needle in my hand and it hurt—when I was in the hospital. But I read somewhere that if you relax, it won't hurt as bad. It worked! And I thought about how Jesus was crucified, I bet that hurt worse! Jesus was nailed to the cross! So then I could sleep. Later they said it wasn't put in right, that's why it hurt so bad. So I'm teaching myself a lot of things. As you get older, you don't have so many things . . . you don't have boyfriends to think about, you don't have good clothes to think about. But you think about something that is important, to me it's important. You know I have a home, I think about my home, and I have a few things that I own, and I think about that. But I never think about something that happens fast, like a sudden death of my children, I try not to think about it, but sometimes it comes! Sometimes I get scared, a lot of things scare you. A lot of things mess up your mind, you think of something bad, or you're mad. There's nobody there to . . . know what I'm thinking, to know I'm mad, to know that I'm scared, or to know that I'm sad. No matter what you have, it still comes to you, [slowly] you feel sad, you feel alone, you want things . . . but it goes away, it doesn't stay with you a long time. Or you want to do more, you can't do more if you try to get going, trying so hard to do more or have more or earn more, or whatever it is. It doesn't happen, so you have to accept. That's life. That's all right!

Even things out there, it's dry and hot, and dusty, but still it's beautiful to me! Because I understand that if I was a tree, I'd be looking like that, because there's no rain! If I was a bird, I'd be like the birds now, begging for food or begging for water. I'd be doing the same thing if I was a bird!

I think about it, and I thank the Lord that he has given me this. I'm not really looking for more, this is enough for me. If I have to have more, God will arrange things for me. Like sometimes I don't have any money, so money will come somehow, I'll get money somehow. So I don't go out and ask for money. Like right now I don't have any soap, so I have to get soap [laughing]. So things happen, even little things! I have a lot of knick-knacks, sometimes I talk to them. And what's in my house, everything has names, that's always my hobby, too. My horses have names, everything's got names.

"I think I liked Nightmary the best," I said.

"Yeah, and Antone, Chakobatsi, Roxanne, Joslyn, Faith, and Hope, Chulia, Misty, Tanga—Lucinda names him Kiowa. Nightmary's dead, and Chato, too."

"And your dogs."

"My dog is Norberto. Huito. And Nadine. And now Graveyard," Frances said, laughing.

"And that one that was half-coyote that you used to have in town. She used to howl!"

"Lady, she died a long time ago. When we first met."

"And your dolls on the fireplace, they all have names, too."

"We call Mrs. Tortilla, and that's June, and Augustine with a little hat. And that's John and Amelia, the little girl. And Mary, and Roslyn with the little cap, and Ramona, the long-eared rabbit, right there. And the one that's Rolling Wind, that's sitting with all the ducks."

"And your turtle?"

"Domingo. His name's Domingo."

Afterword: Life/History

Life

All the things in nature, it all works together. Like you hear about a flower, we call it *taṣ ma:hag* [desert lupine].[1] The leaves are like this [Frances gestures with her hands to show the open leaves]. So when the sun comes up, it's like this, and it goes, goes, and goes, then by evening the leaves are closed. I believe that, because that's what I was told. And the flowers will bloom when their time comes. Just like the baby will be born when its time comes, not when the doctor says it's gonna come. I believe because I was told a long time ago. I believe because it happens right in front of my eyes!

And there's a lot of things we can tell from the moon. We have different names of the moon[2] and we can tell, like, um, what position the moon is in when a woman gets pregnant. The Indians will know what position the moon will be in when the baby is born. If it's a full moon, if it's the first quarter or the last quarter, or if it's the end of the moon, when the baby's born, they take the baby to eat the clay. Nowadays you go to the doctor and the doctor will say two weeks, or the first part of the month you'll get the baby. It doesn't work that way because they are not going by the moon. And the moon tells us when the woman gets her period. The moon is always the one to tell the date.

The moons tell us the different things we are supposed to do. Like the summer moon is called "short planting," and the next moon will be called "dry wheat moon," or "little cooler moon," because it's getting a little cooler. And the next moon is called "winter moon." Then we have "waiting moon"; I forget the February—I'll think about it. March moon is called "green and blue moon"; April moon, "yellow moon"; and May is called "hungry moon"; June is "harvesting moon." July—I already told you about July. July is called "planting moon"; August is "short planting." So I give you all the names of the different moons. Like I told you, the moons tell us the different things we are supposed to do.

All those things, that's what the moon is there for. It is to light the darkness. And now, the white people, they go to the moon. It's the old saying, the people are so smart, the white people are so smart, and we never will catch up with the white people because it isn't meant for us. That's why they're so smart. They didn't have any language, so they gave them a piece of feather, so they wrote their language. That's why they are so smart, because they can write. They can see through a lot of things. And they go to the moon and they say there is another place up there, and all those things, and maybe they are so smart that they are the ones that are going to end the world. The white people are so smart, they are getting smarter and smarter, but they are going to end the world. That's what my grandfather said. Maybe things have changed because people have been bothering the moon. They never said anything in our legends that someday the people will go to the moon. They never did say anything about it!

And things happen now, seeing the year, the summer doesn't come when it's supposed to, the spring doesn't come when it's supposed to, winter doesn't come when it's supposed to. We don't have that much rain, we have spotted rain, it rains here and it rains over there because the world and the sky and everything up there has been bothered. It's the old thing—if you bother them too much, the world's gonna end.

April 14, 1997
I visited with Frances yesterday, because I had a plan to go on a hike with her grandson Jimmy. We met for lunch, and had a few minutes alone while the tamales were warming in the oven. As she faced me at the kitchen table, Frances's uncharacteristic directness took me by surprise. She looked at me and said, "Thank you, Debbie. You have been the best friend, you have always been there for me, when I need medicine, when I need a friend. You know, when you were gone. . . . Where did you go? Oh, that's right, to Washington. One day while you were gone, I was feeling lonely and I thought of you. As I thought of you, a flower seemed to open in my heart. It opened."

It was not like Frances to speak this way, and I felt embarrassed. Frances tried to joke a little afterward, but I could feel the heaviness in the air. I felt it with Frances's grandsons as we were eating, too, felt it draining us.

The hike into the vast desert I had been visiting for twenty years was as shining and beautiful as it was comforting. We rode in Jimmy's pale blue Dodge—

a real reservation car—rusty, unlicensed, personable; and then hiked to the top of a small mountain. I needed the red earth and the desert breeze that day, for there was something very wrong, and no one was talking about it.

The desert border earth at San Pedro, like the Children's Shrine, is a place of sacrifice and redemption, of birth, tragedy, and sometimes death. At home the next day, I was still feeling shook up. "I am too old for this!" Frances exclaimed on the phone. The medicine woman knows there is something amiss in the village, the neighbors see lights and hear sounds in the night. Could this be it? "Children must be raised with discipline," Frances admonished, "discipline and love." It was not clear to me then that Frances had a premonition, a strong feeling that something was going to happen to someone she loves.

May 23, 1997
One day, out of the blue, Frances expressed her desire to travel to Ge Pi:ckim, the birthplace of her mother. Amelia Lopez died when Frances was about one and a half years old; she was sick, they said, having never recovered from childbirth. Her people spoke a different dialect than her father's people; they also spoke "Mexican [Spanish]."[3] Their histories, too, though intertwined, were different, for the O'odham to the south had been heavily missionized by the late seventeenth century, and ranchers and miners were encroaching on their land by the early nineteenth century.[4] By the time of Frances's mother's birth, most of the southern O'odham who had not relocated to the United States were becoming assimilated into the ways of the Mexicans, and were increasingly impoverished. Those on the Arizona side had been influenced by Catholicism later than those to the south, and, unlike their relatives in Mexico, the Arizona O'odham had a reservation (since 1916), and receive health, social, and educational benefits as members of the Tohono O'odham Nation today.

Frances has had regular contact with Mexico since she was a child. Crossing the border with ease, Frances and her grandparents used to meet relatives from farther south in Nogales and Magdalena. At the fiesta for St. Francis in Magdalena, people would board their horses, eat, and camp with O'odham from their home community. They would meet relatives from distant villages at their camps and favorite hangouts, too. Frances met her grandfather, Antonio Lopez, there twice, and later, Jesus Antonio, who relocated to New Fields with Frances's assistance.

We had heard Frances talk about Ge Pi:ckim before, but only recently

The Yaqui hands, photographed across from Tiburón Island on the Gulf of
California near Hermosillo.

*learned that her mother was only part-Seri. At the time we assumed Ge Pi:ckim
would be a Seri village. I telephoned a colleague who had worked with the Seris
for many years, but she had never heard of Ge Pi:ckim and could not locate it
on her maps. In passing, I mentioned the name of Frances's grandfather, and
she recalled that she had seen an O'odham named Antonio Lopez in an old
photo. In fact, the photo had been published in an article she had written for
the* Southwest Journal of Anthropology *a few years earlier.[5] Over coffee the
next day she told me the bizarre and unsettling story of the Yaqui hands.*

*She explained that for many years the Seris, like the Yaquis, were regarded
by the Mexican government as a military threat. The Yaquis fought a two
hundred-year war to save their land and, as a result of their persistence, have
never been defeated, by Spaniards or Mexicans.[6] As late as 1927, the Yaquis
had a strong standing army. At the time this photo was taken, in 1904, there
were only a few hundred Seris along the Gulf of California, just west of Hermosillo, near where Frances's mother is supposed to be from. By that time many
Yaquis had been killed or deported to the Yucatán, their property confiscated
by the military. Still, pockets of resistance remained. The Mexican infantry,
including several hundred mule-riding Tohono O'odham, were ordered by the
government to capture Yaquis hiding among the Seris on Tiburón Island.*

Because the Seris at that time didn't speak much Spanish, there occurred a grave misunderstanding. After being ordered by the Mexicans to bring back the Yaquis from their village ("so that your people, 'the relatives,' would live"), Manuela, wife of Seri chief El Pelado, put her hands together and raised them, indicating that she understood her instructions. Federico García y Alva reported, "The governor, like the rest of us, understood that the stinking savage [sic] meant that they would bring the Yaquis with their hands bound. Later on, though, you will see what she meant, which we could not possibly have guessed."[7]

The two women returned three days later, carrying a pole with eight pairs of hands dangling from it like a flag, or an offering of peace. The two Seri women, probably with the help of several Seri men, had found the Yaqui men and women on the side of a mountain preparing agave for roasting. The Yaquis were killed with stones, then their hands were cut off at the wrists, strung up on a pole, and carried back to the governor.

I looked closely at the photo. The two Seri women were in the foreground, and one of them was carrying a small baby. The older one, Juana, was holding the pole, smiling; the others were more serious, their eyes veiled. The Seri women were standing on the beach with the ocean and mountains in the background. Behind them in a receding semicircle were the infantry, the governor, and the scouts; ten men in all, posing as if to say: "Here we are with these hands." The photo conveys a feeling of futility, because the Seris had been ordered out to do this loathsome thing, to kill their friends. The "savagery" of the Seris, according to the Mexican account, was blamed for the "misunderstanding" that had occurred. The fact is that the Mexicans, like the Spaniards before them, often massacred Indians, and the two Seri women were raped repeatedly by the army upon their return.[8] The scenario presented a descent of the human condition into a relentless horror that blamed the victims, pitting friends and neighbors against each other and brutalizing native peoples, especially women.

In the morning I drove out to the reservation, where Frances was anxiously waiting. She looked at the photo for a long time in silence, and then looked at me questioningly, pointing to Antonio. I nodded. (I had also picked him out, for there is a striking family resemblance.) I explained the photo as my colleague had done for me. Frances's reaction was, "Yuch, I hope it's not him" [laughing]. But it could be, she said; he was an older man when she saw him (in 1922). The photo was too small for us to make the man out clearly.

I called my friend and arranged to photocopy the original photo. In the larger copy I could see that someone had written on the bottom, "Antonio Lopez, tracker, best in Sonora!" So I made three laser copies, as clear as the original, and took them out to show Frances.

Frances became visibly disturbed, her silence lasting for several minutes. We spent the rest of the day going back and forth about it, laughing at ourselves. Frances called her daughter Juanita in Ohio, to tell her about it, and showed the photo to her grandsons. After lunch, Frances announced jokingly, "Well, I guess we'll have to claim him!"

Frances arranged a trip to New Fields, near the Mexican border just south of Sells, so we could talk to her cousin Jesus Antonio Lopez. He might know where Ge Pi:ckim is, and if the man in the photograph was their grandfather. Before going to see Lopez, I learned that Ge Pi:ckim is the Tohono O'odham term for old Hermosillo, the Spanish presidio, Pitic. Pitic is the southernmost pre-1800 camp of the O'odham; by 1900 it had become a colonial settlement, a military garrison. It made sense that Antonio Lopez would be from there — acculturated, political, and savvy. No wonder we couldn't find Ge Pi:ckim on the old maps. As Joe Garcia put it, "Until the old people die, it'll be known as Ge Pi:ckim — but now they are gone."

Ge Pi:ckim. That's where my mother was from. I was born in December and I guess it was cold. I was born in a tent. She never got well. Mother came because they were so poor. Somebody said Ge Pi:ckim is a town now. I heard they [the O'odham] moved to Caborca, that there are only a few left there.

My mother and father met in Tucson, my father used to hang around like the young men do, but he was always on horseback. She stayed with her godmother; she did domestic work. That lady, the godmother, she doesn't drink like the women do now, but she drinks, so the people gathered there, I guess my father goes to her house. They called her "Merci," Merci. I don't know how they would say it in English. She was O'odham from Sonora, married some O'odham from here that she met in Magdalena. She lived here all her life; she was old. My grandmother knew her real well, she would interpret for her, because she didn't speak Indian too good. My mother died a long time ago, and her mother was already dead before she came to America. My grandmother used to call me "Seri" [ṣe:l]. I never knew why, but she told me later that my mother told her that her great-grandmother was Seri. I used to feel that they were bad people, until I met a man from Hermosillo and I asked him. He said, "They're like any people, some are good, some are bad. Just like we are!"

I don't know much about my mother's father. His name was Antonio Lopez. They say his gun was his food, so I thought he was a hunter. His nickname, Ge Wu:lo, "Donkey," it means hard worker. Mother was very hardworking, too—when somebody came in, right away she would get up and put away the horses. My grandmother loved her. I heard her brother was murdered when he was eating lunch, and another was killed in a car accident in Hermosillo.

When we go to Magdalena, the people usually come in on wagons. Some people come in on horseback, so they have fields and they have *ramadas*, and they even have houses for the people to stay in. I don't know how much it costs, but we used to do that. So when my mother and my father got married and they stayed with my grandparents, and my grandparents were going, my mother told my grandparents, "If you see my father, tell them I am over here and I am married, and I have a little girl." And, ah, she told them which side of the church the field was where they always stayed, whether they came in on a wagon or they came in on horseback. I guess they were there. So my grandmother and grandfather went over there. My grandfather was already drunk, and he was asking straight out, "We are looking for Ge Wu:lo," he said, "my daughter-in-law's father." He was so *proud*. So he was saying that, and somebody said, "What does she [my mother] want over here?" I guess he must have heard that somebody was asking for him. So he came, looking for my grandfather, and he came. So they go over there and they meet, I don't know how many times. So after my mother died, and when I got bigger, they took me over to meet him.

Then later in the years . . . they always said that our people in Mexico are very poor, ya know. The O'odham are very poor. But my grandfather didn't look poor, he had a nice jacket with all the fringe on it—that's all I remember—and a straw hat. So it must be the second time that I went after my mother died, and my grandfather told my other grandfather that my mother was dead. Then later on, we went again, and I saw him again. That's why I remember the first time I saw him, I don't remember the other times how he looked. He had a mustache, he looked like a Mexican. He was outspoken, a proud man. The more I look at him, the more I see my grandfather. But I'm not gonna say he's my grandfather. It'll be me, I'll be on the safe side.

Later, Frances continued.

The second time we went again, he said they wanted to take me back to there. He wanted to take me back after my mother died, because a girl will go to her mother's people. That's the way it was. He said, "I got my chief and I want him to fix it so I can take her." A chief, a representative or something. I didn't want to go. He was older when I saw him, he was stooped over. My grandmother cried the whole way back after that. She was scared. I heard that he died, I don't know when—a long time ago.

Talking about the times, I just remembered another story my grandmother told me. One time my mother and my father were going to town, so they had a buggy and they were going. My father always carry a shotgun. So they were passing by two ranches, now it's called Happy Jack's, and the other is Big Seconbina,[9] so they passed the men. And one of the men met them and wanted water. They must have gone back to tell the others that there was a lady with them; so they chased them. I was a little baby, and my father said she dropped the baby—me—down, and my father got his shotgun and was shooting back. So they went back.

I didn't know how far we would travel to New Fields, but it ended up being less than an hour from San Pedro. It was a shimmering day, one of those bright desert mornings when the sun casts brilliant light and bold shadows on the earth. We had an incredible view of Baboquivari, the Tohono O'odham sacred

mountain—I had never seen it from that side. The few houses and churches that we passed were barely noticeable, the desert was so bright. Frances broke our silence. "It's around here." We were less than a mile from the unmarked border, a barbed wire fence in a desolate desert. "Look for the house on the right," she said, as we quickly veered onto a long dirt driveway. An old man stood up from his seat under a large mesquite tree in the distance, smiling as he walked toward a house and car. Three women, huddled together by an older adobe home in the back, were wearing Mexican rebozos *and sitting under a* ramada—*a picture postcard of old Sonora. Some of the walls and doors were decorated with dried flowers and crosses, like Yaqui homes before the tribe started to build the brick homes in the 1970s.*

Greeting us was Jesus Antonio Lopez, a white-haired spitting image of the man in the photo. His daughter was with him, and another woman, a friend. The friend was the only O'odham who could speak English, although she claimed not to. Fascinated, I asked, "Do you speak O'odham, Spanish, and *English?" "No, not really. Only Indian. I'm a Papago Indian," she said proudly in English, laughing. She walked across the border daily. It was only a fence, and usually no one was there.*

Frances had brought the photograph, and quickly pulled it out to show Lopez. They spoke for a while in O'odham, but it was clear that he was acknowledging recognition. Antonio Lopez was not his grandfather, but his father: "Sí, es él, mi Papá, that's him, Ge Wu:lo." His father had been a sergeant in the Mexican army, tracking and fighting Apaches and Yaquis. "He did a lot for his people and was a good man. He did what he had to do and believed in what he was doing. There's a school named after him down by Hermosillo," Lopez said matter-of-factly.

I got together with Frances twice during the next week; we spent all day Thursday driving around Tucson, running errands. Frances had me make seven copies of the "family photo," and we took one to Frances's daughter Linda, in South Tucson. Visibly intrigued, as we were, Linda must have looked at it for an hour. I asked her if the photo bothered her, and she said no, that the man had to do what he had to do at the time, and those were violent times. No, she was just trying to see him as a member of the family, she said. The photo captivated just about everyone who saw it, encapsulating as it did the violence, chaos, and confusion of that period. All the key players were there: the gov-

ernor of Sonora, the head of the armed forces, the O'odham scouts with their guns and bandoleras. And the two women, somehow relieved that now, by their act, the Seri people would be spared.

June 5, 1997
Five days have passed since we learned that Frances's son, Floyd, had passed on in Ohio. It has been an intense, tiring, yet somehow completing five days, for we, Frances's community, have buried her son.

    I think it was a Wednesday. Having left my little girl with a friend, I arrived at San Pedro at about ten in the evening. Four of Frances's daughters were sitting in a circle with Frances and her half sister Millie. Frances was sitting on the couch, bedraggled and worn, crying. We hugged and cried, as is customary, and sat in silence. Florence had a pen and paper, and after explaining what had happened, the group proceeded with their task of putting together a list of all that there was to do. They were discussing who would buy food for the workers, Jell-o and fruit cup, who would call Willard (a neighbor), the tribe, and who would buy the flowers and ribbon. The meeting went on for two or three hours, interrupted periodically by the coming of visitors—close family like Frances's half brother Johnny from Casa Grande and her half sister Nellie, and a neighbor.

    The girls had made some food earlier, and Frances's granddaughters Amelia and Sonya were doing the dishes; later, they milled about on the fringes. Florence had driven out to tell Frances; she had been making tortillas under the ramada with her daughter Mildred. That was hours ago. By midnight, people were leaving; they would return the following day. I stayed, and Frances and I cried together before we went to bed.

The morning came quickly and was too quiet. Frances had gotten up earlier and opened the doors to let the breeze in, and then had gone back to bed. Upon awakening, the first thing I saw when I looked out the front door was Antonio, his large silhouette filling the doorway. He was a tall horse, standing there waiting for corn or watermelon, begging like a dog. I laughed, took some food from a can of scraps, and went outside to feed him. Looking up, I saw Tina, James's blue Corvair (Frances had named it), and looked inside. James was asleep in the back seat. He had made it home, he had heard. He opened his eyes for a second, muttered something affectionately, and went back to sleep.

I went back inside to get breakfast, and people started coming, crying together and then sitting in silence. It had been resolved that Juanita would bring Floyd from Ohio on Saturday, and that the wake would take place Sunday night. The family was anxious to get Floyd to Arizona, to rest at San Pedro, feeling that he had been alone too long, his spirit uneasy. . . . He had been in Ohio for almost forty years. This was Thursday. We went to bed early that night, outside because it was hot.

I moved into the house in the middle of the night because the dogs were keeping me awake, playing like there was nothing wrong. I felt a little uneasy sleeping in the sewing room with the Blessed Mother altar where Floyd's spirit had been fed. Having slept well, I asked Frances about it the next day. She seemed surprised that I asked. I think it was quite natural to her that the spirit world would be with us.

Friday night I returned with my daughter, along with the rest of the family, and stayed until Monday morning, when the burial was completed. Three days passed in a whirl of activity, much of it now a blur. We visited a lot, and laughed, sometimes forgetting for a brief instant why we were there. I felt like one of the family. I loved the way these women mothered my child. I loved the community we shared in our united effort to support Frances.

We started eating in the feast house on Friday morning, feeding the workers at five, before the men began to dig the grave. Frances's daughter Juanita came from Ohio with the body on Saturday, with Floyd's personal effects. Floyd's mother and five sisters cried together as each item was brought out, cried their eyes out. The men, grandchildren, and I stood awkwardly around the perimeter. Juanita said a beautiful prayer at dinner in the feast house, where neighbors and family had prepared the meal. There was some joking, too—there's often joking after the tears. The next day more people came to help.

We started cooking for the wake on Saturday, and that went on. The first foods that were ready were served to Floyd on the vanity in Frances's sewing room, with the statue of Blessed Mother and a candle flickering to accompany the family's prayers, to light Floyd's path home. Blessed Mother was now joined by Floyd's patron saint, San Francisco—it went everywhere with him. Floyd's spirit was offered generous helpings of food that crowded the vanity next to the candle: fruit salad, chile, coleslaw, three kinds of beans, tortillas, lemon-

ade, and cake with fruit cup. There was a candle left burning in the grave that night, and one in his apartment in Ohio, left earlier in the week. These were for his spirit, which was believed to be wandering about, seeking its peace.

When she awoke, Frances told me about her dream. Floyd had come to her, laughing, in the room where the food offerings were. It chilled her, she said, for the scene was hyperreal, like electricity. Frances felt it was a message from him, telling her that he was happy.

Frances and her daughters were in strong spirits when they left to pick up Floyd in Tucson. Down by the church the late afternoon wind was howling as the church bell began to ring. Soon a blue truck became visible, Johnny's truck, with two grandsons standing on either side of the casket, Floyd's body came home. Someone had made a cross for the grave and decorated it with a large spray of red flowers. The men carried the casket into the church, where a simple bouquet of white flowers and candles were placed next to it. A young priest wearing pants and a T-shirt appeared, and then donned the simple brown robes of a Franciscan priest.

The Franciscan celebrated a heartfelt Catholic mass, ending with "How Great Thou Art" sung in O'odham by a choir playing guitars. Two of Frances's grown grandchildren gave moving readings. We shared Communion, and after the priest left, Floyd's casket was moved outside for the outdoor session which would last all night, without a priest. The new, all-ladies choir said the rosary and sang hymns taught by the Spaniards a hundred years ago. The family seemed solemn, in a focused, trancelike state, listening to the chants. Visitors came to pay respects to the family and the deceased, laying candles, wreaths, and flowers on the altar next to Floyd's photo. Floyd was a big man, full-faced and smiling.

Most visitors left after the large meal at the community feast house, going home to sleep for a few hours while close family and community kept vigil, listening to several more choirs from neighboring villages. At 4:30 a.m. we gathered to hear the rosary at the church while the early morning sun began to light up the desert. Cars and pickup trucks were arriving, sending up dust and rays of color. The men of the family took Frances and Floyd in Johnny's pickup, and the rest of us walked or drove slowly in a long and solemn procession to the cemetery. Floyd's sisters were clinging to each other and to their spouses, holding each other up as they walked.

The funeral was simple in comparison to the elaborate wake of the previous night. Frances's son-in-law Danny Lopez gave a moving speech about coming home and keeping in touch with your family, exhorting the young to remember who they are. The choir sang Spanish hymns as each friend and family member placed a handful of desert soil on Floyd's casket as it descended into the earth. Frances threw a flower onto the casket. The funerary process had been ritualized from the moment Juanita had been notified, orchestrated through syncopated mourning sequences, interspersed with feelings of community, love, and light humor.

Juanita told me in the morning, "You should have stayed [at the church], Debbie, he came. You know, they sometimes come as owls, an owl came and flew all around here," she said, waving her arm. "It was beautiful." Sonny (Floyd's nephew) sang Jimmy Hendrix's "My Sweet Angel" at the end, after most of us had left.

Looking back, I feel that the intensity of the funeral was, for many of us, fueled by the eventuality of Frances's passing, only indirectly alluded to in conversation. How could we stand up, who would carry us? Custom demanded a lot from each of us, and it seemed to work, for after it was all over, Frances said to me, "I think now, maybe, I can go back to my life, to the business of living." But time passed, and still she couldn't.

History

The O'odham's placement on their land is no small thing; the people have a very strong and ancient tie with this land, in spite of the ways in which the bounty of the land and of its people has been stripped by forces beyond their control. The Tohono O'odham are generally a peaceful, humble, and friendly people with an awesome respect for living things. This point lies at the heart of Frances' teachings and her style of living in this world.

Despite its surface tranquillity, the reservation can be a rough place—sometimes violent, often unpredictable.[10] Strewn along sixty-four miles of a heavily patrolled international boundary, the reservation has become a border front line between two large nations, as drug trafficking and illegal immigration increase their impact. A region with a turbulent history, the reservation has long been a frontier, contested and lawless.[11] It is a little-known, desolate segment of the U.S.-Mexican border, and few people are familiar with the fortunes and misfortunes of the Tohono O'odham there.

To live on the reservation today means to be familiar with poverty, alcoholism, drug abuse, unemployment, violence, suicide, and poor nutrition and health (including one of the highest diabetes rates in the world). These circumstances did not arise overnight. They are the result of a complex set of historical processes, including several centuries of conquest, economic racism, the forceful imposition of both ill- and well-meaning programs, and a focus on short-term solutions. The problem has to do with a history of lack of control over the forces of change, and a lack of participation and community control over resources as mechanisms for economic progress, because, until recent times, the impetus for change has usually come from outside.[12]

The most far-reaching events that have altered Tohono O'odham lives in recorded history are forceful colonization by Spain, Mexico, and, most recently, the United States.[13] Seeking to expand their colonial empires, the Spaniards first explored O'odham country in 1539, but did not extend their exploration into the northern Sonoran desert for another 150 years. In 1687 the Jesuits introduced cattle, horses, and wheat, along with disease and warfare which accounted for untold decimation of Indian populations.[14] Later, the area was settled by soldiers, missionaries, prospectors, and immigrants en route to California who exploited natural resources such as minerals, copper, and grazing lands. In 1854, following the Gadsden Purchase, O'odham land became divided between Mexico and the United States. Flu, smallpox, and tuberculosis epidemics hit the Tohono O'odham in the early 1900s. Apache warfare, lasting from the late seventeenth century until 1886, changed the face of the region, forcing the O'odham into larger villages, and delaying the Spanish advance into the area. According to Thomas Sheridan, until the late nineteenth century, the state of Arizona was a frontier, "a contested ground, a place where no one group—tribe, nation-state, or empire—held uncontested sway."[15] When the United States finally defeated Geronimo in 1886, the frontier era came to an end. On the O'odham reservation, this turbulent history continues to have an impact on people's lives.[16]

At the time of Frances's birth in 1912, the Tohono O'odham way of life had become drastically transformed. By the end of the nineteenth century, the Tohono O'odham had already entered the cash economy, obtaining cash for labor *on Mexican and American ranches, plantations, and mines. Cattlemen and miners had been homing in on Tohono O'odham land—cutting timber and overgrazing cattle, leading to erosion and flooding after the desert monsoons. Like Frances's father, many O'odham learned cattle ranching while working as cowboys, and were ranching their own lands, gradually abandoning hunting and farming for wage work in the mines as the land became less productive.[17] These changes moved the people from a self-sufficient subsistence economy, dependent on desert resources, and placed them in a position of dependence on the cash economy. The O'odham became vulnerable to the ravages of that economy while their only economic insurance—ranching and farming—became dependent on an already ravaged environment. Winston Erikson provides an apt summary of what was going on at the time:*

> *As the O'odham entered the twentieth century, they found themselves in a situation where they were less able to sustain their old way of life based on farming and gathering. Increasingly, they turned elsewhere to make a living. Some turned to raising cattle, but this could not be successful over the long run because the grasslands could not support enough cattle for everyone to make a decent living. Others looked to employment as cowboys, railroad laborers, construction workers, and domestics. There was never enough employment available to make a good living, but with their traditional skills, supplemented by the available wages, they were able to survive.[18]*

At the turn of the century, thousands of Tohono O'odham were migrating from Mexico, where conditions were getting worse.[19] Frances' mother, Amelia, would have come to Tucson from Hermosillo sometime between 1909 and 1911, during the tumultuous dawn of the Mexican Revolution.

By force of law, in 1916 Tohono O'odham living in the United States were confined to the reservation, on land roughly equal to their original homeland in what is now the United States—totaling almost three million acres. Wells were introduced to encourage cattle ranching, and many O'odham began living year round in villages and farming homesteads. More man-made drought years in the 1910s, 1920s, and 1930s brought an increasing migration to Tucson and other Arizona cities, at the same time the ancient subsistence practices of the Tohono O'odham were gradually being abandoned. Cataclysmic habitat destruction, biotic depletion, and linguistic acculturation have led to the rapid loss of culturally encoded knowledge about the natural environment, eclipsing traditional ways and language by the 1920s and 1930s.[20] *Frances's grandparents on her father's side, living in Arizona, were among the last to practice subsistence farming full time.*

The 1930s were a watershed of change for the Tohono O'odham. During the Roosevelt administration, the Civilian Conservation Corps's Indian Division (CCC-ID) was established by the federal government to create wells, waterholes, fences, and roads to facilitate O'odham cattle ranching. In 1934 the Indian Organization Act provided a tribal constitution and bylaws to replace the traditional clan-based forms of governance. It was an unstable, artificial political system based on a foreign, imposed concept of government with ideas of private property, progress, and assimilation.

Frances's story describes her gradual entry into the world of the Milga:n. While she was a child living at S-koksonagk, the men in her family became increasingly involved in activities away from home. They worked at the mines for part of the year, and later with the CCC and Southern Pacific Railroad. As a teenager Frances was sent to boarding school, where she was required to wear a uniform and was forbidden to speak O'odham. After Frances married, she traveled with her husband, keeping camp at the CCC and later working in town. In 1941 a major drought killed most of their cows, causing Frances and her husband, Jose, to abandon their family fields at San Pedro. Like many others, they left children behind and found menial work in hotels, restaurants, and the homes of wealthy Milga:n in Tucson. By 1936 there were three hundred Tohono O'odham living on the outskirts of Tucson in a town of twenty-four hundred, a Mexican frontier town experiencing steady migration from the reservation since the early 1900s. Wage labor constituted 27 percent of Tohono O'odham income by 1937, and 56 percent ten years later.[21]

With little education, Frances and Jose were forced to work for low wages, enduring social and economic pressures which served to exclude them from the higher ranks of Milga:n society. Living in Tucson barrios with other poor, they worked, worshiped, and raised their children. Many adults drank heavily and were regularly in and out of jail. After her husband's death, Frances opted to remain in Tucson, washing, ironing, and cleaning, selling baskets and tortillas, and later, demonstrating basket weaving. Urban Tohono O'odham were distinct from other city poor in having a tribally owned land base. For Frances, like many O'odham, residence in town was temporary; the reservation was regarded as their permanent home. Even today, many O'odham live between

Tucson and the reservation, maintaining social ties in home villages that they can go back to when times get rough.

Like the diets of other O'odham her age, Frances's diet has changed drastically since her childhood at S-koksonagk, where she ate mostly home-grown and gathered desert foods. Today Frances's diet consists of some traditional food—cactus buds, squash, and gruels. But it also includes a lot of the foods introduced by the Spaniards—lard, beef, white flour, sugar, and coffee—and commodity foods introduced by the government. Pinto beans, introduced as a commodity food, replaced tepary beans and are a mainstay of the family's diet. Frances and many of the adult members of her family live with diabetes, a bodily effect of the long-sustained, drastic change in diet that her people have undergone.

Today the Tohono O'odham have one of the highest incidences of adult-onset diabetes in the United States, fifteen times the national average (over one in eight O'odham), and it is increasing, along with kidney failure, blindness, obesity, and arteriosclerosis. An insidious form of childhood diabetes is currently developing on the reservation. Recent research has shown that the same foods that have been eliminated from Tohono O'odham diets have been proven to control diabetes, including beans, mesquite-seed gum, prickly pear pads, and plantago seed.[22] It seems that Tohono O'odham bodies were adapted to a specific desert diet that maintained a necessary balance for them in variable crop years.

Rapid change and looming environmental, cultural, health, and fiscal issues continue to exert tremendous pressures on Frances's people. The reservation where Frances lives is a third culture within and between two large nations, the forcible impact of which has forever changed the Tohono O'odham. Most recently, stepped-up drug trafficking and illegal immigration have had a visible impact—the increased presence of the Border Patrol in the area—and have set severe limits on O'odham movement between the United States and Mexico. And even with the advent of sophisticated tribal initiatives, like legal gambling and tribally owned utility and telecommunications companies, unemployment, alcohol-related tragedy, and violent death continue. As I write this, I am reminded of phone conversations we've had in recent days, "conversations from the battle zone," I have come to call them, the world out of order. Just this week I called and immediately heard the familiar sadness in Frances's voice. "What's wrong?" I asked. "You sound down." "Remember Winfred? Lived over *there by Jimmy? Died," Frances said sadly. "How?" I asked. "From the same thing that's killing all the young people. Cirrhosis," she whispered. Not too long ago I called and Frances couldn't talk. "What's the matter?" I asked. "Gunshots," she answered, "I have to go. I'll call ya later, okay?" Just a few days ago Frances called to tell me about a distant relative from town who killed his girlfriend and her son, and then himself. These are just a few of many tragedies that Frances and her people have lived with in the years since I have known her. And then the family returns to their everyday lives.*

Life History

Frances's talk about her everyday life sheds light upon broader historical struggles, migrations, and transformations from the time of her birth in 1912. Her story is one of few written works focusing on rural life on the border and the migration from the reservation ranch to the barrios, and back to the reservation.[23] It places woman squarely center stage, and thus is part of a movement recognizing the increasing importance of women's narratives to our understanding of history.[24] It is radical and extraordinary to hear from a Native American woman like Frances, in her own words and from her own point of view, to enter the complex and sensitive aspects of her life experience, her imaginings, and her sorrows. Frances's story situates itself as a Native American woman's narrative, the work of a unique, creative individual. This is the ultimate promise of life history: that the meaning and style of one person's life is communicated—here, in the details of day-to-day living.

An O'odham elder, Frances is concerned with the message she leaves for the children to come. Her words reach deep into her people's past and forward into the future: "Well, here's a song (or story) about that," Frances says, powerfully communicating her meaning through songs and stories "from the Beginning." Her dreams and premonitions reach forward into the future, serving as guideposts and warnings. Frances's style of embedding these songs, legends, and dreams or prophecies, so common in oral cultures, brings the power of other places and time frames into the present. This points to the cyclic nature of time and reality, and to what endures, like the value of human life and the things God gave us to live on this Earth. Songs and legends are powerfully performative—multisensory and dramatic in delivery, communicating through feeling and the body. They intensify Frances's meanings and enhance our experience of the telling. Within them lies the power to transform.

Frances's story is a living record of how one person has experienced and settled her life in what has been, for many O'odham, a time of turmoil and imbalance. It is in the details of her everyday life that we see how Frances has negotiated between her O'odham identity and an increasingly dominant Milga:n culture. And how, living a life between the reservation and urban barrio, Frances has created an identity, a world of sense and meaning with her people's teachings at the core. It is a story of an individual life lived well, a work of reconciliation and of hope.

Appendix A: Inscribing Life History

Yeah,
I read those books written about the O'odham
.
[in a high pitch] A lot of things that was made up!
And a lot of things that was just . . .
Sometimes
it's HOPI.
Like the marriage is HOPI.
I read that.
A lot of things is all right
and a lot of this is made up
.
That's why I never thought it was so good and I hear everybody say
"Yeah it's so good."
I don't know what's so good about it.
Well, they do that
sometimes they write, they get
maybe from San Carlos or from somewhere and put it in!
That's why
I'm gonna tell the truth
no matter what
.
But it's gonna be
OURS
cuz I'm not gonna mixing with anything.
    (1987)

The following sections are written for the reader interested in the nuts and bolts of writing life history. Though each collaborative process is different, this type of work often involves an inherent tension around the positioning and expectations that collaborators bring to the work. I did not expect any difficulties to arise; I thought we would get to work, and that would be it! As it happens in life, what we plan and the way things turn out are often very different. But our journey has not been for naught. Working together has changed us both; much has happened in our lives and families during the last twenty-odd years. As I write this, Frances is eighty-four, precisely twice my age. Our friendship has grown as we have worked together and, over the years, our lives have become intertwined. In this section we talk about the process of inscribing our litera-tures and our relationships, both for ourselves and for our readership, and for those who may someday attempt to trace the dance of our collaboration.[1]

Working Together

No more elegant tool exists to describe the human condition than the personal narrative. Ordinary people living ordinary and not-so-ordinary lives weave from their memories and experiences the meaning life has for them. These stories are complex, telling of worlds sometimes foreign to us, worlds that sometimes no longer exist. They express modes of thought and culture often different from our own, a challenge to easy understanding. Yet, these stories are also familiar. It is just this tension—the identifiable in endless transformation—that is the cur-rency of personal narratives, as they reveal the complexities and paradoxes of human lives. —Marjorie Shostak[2]

Our most intensive work together occurred during the taping sessions, a process extending over ten years. Most of our early work together took place rather spontaneously and at Frances's lead, but when Frances and I were living together in 1987, things were different. In the past we mainly worked when the spirit moved us, but now I was coming to "collect" stories from Frances's life, living with her for three months. What follows are selections from the journal I kept during that time. These pieces highlight the disjunction between each of our styles of working, and some of the lessons I learned from Frances's way of doing things in the process. It was hard for me to overcome the individual-ism that was such a part of my approach to the project. Frances was always busy with family and community activities, her words had their own times and rhythms. These had to be carved out of life with care.

February 20, 1987
It is much harder to work this way, to live together with the expectation that we will work every day. Frances only rarely says, "Get the tape, I have to tell you something," like she used to. And it's hard for me to initiate, because Frances is my elder. She's supposed to take the lead.

Frances has a very busy life. She worries about her grandsons, teaches in town, goes to meetings several times a week, helps at the church, cooks feasts, bakes bread, baby-sits for grandchildren, makes baskets for anthropologists and priests. It took us one month to do three tapes!

I feel uprooted, frustrated; I'm waiting and waiting and not getting any-where. It is hard to plan, Frances just waits to see how she feels. Taping stories is not her favorite thing; it's certainly not the most important thing. Frances's priorities are different, like cooking for the boys, or resting. I don't think she is feeling well, her blood sugar is out of sync.

February 24
This morning we had a good talk about the project and about our relationship. Frances admitted that it's hard to have someone living there, and expressed concern about her state of mind and health. Her diabetes was bad, having me there was stressful for her, and there were things going on in the community . . . (alluded to only indirectly).

The death topic comes up a lot, as Frances has been going to a lot of funer-als lately. And Lorenzo is dreaming about me, something about medicine (he won't say). Sometimes I think he thinks my presence is responsible for things going wrong, but maybe I am imagining this.

It is difficult to get Frances to talk about what is bothering her. She says she feels that we are prisoners of our beliefs, that our thoughts, imaginations, and dreams create our world. Last night we lay on her bed and she spoke to me openly about her premonitions. Later she sat outside with Lorenzo and called to me to come hear two owls, one big and one little one. We listened and could hear them, but although they were close, we couldn't see them. I could feel their fear, for the owls are spirit messengers and, sometimes, harbingers of death. She told me about a roadrunner chasing Lorenzo, then the next day someone died. Frances has had a lot on her mind lately.

Today Frances spoke about her confusion, how she believes but she doesn't, how there is no hope to really know about things of the spirit world. Like her grandfather said, we can never go back to the way things were. I think she wanted to talk because she was scared. It's been two years since she re-members the owls coming to the village; Frances got so sick she almost died. There's this uncertainty of believing what she doesn't want to believe, of the old ways having such force while things have changed so drastically. While she has changed.

I have come to think that Frances's perpetual state of hopefulness is strongly related to her basket weaving. The only time that Frances gets really depressed is when she can't make baskets, like when her finger gets infected (this is related to her diabetes). Frances looks forward to sitting down to make a basket, and now that she is older, it keeps her going.

More than anything our book is a dialogue, written collaboratively. I am the sometimes absent conversant/participant, clumsy interlocutor, but there it is, shared between us. And then there's that third person, the tape recorder— the book, written for her kids, her people, and "those white ladies in town." I went to sleep last night feeling very uprooted, out of place in both of my worlds.

March 2

"This bird is singing to the Earth," Frances told me poetically. There's a full moon, and a symphony of animal sounds. There is the trip to the emergency room, Lorenzo's congestive heart failure.

March 6

We joke a lot about ghosts of people like Pancho Villa, especially when Americans come to visit. Frances says, "We don't believe in ghosts, but we do in spirits." I'm not sure what that means.

Frances is teaching me things about the spirit world, about being indirect, about being what she calls "real," which, I think, has to do with being present in the moment. Sometimes it is difficult to follow when she talks by analogy. She often tells me what she wants indirectly, surprising me with the candor and strength of her message:

> I don't really believe in dreams, but sometimes the dream is so clear, so sometimes I think it is true. The other night I dreamed that a tall man in shorts came in with a notebook and he asked me if I wanted to die, and I said, "Of course not, I'm afraid to die," and then he marked something and he turned around to my friend, Lorenzo, and asked him if he wanted to die, and he said, "Yes." Then he turned around to me and said, "Well, you're going to live to be ninety." Then I looked at his shoes, they were so raggedy and the toe was peeping out. And I was wondering all day why I dreamed that and I remembered it, and what it means. I don't usually remember my dreams so clearly. I was in bed, dreaming I was laying on the couch and Lorenzo was sitting in the chair. My recent life is almost the same, get up in the morning and do cooking.

If I'm lazy, I don't do anything, I just do things that has to be done. And, um, if I really feel like working on baskets, I'll just soak the yucca and wait. Sometimes I don't get to it until afternoon. And um, some days I work and some days I play. But I'm not the kind of person who goes to somebody's house and sit and talk. That's the way I am from way back. Because I don't have enough things to say, and I don't say things that I feel they won't be interested. I don't like to talk for just the sound, without meaning anything to them, when it's not part of their ways.

And I don't try to make things interesting, I don't add anything, I just talk about things the way it happens. I don't lie, but sometimes I say I don't know, but I just don't want to talk about it. If I don't feel like talking about it, I don't talk about it. It just goes on like that. And another thing, I don't just come out and ask for all the details, I just . . . slowly, little by little. It's a lot easier than asking a question straight out, it just loses something! That's why the people don't get the straight answers.

March 15

The taping process is going a bit more smoothly. I've taken to keeping a list of aspects of her life we've discussed, or those I've participated in and appreciated, and after a few days of not working, Frances asks me to run through the list. Then she chooses something of interest, something that is compatible with her mood, thoughts, and preparation. Clarifying details and checking facts is the most difficult. These sessions are fraught with complications—lost tapes, secret knowledge, disappointments, seasonal (snake) limitations, poor health, and family and community obligations. Frances's mood has to be right for her to say what she's saying, or she won't say it!

This process is very tiring for Frances, she says she gets tired of talking about herself. She puts herself down if I try to praise her. Frances has been set apart by other villagers for having Milga:n friends, for having me here. And in the process of reflecting on her experiences, she is dealing with some unsettling topics.

March 21

I think of Frances as my grandmother, Hu'uli, and she says she thinks of me as a daughter. We talk a lot about spiritual things, the Earth and the animals, topics that inspire us, interests we share. She doesn't often say thank you, and gets mad when I say something sounds good or is interesting. But she lets you know she notices when you help her. Frances is very accepting of me, I can be myself with her.

March 24

In spite of our difficulties, we have a lot of fun! I love our jokes about the coffee pot being jealous of the pan, and how hard it is to get it to boil. I love the way Frances names her dolls, animals, objects in her house. Through play, I am learning how events have life, bring things into creation or negate those things, or join with new things, transform them. A coyote standing near the house or an owl coming close can bring death, power, or food. Curses and dreams, too, have life—these are events because they are part of you. They bring songs, which bring power; they tell you to do things.

But being here, things are way out of my control, I'm just waiting. Frances is busy, tired, sick, resting, not in the mood, disorganized, mad, and waiting on me, too. I think she sees me as directing things, but how can I tell my grandmother what to do? I tried meeting the same time every day, but that turned out to be impossible.

Well, like Frances says, if it's not real, it won't come out—the time has to be right. So I need to just be there. Is this what it is all about? I keep asking myself what is this thing that we are doing? Frances' life is 100 percent devoted to family.

March 28

What is this experience of hers that is different than mine, and that is working disjunctively with mine? Never draw attention to one's self. So how can we do life history? Does Frances really want to do this?

April 3

Frances told me today that she doesn't feel the same about the book as she did in the beginning. It got worse when I started making lists and asking a lot of questions. We worked best when I simply listened, and she would talk deeply from her heart.

Frances and I wrote over half of the book during this period. Things got progressively better as I learned to be more flexible, learned to listen and wait as

Frances responded to the ongoing contingencies of her life. I came out of this experience realizing how hard Frances's life can be. Frances was seventy-five years old, and during those three months many of the people she had become close to were dying. These were the tragedies so familiar to people on the reservation: the car accidents, suicides, cirrhosis, domestic abuse, and the severe diabetes that causes Frances so much suffering. Despite her sense of humor and positive outlook, Frances taped many of her stories within a state of thoughtfulness and loss.

English and O'odham

"English kills the meaning. You have to speak Papago to really understand," Frances said one day when I asked her to tell a story in O'odham. She said she preferred to use English with me, and resisted my attempts to get her to speak in O'odham (I was thinking, naively, that we'd translate them into English later). The use of English was necessary, for I did not speak O'odham.

The following conversation took place in the middle of that spring of 1987, as we were beginning to work out some of the nuts and bolts of collaboration. Sitting at the kitchen table one midmorning in March, I was wondering if we couldn't do more of the recording in O'odham.

"Do you want to do some of our recording in O'odham?" I asked.

"Papago is a different dialogue. There's no place to squeeze in, it just goes on and on and on—it just goes. It has its own words, its own sounds, the own person telling it—it just goes. It fixes itself to drag on if you want it to drag on. If you want to really [say something], it has to come from your feeling, it has to come from your heart. You can't just make yourself say it. It's like telling a story. You can't just say, 'Well, tell the story.' You can't do it. Well, maybe somebody else can, but I can't."

While the songs and a few of Frances's monologues are in O'odham, if she was going to speak to me from her heart, she would have to speak to me in English. Emergent meaning inheres in the dialogue between us, and an imagined, primarily English-speaking, audience.[3] Although O'odham is her first language, Frances has become quite fluent in English. English is the language Frances uses when she speaks to members of my generation—her younger children and many of her grandchildren.

I think what Frances meant when she said that English kills the meaning is *that certain things may be left out, that in telling the legends in English, for example, there is an inevitable loss in eloquence, style, and detail. Content, too, may be different. But the reverse is also true; what is said in English might not have been said in O'odham (and probably would not be said in the same way). In primarily employing English, the book may detract from the movement in favor of Native American literature rendered in the native tongue and bilingual works, a shortcoming of our work because I was not able to learn O'odham. The use of English, however, has one major advantage over translated works: it simplifies the collaborative process, avoiding the third-party interpeter/translator.*[4] *What the reader sees in this book is a compilation of the original version as it was spoken by Frances, using her own words to express her meaning.*

Inscription: The Division of Labor

They didn't have any language, so they gave them a piece of feather
so they wrote their language.
That's why they're so SMART,
because they can write.
   (1981)

This is a story I read somewhere. Once upon a time the coyote was walking, he was hungry and he met up with this [mountain] lion. So this lion started to grab the coyote, so the coyote said, "Don't eat me up, I'm following a horse, so just go with me, we'll follow the horse. When we get the horse, we'll both eat it." So the lion came and they went, and they went on, and on, and on until they came to a pasture. And there was a white horse. The coyote said, "Here's the horse right here, that's what I'm following." So he went after it, and the horse saw the coyote and the lion, so he was all ready. And so the coyote went toward the horse and he said he was ready to kick. He went back and said to the lion, "You go and grab the horse. There's something written on the horse, I don't know what it says because I can't read." And so the lion went and said, "There's nothing there!" "Get closer, it's there," said the coyote. So it went closer and the horse kicked the lion in the head and killed it right there, so the coyote ate, and ate, and ate until he couldn't eat any more. And that was the end. When he was eating, he said to himself, "Thanks to my father, he didn't send me to school!" [1987]

Frances is keenly aware of the literary inequality between us. We were talking about the editing process in 1981, and I asked Frances how she wanted to be involved.

I'm just saying this—
  if I was doing this
  if I was doing this,
I'd know
where to put the words,
because I'm doing it.
I'd listen and hear, and if that's not right,
I'd take it out and put it in
and take it out

If I was doing that, but I'm not doing that
I'm just telling YOU

It may be MY book but I'm not doing that.
I'm just telling YOU,
so it's up to you whatever you think

So you don't want to edit this together?

No.
Um mmm.

It's a lot of work . . .
it's tedious.

It isn't that it's a lot of work

it's just the way I feel
it's not the word, it's the feeling
  it's the way I FEEL

Like I read something
and it doesn't sound right
  and I think
"maybe it sounds good to her
because she knows more about writing than I do."
  (1981)

*Who knows what direction this book would have taken if Frances had writ-
ten it herself? But she probably wouldn't have without some urging.[5] Frances
was always saying, "I'm not so special!" Although it was clear that she wanted
to do this, Frances often felt awkward being the constant subject of our work,
especially after she saw her story in writing. After reading the first draft, she
commented, "This is my life! It's not that interesting, but maybe it will be when
I'm gone. Because all of this is just written, I find myself repeating myself. And,
like . . . let's don't say any more, [forcefully] 'It's very good!' The Indians don't
use that. The actions shows, not the words."*

    *Frances's story is written in the style of a Euro-American genre called life
history—biography, and/or autobiography in interviews and/or written
form.[6] Our work is both biography and autobiography, for we both talk about
Frances's life. "Bicultural composite compositions," jointly authored works such
as ours, are written in the boundary between cultures; here, between Milga:n
and O'odham sensibilities.[7] This combination of sensibilities inheres both in
Frances's voice—speaking in English to an English speaker—and in the dialogue between us. Frances and I decided early on that the book would be written in Frances's words, with some bilingual material. I would do the writing
and editing, and provide commentary. The book would be jointly authored,
unlike "as told to" works with the scholar as sole author.[8] So Frances spoke
and I wrote. Frances decided when and how much we would work and, for
the most part, what topics would be covered. I had some input, choosing topics
that were interesting to me, and directed some of the work we did on religion,
for example, using a question-answer format. After the tapes were recorded,
I transcribed them and, following Frances's direction, attempted to order the
material chronologically ("to get rid of repetitions, putting things here and
there, where they should go"). This meant cutting and pasting several hundred
pages of original text. Fortunately, Frances's themes repeated themselves, and*

most sections fell together easily. Though my interests and interpretations have inevitably had their impact on the content and direction of the work, the collaborative process was guided first of all by Frances's criteria, including choices concerning inclusion and exclusion of topics. I exercised a lot of freedom in arranging her words from the original corpus, sticking to her chronology and the guidelines she offered. I provided commentary, from my own point of view, to fill out some of the historical contexts of Frances's story, but tried to avoid analyzing her words or subsuming them beneath mine, as many of my predecessors have done.

At Wisconsin, I read everything I could get my hands on about life history and oral literature. I carefully listened to Frances's words on tape at a linguistics lab where I recorded Frances's voice in both English and O'odham. I wanted to get a feel for the rhythms and cadences of her speech, enough so I could capture a sense of her spoken word on the written page. Others had been using the poetic format for oral texts, so I decided to try it, for what is poetry if it is not words spoken out loud, in performance? Because form (as well as content) influences meaning, I employed a poetic format in section and chapter headings to evoke the original oral context. What is not made accessible to the reader is the repetition and redundancy of the original texts. Because they were primarily oral, told over numerous sittings over many years, they seemed discontinuous when written. Within sessions, however, Frances's narrative was quite coherent.[9] This simplified the editing process, rendering it easy to keep the original sections together.

One of the major challenges I faced in the editing was trying to retain Frances's individual style of speaking while editing for ease of readability for a primarily English-speaking audience. I opted for minimal grammatical editing, correcting grammatical constructions when necessary, while giving priority to the authentic presentation of Frances's style of speaking in her O'odham English dialect. For example, I corrected some, but not all, of the lack of final –(e)d in past tense, omission of final –(e)s in the regular noun plural, and subject-verb agreement errors, and confusion in gender distinction. Embedded songs and stories were kept in their original contexts. Once the editing was completed, I worked to contextualize the conversations, attempting not to intrude upon Frances's story as she had told it and not to analyze it for purposes beyond her own. As the style and significance of the work emerged, we came to share a similar emphasis on personal experience—exegesis as it illuminates *through reflection, rather than explanation, and to "tell things are they really are."[10] Frances gave me freedom to write my sections, and, in time, I developed a voice that I felt would complement Frances's tone and intentions. After Frances read the final draft, she commented, "I like it. You tell the truth. We always said we were gonna tell them the truth! The way it really happened!" Frances and I were in close contact throughout the editing and writing stages, a period spanning several years. Frances read and commented upon drafts, and made changes. Frances's children also received copies of the manuscript and made comments. Frances retained veto power throughout the process.[11] Our efforts to clarify and equalize our collaboration do not negate literary, economic, age, and cultural differences that exist between us. But it is, in part, these very "differences" that have made this book what it is, while deepening our friendship. There is something uniquely powerful in stepping outside of our taken-for-granted realities, in working within difference, between cultural worlds. These worlds end up being not very far apart, after all.*

Appendix B: A Partial Outline of the Original Transcript

Tape 1

The first tape was recorded by Hazel Salzman in the late 1970s, and was given to Deborah in 1981.

I. The Wi:gita
II. Growing up
III. Grandparents
    A. Trees
    B. Food
    C. "Weird things that happened"
    D. Grandparents' preaching
IV. Nawacu jogs
V. Marriage and in-laws
VI. Parents and grandparents
    A. "My mother's death"
VII. Leaving the children behind: the bad year
VIII. The cricket song for Amelia
IX. Power, stories, being Indian: struggles with beliefs
    A. Death clothes
    B. Dreams
    C. "Things I don't understand"

Tape 2

Tape 2, a short tape, was recorded for Hazel in the late 1970s.

I. Songs
II. Friendship, stories
III. "The old people are gifted"

Tape 3

Tape 3 was recorded for Hazel in the late 1970s.

I. "There is no time for stories"
II. Indians and whites
    A. White man's disease
    B. Changes in food
    C. The moon
    D. "White man is so smart, summer doesn't come . . ."
    E. War nurse's prayer
III. The kickball story

Tape 4

Tape 4, the last of Hazel's tapes, has a few sentences on it about getting some old pictures enlarged.

Tape 5

Tape 5, entitled "Papago Enculturation into Christianity," records a speech delivered to the Religious Education Conference of the Catholic priests in Tucson, 1982.

Tape 6

Tape 6 was recorded in several sittings, sitting at the kitchen table at San Pedro in the fall of 1981. Most of these topics were initiated by Frances, with occasional prompting from Deborah to tell the stories in as much detail as possible.

I. The boy from Seranaki and a related legend
II. Getting lost in the desert: Pancho Villa
III. The Wi:gita
IV. Water

V. A child born to a man
VI. Apaches
VII. Purification
VIII. Beans and animals
IX. Nawacu and I'itoi
X. Going back to the old village
XI. Grandfather
XII. The owl sickness and other illnesses

Tape 7

Tape 7, a continuation of tape 6, also was recorded at San Pedro during several sittings in the fall of 1981.

I. The owl sickness
II. The bad year
III. Cows and horses
IV. Religion: old and new
V. Apaches
VI. Midwifery

Tape 8

Tape 8 was recorded in the winter of 1985 during my visit from Wisconsin. The topics included in the first part of the tape were initiated by Frances, with efforts by Deborah to fill in details during the final sessions.

I. Legend of the twins
II. Going to school
III. "My husband, Jose"
IV. Going to the dance
V. The roundup, horses
VI. White people and education
VII. Sex and drinking

Tape 9

Tape 9 was recorded in San Pedro in 1981 and 1985 during my visits from Wisconsin.

    I. Mixing I'itoi and God
       A. Grandparents
       B. Dreams
       C. Being a runner

Tape 10

Tape 10 was recorded by Frances alone on May 5, 1985, and consists mainly of the story of Lorenzo's horseback riding accident.

The 1987 Series

The 1987 series was recorded between February and April 1987. Each tape includes several sittings that were recorded primarily in Frances's kitchen at San Pedro; some recording was done in the car, en route between Tucson and San Pedro. Deborah was residing on the reservation at the time.

Tape 87.1
Most of this material was chosen and ordered by Frances.

    I. Growing up
    II. School
    III. Men
    IV. Womanhood
    V. "My marriage"
    VI. "My mother and grandmother"

Tape 87.2

    I. Obtaining power
    II. Telling stories

III. The bad year
IV. Tucson
V. Frances's in-laws
VI. Farming
VII. Two hands

Tape 87.3

I. "My health"
II. The little girl
III. Dreams and stories
IV. Midwifery
V. Writing for the kids
VI. The owl sickness
VII. Farming

Tape 87.4
This short tape concerns village meetings.

Tape 87.5

I. "My funeral service"
II. People who have died recently
III. "Jokes about my basket-weaving tools"
IV. Dreams
V. Childhood and superstitions
VI. "There is no time"
VII. "My story is not so special"
VIII. Medicine men and dreams
IX. Going blind

Tape 87.6
Deborah initiates the topic of Frances's saints, and, with great enthusiasm, Frances initiates the topic of "bad things she's done." The fifth topic, married life, was recorded in the car, as a conversation between us.

I. "My shrine"
II. Saints, hair, old beliefs

A. Catholicism
B. Prayers
III. "Bad things I've done"
IV. Drinking
V. Married life
A. Working at the mine

Tape 87.7
The beginning of the tape was recorded in the car on a Tuesday morning, as we were going to basket-weaving class. The horses have been fighting and Lorenzo is not feeling well.

I. Horses fighting
II. How Frances started her shrine
III. Questions and answers about childhood
IV. Things that connect
V. Lucious died
VI. "My dreams"
VII. Grandparents

Tape 87.8
Most of this tape is a monologue recorded by Frances at home, alone.

I. "My health"
II. Stories
III. Midwifery
IV. Being a simple person
V. Grew up different
VI. Indians and whites
VII. The moon

The "U" series

The "U" series consists of a lot of new material as well as questions and answers directed at filling in details from previous recordings. This is the final set of tapes recorded during our three months of living together in the spring of 1987, and includes strong statements by Frances about what she wants the book to look like.

U1

    I. Childhood
    II. Legends
    III. Lorenzo's songs
    IV. Peeping at graves
    V. Legends
    VI. Foods

U2

The tape begins with Frances speaking somberly about how she grew up. The rest of the tape consists of questions and answers about religion and miscellaneous topics, to fill in details.

    I. Growing up
    II. All Souls' Day
    III. Having babies
    IV. The owl
    V. Desert plants

U3

U3 is primarily directed by Frances and includes some songs with Lorenzo.

    I. Lorenzo and songs
        A. Cowboy songs
        B. Other songs
    II. Eating
    III. Family life
    IV. The white man

U4

    I. Women and power
    II. Men
    III. Underhill

IV. Religion and medicine men
V. Baskets
VI. Friendship
VII. Childhood
VIII. Farming

U5

I. Singing
II. O'odham language

U6

I. "People let you down."
II. Arguments between married couples, Jenny
III. Changes

U7
Deborah asks questions.

I. The San Pedro church
II. All Souls' Day
III. Grandparents' religion

U8
Frances initiates topics.

I. Medicine men
II. Sleeping outside
III. Dreams
IV. Medicine men
V. Money

Ten short tape recordings were made between 1990 and the present in order to keep the book up to date (for example, Lorenzo's accident and death). The story of Frances's husband's death was recorded in 1996.

Notes

Preface

1. "Is there anything you want to say about writing the book?" Deborah had asked.

2. O'odham baskets are currently made from bear grass, yucca, and devil's claw.

3. Lorenzo (pronounced "Loli:ñso") figures prominently in the book because he was around during the time that it was being recorded. This may give the reader the impression that Lorenzo's role in Frances's life was more important than that of her husband, which was, of course, not the case. Jose had died decades before the book was written, and is present in spirit.

4. Until recent years the Tohono O'odham were called Papago, by outsiders, and Frances often uses this term to refer to her people. In their native language, Frances's people have always called themselves Tohono O'odham, "the Desert People." See Bernard L. Fontana, *Of Earth and Little Rain* (Tucson: University of Arizona Press, 1989), pp. 37–38, for a discussion of the possible origins of the term "Papago" from the Spanish *Papabotas* (Pima bean eaters).

5. The poetic approach foregrounds discourse as lived practice, performative practice in which meaning is constituted in the speech event. In the spoken event, words are combined with gesture, loudness and intonation, breath groups, tone, and other sound features. We chose to employ the poetic format primarily in introductions to chapters and parts in order to evoke the oral context of telling, to provide a sense of Frances's emotive style, and to help the reader to grasp the relationship between aesthetic form and content. See Dennis Tedlock, *The Spoken Word and the Work of Interpretation* (Philadelphia: University of Pennsylvania Press, 1983); Joel Sherzer, "Poetic Structuring of Kuna Discourse: The Line," *Language and Society* 2: (1982): 371–390; and Dell Hymes, "Discovering Oral Performance and Measured Verse in American Indian Narrative," *New Literary History* 8 (1977): 431–457.

6. Frances's story is written in the style of a Euro-American genre called the life history. L. L. Langness, *The Life History in Anthropological Science* (New York: Holt, Rinehart and Winston, 1965), defines life history as "an extensive record of a person's life as it is reported either by the person himself or by others or both, and whether it is written or in interviews or both."

7. There have been fewer jointly authored life histories of Native Americans than single-authored ones; John (Fire) Lame Deer and Richard Erdoes, *Lame Deer:*

Seeker of Visions (New York: Simon and Schuster, 1972), was an early exception. More broadly, works about the O'odham have been innovative in this regard. See, for example, Donald M. Bahr, Juan Gregorio, David I. Lopez, and Albert Alvarez, *Piman Shamanism and Staying Sickness (Ká:cim Múmkidag)* (Tucson: University of Arizona Press, 1981); and Ruth M. Underhill, Donald M. Bahr, Baptisto Lopez, Jose Pancho, and David Lopez, *Rainhouse and Ocean: Speeches for the Papago Year* (Tucson: University of Arizona Press, 1979).

8. See, for example, Frank B. Linderman, ed., *Pretty-Shield: Medicine Woman of the Crows* (Lincoln: University of Nebraska Press, 1972); *Black Elk Speaks: Being the Life Story of a Holy Man of the Oglala Sioux*, as told through John G. Neihardt (Lincoln: University of Nebraska Press, 1932); and Nancy Oestreich Lurie, *Mountain Wolf Woman, Sister of Crashing Thunder: The Autobiography of a Winnebago Woman* (Ann Arbor: University of Michigan Press, 1961). A form of authorship that is increasingly found is the "in collaboration with" style — for example, Julie Cruikshank in collaboration with Angela Sidney, Kitty Smith, and Annie Ned, *Life Lived like a Story* (Lincoln: University of Nebraska Press, 1990). Key references on Native American life history include Arnold Krupat, *For Those Who Come After: A Study of Native American Autobiography* (Berkeley: University of California Press, 1985); David Brumble III, *American Indian Autobiography* (Berkeley: University of California Press, 1988); and Hertha Dawn Wong, *Sending My Heart Back Across the Years: Tradition and Innovation in Native American Autobiography* (New York: Oxford University Press, 1992).

9. Native American literature is one of the most self-conscious fields in its contention that oral tradition is literature. See, for example, Larry Evers, ed., *The South Corner of Time: Hopi, Navajo, Papago, Yaqui Tribal Literature* (Tucson: Sun Tracks, University of Arizona Press, 1983); and Arnold Krupat, *The Voice in the Margin: Native American Literature and the Canon* (Berkeley: University of California Press, 1989).

10. See Appendix A for details concerning the processes of recording, editing, and collaboration.

11. See Appendix A for more discussion of language use.

12. See Albert Alvarez and Kenneth Hale, "Toward a Manual of Papago Grammar: Some Phonological Terms," *International Journal of American Linguistics* 36:2 (1970): 83–97.

Introductions

1. See Appendix B for a summary outline of the topics covered in Hazel's tapes.

2. Frances used to attend the Wi:gita at Ge Aji. The ceremony is still performed

today at Kitowak, in Mexico. For a description of the ceremony at Kitowak, see Bernard L. Fontana, *Of Earth and Little Rain* (Tucson: University of Arizona Press, 1989), pp. 99–102. Several Wi:gita songs can be found in Ruth Underhill, *Papago Indian Religion* (London: Columbia University Press, 1946), pp. 135–164.

3. Frances is referring to Ruth Underhill's book, *Papago Indian Religion*.

4. The *Ho'oki agita* are Tohono O'odham legends about powerful beings.

5. See the introduction to Part V for a discussion of Frances's abbreviated legends, or "little stories."

6. The taxonomic classification of this plant is *Lycium*. The taxonomic classifications of O'odham plants and animals that appear here are from Amadeo M. Rea, *At the Desert's Green Edge: An Ethnobotany of the Gila River Pima* (Tucson: University of Arizona Press, 1997).

7. Frances says the gourd is called *wako* in O'odham (Pima, *vako*, or bottle gourd: *Lagenaria siceraria*).

8. Frances refers to the districts demarcated by the federal government in 1934.

9. The question of how long the O'odham have been in the area continues to be a subject of controversy. For a brief summary of the issue, see Lynn S. Teague, "Prehistory and the Traditions of the O'odham and Hopi," *Kiva* 58:4 (1993): 435–454.

10. For detailed information about O'odham plants, habitats, and cultural systems, see Amadeo M. Rea, *At the Desert's Green Edge*. The Gila River Pima (Akimel O'odham) are close relatives of the Tohono O'odham and share many characteristics. For more information on the desert ecology of the Tohono O'odham, see Gary Paul Nabhan, *Gathering the Desert* (Tucson: University of Arizona Press, 1985); and Bernard L. Fontana, *Of Earth and Little Rain*, pp. 10 –19.

11. See the Afterword for more discussion of this history. Also, note that in this book O'odham place names are spelled phonetically to reflect pronunciation.

12. Though this point has been made many times, Wong argues that the telling, creating, and enactment of personal narratives through stories, pictographs, and performances of Native Americans predates colonization. See Hertha Dawn Wong, *Sending My Heart Back Across the Years: Tradition and Innovation in Native American Autobiography* (New York: Oxford University Press, 1992).

13. Whereas this general argument about culture has recently come into vogue, Frances's story quietly shatters reified images of "traditional" Native American life, without the essentializing tendencies of some of the recent work in anthropology, history, literary studies, feminism, and cultural studies which seeks to address the production of knowledge. The reader interested in learning more about the Tohono O'odham should see Winston P. Erickson, *Sharing the Desert: The Tohono O'odham in History* (Tucson: University of Arizona Press, 1994); Bernard L. Fontana, *Of Earth*

and Little Rain; and Gary Paul Nabhan; *The Desert Smells like Rain* (New York: North Point Press/Farrar, Straus & Giroux, 1982).

14. This is also true for most O'odham who recorded their life stories. See, for example, George Webb's *A Pima Remembers* (Tucson: University of Arizona Press, 1994; (first published 1959) and James McCarthy's *A Papago Traveler* (Tucson: Sun Tracks and University of Arizona Press, 1984).

15. Once we met, the fact that I was training to be an anthropologist had less and less to do with our relationship, for I decided early on that I could not *study* Native Americans. I felt too at home; I didn't have the requisite distance.

16. For a discussion of stereotypes of Native Americans, see Roy Harvey Pearce, *Savagism and Civilization: A Study of the Indian and the American Mind* (Baltimore: John Hopkins University Press, 1965); and Frederick W. Turner III, ed., "Introduction," in *The Portable North American Indian Reader* (New York: Viking Press, 1973).

Chapter 1. Simple Things

1. Frances's family didn't keep birth records at that time.

2. Frances told me, "My father went only by his Indian name, Si'al Memḍa, until he was supposed to go to China. Women would make pottery and men, bows and arrows. . . . So before they were going to go, they needed an American name, so he says 'John,' and there was another man there named John Blaine, so he said it was his uncle — it wasn't really — and that's how he got his name, John Blaine."

3. The only mention that I have ever found of S-koksonagk in print is in Richard Jones's doctoral dissertation. The paragraph reads:

I remember a man named (U'o'aha) "Painting Himself" who originally lived at Chiawuli Tak [Frances says Ko:m Wawhai], but he moved way up to a place called 'S-kokosonak' [*sic*]. As far as I know, his was the only family there. He had his farm there. He moved down to Schuchk about 1931. They moved into that old Mexican ranch house at Santa Rosa Ranch. His name was Jose Fransisco, U'o'aha. ("An Analysis of Papago Communities: 1900–1920," University of Arizona, 1969)

4. The taxonomic classification of hedgehog cactus is *Echinocereus engelmannii*.

5. The taxonomic classification of fishhook cactus is *Mammillaria thomeri*.

6. We found out later that *Ge Pi:ckim* is the O'odham word for Pitic, or Pitiquito, old Hermosillo (see Afterword).

7. Frances is referring to the community surrounding the mission at San Xavier del Bac on the Tohono O'odham San Xavier Reservation. The mission was founded by Father Eusebio Kino in 1696. It was at first a cattle ranch and later was settled by missionaries.

8. Pancho Villa was a controversial figure in the Mexican Revolution whose legendary exploits continue to be encoded in myth and story.

9. Deep inhalations such as these are common in O'odham speech. They are marked here to evoke the intensity of feeling that accompanies some of Frances's statements.

10. This story is a redaction of the legendary story of La Llorona, popular throughout the region and Mexico.

11. Baboquivari is the sacred home of the legendary I'itoi, or Big Brother.

12. Frances is referring to a dance held in one of the villages in honor of the village's patron saint. For more information on Christian fiestas among the Tohono O'odham, see Alice Joseph, Rosamond B. Spicer, and Jane Chesky, *The Desert People: A Study of the Papago Indians* (Chicago: University of Chicago Press, 1949).

Chapter 2. Spring Spinach

1. Spring spinach (*o:poñ i:wakĭ*) is a wild plant that grows near the road and water holes. Its taxonomic classification is *Monolepis nutalliana*.

2. For more information about these desert foods, see Gary Paul Nabhan, *Gathering the Desert* (Tucson: University of Arizona Press, 1985); and Carolyn Niethammer, *American Indian Food and Lore: 150 Authentic Recipes* (New York: Collier Books, 1974).

3. See Gary Nabhan's *Gathering the Desert* (1985) for an outstanding discussion of the yearly round of farming and gathering, from making saguaro cactus wine near the mountains to growing beans and squash (and many other plant varieties) in the floodplains and harvesting desert greens along roadsides and in O'odham fields. Frances, by the way, eats her spring spinach fried with eggs.

4. The taxonomic classification for *s-siw ʼu:s* is *Rumex hymenosepalus* (wild rhubarb).

5. Frances told me later that she is referring to the plant called *segai* in O'odham, which Rea identifies as *Larrea divaricata* (creosote bush). It is not uncommon for O'odham to call creosote "greasewood."

6. The taxonomic classification of *a'uḏ* is *Agave palmer*.

7. Frances's Indian kitchen is an outdoor kitchen consisting of a *ramada* with an outdoor stove and storage shelves.

Chapter 3. Met My Womanhood

1. "*Pici-pikime*" is the sound of the quail.

2. In the olden days the girl's puberty ceremony, called *wuaga*, often lasted as

long as a month. See Ruth Underhill, *Papago Woman* (New York: Holt, Rinehart and Winston, 1979; Prospect Heights, Ill.: Waveland Press, 1985), p. 61, for Chona's earlier account of the ceremony.

3. For more information on the Apache wars, see Ruth Underhill, *Papago Indian Religion* (London: Columbia University Press, 1946), pp. 165–210.

4. Owls are considered messengers from the dead. See chapter 9.

5. The Phoenix Indian School was established as a boarding school for Native Americans in 1891 by the United States government to teach the English language and mainstream American values to Indian youth.

6. Lorenzo died in 1992 (chapter 10). See also chapter 6, "Alone."

7. This kind of community cooperation can be seen in community wakes and funeral rituals today. See the Afterword for a description of one such event.

Chapter 4. San Pedro

1. Frances is referring to parent and daughter villages, between which marriage arrangements were commonly made. For more information on the social organization of the Tohono O'odham, see Ruth Underhill, *Social Organization of the Papago Indians* (New York: Columbia University Press, 1939).

2. The Civilian Conservation Corps's Indian Division was established during the Roosevelt era to encourage cattle ranching.

3. Sells is the agency town on the main Tohono O'odham reservation.

4. For more information on Tohono O'odham employment at the mines, see Henry F. Manuel, Julian Ramon, and Bernard L. Fontana, "Dressing for the Window: Papago Indians and Economic Development," in Sam Stanley, ed., *American Indian Economic Development* (The Hague and Paris: Mouton, 1978), pp. 511–577.

5. For detailed descriptions of the fiesta for St. Francis at Magdalena, see Bernard L. Fontana, *Of Earth and Little Rain* (Tucson: University of Arizona Press, 1989), pp. 103–109; and Gary Paul Nabhan, *The Desert Smells Like Rain* (New York: Farrar, Straus & Giroux, 1982), pp. 113–119.

Chapter 5. The Bad Year

1. For more information on the changes in the O'odham environment during this period, see the Afterword. See also Elizabeth Tooker's "Papagos in Tucson: An Introduction to Their History, Community Life, and Acculturation" (master's thesis, University of Arizona, 1952).

Chapter 6. Alone

1. *Cascarones*, a form of folk art common to the region, commonly consist of eggshells filled with confetti and decorated with colorful strips of tissue paper.

Chapter 9. The Owl Sickness

1. For a detailed discussion of animal forebodings, see Donald M. Bahr, Juan Gregario, David I. Lopez, and Albert Alvarez, *Piman Shamanism and Staying Sickness (Ká:cim Múmkidag)* (Tucson: University of Arizona Press, 1981), pp. 49–64.

2. Frances has adult-onset diabetes, commonly found among her people. See the Afterword for a discussion of the changes in diet that have brought the disease to epidemic proportions among her people.

3. Smallpox was one of the diseases introduced from Europe.

Chapter 10. Lorenzo

1. For some O'odham, horses (and cowboy work, more generally) are associated with the devil.

2. Songs are an important part of the old ways, associated with just about everything: ritual, dreams, healing, agriculture, religion, and everyday life. See Ruth Murray Underhill, *The Song Magic of the Papago Indians of Southern Arizona* (Tucson: Sun Tracks, University of Arizona Press, 1938; 1993); and Frances Densmore, *Papago Music, Bulletin of the Bureau of American Ethnology* no. 90 (Washington, D.C.: U.S. Government Printing Office, 1929).

Part IV. God and I'itoi: Introduction

1. For more information on Tohono O'odham religion and ritual, see Ruth Underhill, *Papago Indian Religion* (London: Columbia University Press, 1946); Ruth M. Underhill, Donald M. Bahr, Baptisto Lopez, Jose Pancho, and David Lopez, *Rainhouse and Ocean: Speeches for the Papago Year* (Tucson: University of Arizona Press, 1979); and Donald M. Bahr, Juan Gregario, David I. Lopez, and Albert Alvarez, *Piman Shamanism and Staying Sickness (Ká:cim Múmkidag)* (Tucson: University of Arizona Press, 1981).

2. See the Afterword for more discussion of this border history.

3. The Tohono O'odham have not been passive recipients of a dominant culture. Though they were considered "friendly" by their conquerors, they also revolted

against them. See Edward Spicer, *Cycles of Conquest* (Tucson: University of Arizona Press, 1992), p. 129.

Chapter 13. The Church at San Pedro

1. For more information on the Spanish conquest and efforts to convert the O'odham, see Edward H. Spicer, *Cycles of Conquest* (Tucson: University of Arizona Press, 1992).

2. Many of the Yaquis living in the Tucson area are descendants of Yaquis who migrated to the United States during the early 1900s to avoid being deported from Río Yaqui (in Sonora) to the Yucatán. Arizona Yaquis are known among their neighbors for their unique ritual interpretation of Catholic teachings, seen annually in their Pascua (Easter) ceremonies held during Lent. See Spicer, *Cycles of Conquest*, pp. 46–85.

Chapter 14. My Saints

1. At Magdalena, St. Francis Assisi, St. Francis Xavier, and Padre Kino are worshipped as St. Francis.

2. The Chapayekas are members of the Fariseo Society, masked Pharisees in the Yaqui Lenten ceremonies.

3. There are many stories about the O'odham trickster, Coyote. See, for example, Dean Saxton and Lucille Saxton, *O'othham Hoho'ok A'agitha* (Tucson: University of Arizona Press, 1973), pp. 65–128, and Gary Nabhan's account in *The Desert Smells Like Rain* (New York: Farrar, Straus & Giroux, 1982), pp. 75–86.

Chapter 15. Modern Medicine People

1. For a discussion of the slippery concept "Snakes are out," see Part V.

2. The question of whether or not the Hohokam were ancestors of present day O'odham groups remains a topic of heated debate among archaeologists. The O'odham may have replaced the Hohokam, which, as Frances points out, means "gone" in O'odham. For a summary of the debate, see Thomas E. Sheridan, *Arizona: A History* (Tucson: University of Arizona Press, 1996), pp. 11–14; and Lynn S. Teague, "Prehistory and the Traditions of the O'odham and Hopi," *Kiva* 58:4 (1993): 435–454.

Part V. Reflections: Introduction

1. Maria Chona also stated that if we tell what is forbidden, the snakes may bite. Ruth Underhill, *Papago Woman* (New York: Holt, Rinehart and Winston, 1979; Prospect Heights, Ill.: Waveland Press, 1985), p. 9.

2. Frances is referring to the fact that people have begun to leave toys at the shrine.

Chapter 16. I'm Not Sewing, Just Telling Stories

1. Other versions of the story of Ho'ok can be found in Bernard L. Fontana, *Of Earth and Little Rain* (Tucson: University of Arizona Press, 1989), pp. 27-31; and Dean Saxton and Lucille Saxton, *O'othham Hoho'ok A'agitha: Legends and Lore of the Papago and Pima Indians* (Tucson: University of Arizona Press, 1973), pp. 243-304.

2. *Agave deserti.*

3. *Opuntia acanthocarpa.*

4. The story of the Children's Shrine has many versions, each with a different emphasis. See, for example, Saxton and Saxton, *O'othham Hoho'ok A'agitha*, pp. 341-346; and Ruth Underhill, *Papago Indian Religion* (London: Columbia University Press, 1946), pp. 68-69.

Chapter 17. Murder My Dreams . . .

1. For a discussion of dreams and forebodings among the O'odham, see Donald M. Bahr, Juan Gregorio, David I. Lopez, and Albert Alvarez, *Piman Shamanism and Staying Sickness (Ká:cim Múmkidag)* (Tucson: University of Arizona Press, 1981), pp. 49-64.

Chapter 18. A Lot of Things We Don't Know About

1. Most lands are tribally rather than individually owned, held in trust by the government. See Bernard L. Fontana, *Of Earth and Little Rain* (Tucson: University of Arizona Press, 1989), p. 79.

2. Frances is referring to the Central Arizona Project.

Chapter 20. Two Hands

1. As this manuscript was going to press, Frances's daughters took turns caring for Frances as she convalesced from knee and hip surgery. Florence had taken a

leave of absence from her work to be with her mother during the week, and Christy and Linda and their children stay with Frances on weekends. Juanita regularly flies from Ohio to help out.

Afterword

1. *Taṣ* (sun) *ma:hag* (the palm of the hand with fingers), *Lupinus sparisiflora*, is a plant with small blue and white flowers. For more information, see Amadeo Rea, *At the Desert's Green Edge* (Tucson: University of Arizona Press, 1997), pp. 233–234.

2. For a complete list of Tohono O'odham moon names, see Ruth Underhill, Donald Bahr, Baptisto Lopez, Jose Pancho, and David Lopez, *Rainhouse and Ocean: Speeches for the Papago Year* (Tucson: University of Arizona Press, 1979), p. 19.

3. On her father's side, Frances belongs to the dialect group called Totoguañi. Her mother spoke the Hia Ceḍ dialect.

4. For more information on the history of Tohono O'odham living in Mexico, see Bernard Fontana, *Of Earth and Little Rain* (Tucson: University of Arizona Press, 1989), pp. 55–109; and Edward H. Spicer, *Cycles of Conquest* (Tucson: University of Arizona Press, 1992).

5. Mary Beck Moser, "Seri History (1904): Two Documents," *Journal of the Southwest*, 3:4 (1988): 489–501.

6. Over twenty thousand Yaquis live on part of their aboriginal homeland in Sonora today. Thousands of Yaquis have relocated to the United States, where they now have a reservation near Tucson (along with several villages in city barrios).

7. Federico García y Alva, ed., *Album-directorio del estado de Sonora* (Hermosillo: Imprenta Oficial, 1905–1907). Quoted in Mary Beck Moser, "Seri History (1904)," p. 489.

8. Mary Beck Moser, personal communication.

9. "Big Seconbina" is a phonetic rendering of the name of the ranch.

10. Though border studies have recently come into vogue, there has been little written about Native Americans living on both sides. For a brief account, see Gary Nabhan, *The Desert Smells like Rain* (New York: Farrar, Straus & Giroux, 1982), pp. 67–74. For a summary of trends in border studies involving histories of war and conquest, the continual encroachment of global capitalism, and the inequality of power economics, see Robert R. Alvarez, Jr., "The Mexican Border: The Making of an Anthropology of Borderlands," *Annual Review of Anthropology* 24 (1995): 447–470; and R. A. Fernandez, *The Mexican-American Border Region: Issues and Trends* (Notre Dame, Ind.: Indiana University Press, 1989).

11. The reservation has been marginalized as a frontier in a double sense: first, as

a reservation, and second, as a border or boundary between the United States and Mexico.

12. See Helen M. Ingram, Thomas McGuire, and Mary Wallace, *Poverty, Power, and Water Resources on the Papago Reservation* (s.l., s.n., 1985).

13. For a world system perspective on European expansion into Arizona-Sonora, see Thomas E. Sheridan, *Arizona: A History* (Tucson: University of Arizona Press, 1996). The most comprehensive work on the conquest and Southwestern Native American history is Edward Spicer's *Cycles of Conquest*.

14. According to Thomas Sheridan, Indian populations declined 66 to 95 percent between the sixteenth and eighteenth centuries. See *Arizona: A History*, p. 24.

15. Ibid., p. xv.

16. For an interesting discussion of the frontier culture in southern Arizona, see Bobby Byrd and Susannah Mississippi Byrd, eds., *The Late Great Mexican Border: Reports from a Disappearing Line* (El Paso, Tex.: Cinco Puntos Press, 1996).

17. For more information on O'odham work in Arizona mines, see Henry F. Manuel, Juliann Ramon, and Bernard L. Fontana, "Dressing for the Window: Papago Indians and Economic Development," in Sam Stanley, ed., *American Indian Economic Development* (The Hague and Paris: Mouton, 1978).

18. See Winston P. Erikson, *Sharing the Desert: The Tohono O'odham in History* (Tucson: University of Arizona Press, 1994), p. 98.

19. Mexican O'odham are not federally recognized and have no reservations or special land rights. According to the 1979 census, there were fewer than two hundred O'odham living in Mexico. For more information on Mexican O'odham, see Bernard L. Fontana, *Of Earth and Little Rain*, pp. 80–99.

20. See Gary Nabhan, "Foreword," in Amadeo M. Rea, *At the Desert's Green Edge*, p. xv.

21. These data are from William H. Metzler's untitled series of manuscript chapters concerning the economic potential of the Tohono O'odham, copy on file at the Arizona State Museum Library, University of Arizona. Quoted from Manuel, Ramon, and Fontana, "Dressing for the Window," p. 534.

22. See Nabhan, *Gathering the Desert* (Tucson: University of Arizona Press, 1985), pp. 120–121.

23. For a comparable emphasis on the migration of a Mexican-American from the ranch to the barrio, see Patricia Preciado Martin's *Songs My Mother Sang to Me: An Oral History of Mexican American Women* (Tucson: University of Arizona Press, 1992).

24. For further reading about Native American women's narrative traditions, see Gretchen Bataille and Kathleen Mullen Sand, *American Indian Women: Telling*

Their Lives (Lincoln: University of Nebraska Press, 1984); Valerie Shirer Mathes, "A New Look at the Role of Women in Indian Society," *American Indian Quarterly* 2:3 (1975): 131-139; Paula Gunn Allen, *The Sacred Hoop: Recovering the Feminine in American Indian Traditions* (Boston: Beacon Press, 1986); and Susan Stanford Friedman, "Women's Autobiographical Selves: Theory and Practice," in Shari Benstock, ed., *The Private Self: Theory and Practice of Women's Autobiographical Writings* (Chapel Hill: University of North Carolina Press, 1988), pp. 34-62.

Appendix A. Inscribing Life History

1. This style of embedding has been commonly seen in Native American life histories, although the collective stories or songs are not always presented in their original contexts. Although Julie Cruikshank's key theoretical point in *Life Lived like a Story* (Lincoln: University of Nebraska Press, 1990) is that her three narrators use formulaic narratives as essential components to talk about their lives, she does the narratives injustice by placing them in separate, odd-numbered chapters rather than where they occur in the original text. Important connections between stories and experience are thus lost to us, giving us little sense of the "cultural construction of experience."

2. Marjorie Shostak, "'What the Wind Won't Take Away': The Genesis of Nisa — the Life and Words of a !Kung Woman," in The Personal Narratives Group, ed., *Interpreting Women's Lives: Feminist Theory and Personal Narratives* (Bloomington: Indiana University Press, 1989), p. 239.

3. See M. M. Bakhtin, *The Dialogic Imagination*, trans. Caryl Emerson and Michael Holquist, ed. Michael Holquist (Austin: University of Texas Press, 1981).

4. The well-known life history, *Black Elk Speaks: Being the Life Story of a Holy Man of the Oglala Sioux*, as told through John G. Neihardt (Lincoln: University of Nebraska Press, 1932), boasts a complex mediation: Black Elk spoke in Lakota, his son translated, Neihardt reworded the translation, and his daughter transcribed, reworded, and typed the text.

5. There is a plethora of excellent works written solely by Native Americans about their lives. A few of the classics incluce N. Scott Momaday, *The Way to Rainy Mountain* (Albuquerque: University of New Mexico Press, 1979) and *Man Made of Words: Essays, Stories, Passages* (New York: St. Martin's Press, 1997); Leslie Marmon Silko, *Ceremony* (New York: New American Library, 1977) and *Storyteller* (New York: Seaver Books, 1981); and Ofelia Zepeda, *Ocean Power: Poems from the Desert* (Tucson: Sun Tracks and University of Arizona Press, 1995). Zepeda, like Frances, is Tohono O'odham.

6. See L. L. Langness, *The Life History in Anthropological Science* (New York: Holt, Rinehart and Winston, 1965), pp. 3–19.

7. Collaborative works such as this have been the dominant form of Native American autobiography since the turn of the twentieth century. This is gradually changing as more Native Americans write their own stories.

8. Arnold Krupat aptly objects to the term "as told to," because it is patronizing, ethnocentric, and inaccurately reflects the nature of the collaborative process. Quoted in Hertha Dawn Wong, *Sending My Heart Back Across the Years: Tradition and Innovation in Native American Autobiography* (New York: Oxford University Press, 1992), p. 3.

9. Cruikshank's observation that her three Yukon narrators exhibited a discontinuous, rarely coherent presentation may have more to do with the discontinuous nature of the recording process than with the discontinuous nature of women's experience. *Life Lived like a Story*, p. 3.

10. Much of the commentary in life histories written by anthropologists follows an explanatory mode, employing master narratives arising out of scholarly traditions and nonnative concerns in order to analyze, compare, and explain their "data" (i.e., the speaker or her material). Their point is to produce generalizations, a characteristic mode of writing in the social sciences that has only recently come under scrutiny. See Ruth Behar and Deborah Gordon, eds., *Women Writing Culture* (Berkeley: University of California Press, 1995); James Clifford and George Marcus, *Writing Culture* (Berkeley: University of California Press, 1986); and George Marcus and Michael Fischer, *Anthropology as Cultural Critique* (Chicago: University of Chicago Press, 1986).

11. This is unusual in this type of work, where, as Brumble states, "a white collaborator usually decided for his Indian informant what was memorable." See David H. Brumble III, *American Indian Autobiography* (Berkeley: University of California Press, 1988), p. 3.

Illustration Credits

Hector Gonzalez
Frances and her daughters

Frances Manuel
Frances' paternal grandparents
Frances and her mother
Frances as a young child
Frances and her husband

Rebecca Moser
The Yaqui hands

Deborah Neff
Frances' "Indian kitchen"
The church at San Pedro

David Sanders
The desert around San Pedro
Frances' bedroom shrine
Frances and her granddaughter
Frances making a basket

About the Authors

Frances Sallie Manuel is a well-known Tohono O'odham basket weaver, singer, and village elder. She currently lives on the Tohono O'odham Reservation near Tucson, Arizona. She divides her time between family and community, and continues to teach basket weaving in Tucson.

Deborah Lyn Neff was trained as a cultural anthropologist and has worked in both the American Southwest and India. As a Fulbright Scholar in India, she studied ritual performance, symbolism, and the lifestyles of an itinerant lower caste of artist-musicians. Dr. Neff has published articles in numerous journals, including *Social Science and Medicine, Ethnology,* and *Theory into Practice.* Her book *Dancing Serpent* is based on her doctoral dissertation and will be published soon. She currently devotes her time to research and writing, and promoting holistic health alternatives and community.